With Eye and Ear

Azimuth defines direction by generating an arc between a fixed point and a variable, between the determined truths of the past and the unknown data of the future.

With Eye and Ear

Kenneth Rexroth

An *Azimuth* Book
Herder and Herder

1970
HERDER AND HERDER NEW YORK
232 Madison Avenue, New York 10016

For Carol

The author extends grateful acknowledgement to the following periodicals, where chapters of this book originally appeared: *Nation* for "D. H. Lawrence: The Other Face of the Coin," "The Tao of Painting," "The New English Bible," "Greek Tragedy in Translation," "On Translating Roman Verse," "Of Myths and Mythmaking," "Sir Thomas Browne," "The Letters of Carl Sandburg," "Sinclair Lewis," "McAlmon and the Lost Generation," "Citizen Fromm." *New York Times Book Review* for "On Japanese Literature," "Scrolls and Sculpture of Japan," "*The Pillow Book* of Sei Shonagon," "*The Prayer Mat of Flesh,*" "St. Thomas More," "Henry Miller: The Iconoclast as Everyman's Friend," "Leslie Fiedler: Custer's Last Stand," "The Bollingen Series," "Allen Ginsberg in America," "The Authentic Joy of Philip Whalen." *The Atlantic* for "William Golding: Unoriginal Sin." *The New Republic* for "The Mirror of Magic." *Commonweal* for "New Sex? New Church?", "Faith in an Age of Faithlessness," "The Oxford Conspirators," "The Modernists," "The Bourgeois." *Saturday Review* for "Poetry in the Sixties." *Art News* for "Tenth Street on the Grand Tour." *The Chicago Review* for "Coleridge and the Lability of Affect." *Book Week* for "Jack London's Native Sons." *Commentary* for "The Lost Vision of Isaac Bashevis Singer."

Acknowledgement is also made to the following publishers: University Books for "The Spiritual Alchemy of Thomas Vaughan." New American Library, Mentor Books, for "Moll Flanders," "Frank Norris and the Classic Past." The Heritage Press for "Ecclesiastes." Farrar, Straus and Giroux for "Tolstoy's Interior Kingdom." Pym-Randell Press for "Ford Madox Ford." Beacon Press for "*Pagany.*"

Library of Congress Catalog Card Number: 74–129765

Contents

1.

The Spiritual Alchemy of Thomas Vaughan

Alchemy is the one field of past human endeavor which it is almost impossible even to begin to understand. No two modern authors agree about it and no two alchemists agree with each other. Thomas Vaughan is supposed to be the leading "spiritual alchemist" of the entire literature, and yet the majority of modern writers on alchemy deny flatly that such a thing as spiritual alchemy ever existed.

Most of the books which do purport to explain the mysteries of spiritual alchemy are suspect. Their scholarship is shoddy or invented or non-existent, their logic is cracked if not paranoid. Most of them occupy the far outer reaches of occultism, along with theories that the works of Shakespeare were written by a committee of mahatmas on Atlantis, or that the equations which disprove Einstein are embodied in the dimensions of the Great Pyramid. Such books are amusing reading if not too barbarously written—Ignatius Donnelly, for instance, is one of America's most entertaining authors. But Thomas Vaughan is far from being light bedside reading and equally far from being a barbarous writer. He is certainly in deadly earnest about something, and he is almost as beautiful a writer as his brother Henry, one of the greatest poets of the language. Even to begin to comprehend what he is in earnest about requires an extraordinary effort of imaginative projection into a universe of discourse utterly unlike anything to be found, at least in respectable intellectual circles, today.

As a guide, A. E. Waite is not much help. His *The Secret Tradition in Alchemy* is an exasperating, elusive book. It is nothing to put in the hands of a novice, for it itself requires an explanation which, like everything else connected with alchemy, it would seem, is intrinsically implausible.

Waite belonged to a number of "secret brotherhoods" and was the founder and leader of at least one such group. As an initiate into practically every organization of occultists of his day which was not patently lunatic, he was bound by all sorts of solemn vows and oaths of secrecy. His works and his autobiography make it sufficiently evident that he took these vows seriously indeed. He wrote a set of books, treating systematically and one by one the major cruxes or problems of what might be called the scholarship of the occult tradition—the Holy Grail legends, Freemasonry, Alchemy, Rosicrucianism, the Tarot cards, Ritual Magic, the Kabbalah; and a number of important personages in the history of the occult, Raymond Lull, St. Martin, Eliphas Levi.

With the sole exception of *The Holy Kabbalah* where for once Waite's language is very thinly veiled—perhaps for the reason that what he was talking about is sufficiently well known at least to Jewish scholarship—all these books purport to deny what Waite is in actual fact, not so much proving, as quietly exposing to those who have eyes to see. Until you catch on, this device can be, to put it mildly, misleading, and it never ceases to be exasperating. *The Secret Tradition in Alchemy* claims to deny and disprove the existence of a secret tradition. It does nothing of the sort. If that had been Waite's real end in view, he would never had written the book, it would have been, in his language, "work of supererogation." However, it is certainly misleading. It misled Carl Jung.

For years Jung, in all his voluminous writings about alchemy, ignored Waite. In volume XII of *The Collected Works,* published in the Bollingen Series, where all of Jung's writings on alchemy are gathered up, *The Works of Thomas Vaughan* is not mentioned, nor are the original editions under his own name or Eugenius Philalethes. *The Secret Tradition* appears at last, along with four other alchemical works by Waite, including the alchemical works of E. Kelley, and the original editions of Eireneaus Philalethes—works important almost exclusively because of the connection with certain controversies around Thomas Vaughan. This in a bibliography of 540 books and 58 manuscripts. In the essay, "Religious Ideas in Alchemy," the only place Jung mentions Waite by name, he attacks him precisely at a point (the Lapis-Christus parallel) where Waite is covering his tracks.

Why no mention at all of Vaughan? In the whole history of alchemy, this is the one author who really, indisputably, gives away the show, divulges the secret. One would think that Vaughan would have been Jung's favorite author, outranking even Rider Haggard and the Kalevala. To believe that Jung's silence is deliberate and designed, in his turn, to cover *his* tracks, is to tempt oneself with the little paranoias of the crackpots who beset this subject enough as it is. Still, it is surely very mystifying.

Alchemy as a subject is not just mystifying, it is intrinsically improbable. It is as though a textbook of chemistry, another of mining engineering, another of gymnastics and breathing exercises, another of pharmacology, several sex manuals, and many treatises of transcendental mysticism had been torn to pieces and not just mixed up together, but fused into a totally new chemical compound of thought. In fact it is not just "as though," looked at from the viewpoint of twentieth-century scientific world-view, this is pretty much what alchemy is—the humorous description is close to exact.

There is no use trying to explain Thomas Vaughan in our terms; he is inexplicable, and can only be appreciated with the subconscious, like a dream or a surrealist poem. He, and many other alchemists, were in fact favorite reading matter of the surrealists, who appreciated them for their resonance rather than their significant meaning. There is a good deal more to

Vaughan than that, and a good deal more than can be comprehended under the terms of Jungian integration of the personality. Carl Jung's extensive writings on alchemy are illuminating to anyone coming fresh to the subject, but they are inadequate. The flaw in Jung's exposition is his assumption that the alchemists are not talking about anything real. "Man projects himself into his ignorance." A pseudo-science that concerns itself entirely with matters and procedures that have no objective reality must of necessity be really concerned with the unconscious of its devotees. This interpretation differs little from that of André Breton or Eugéne Jolas, and as a matter of fact the Jungians and the surrealists greatly influenced each other's notions about alchemy.

However, as long as alchemy is considered only a symbolic dramatization of the unconscious, works like Thomas Vaughan's little tracts will have only a fortuitous, alogical coherence, the coherence of dream, and will have only evocative rather than communicative meanings to offer us. Not only does Vaughan mean something, but his works form a kind of spiritual autobiography which comes to its climax in one of the more pathetic tragedies of English literature. Waite knew this, though he made no comment, he printed those poignant fragments from the notebooks which tell the story for those who can understand.

Nor is there any point in trying to explain Vaughan in an exegetical way, such an exegesis would only sound crazy to the uninitiated. Since all other alchemical works in Europe are far more "in code" than Vaughan's—which, as I said, really give the show away—I think it is best to lay the whole problem aside and turn to a place where these matters are all made quite explicit. Theoretically this should be India. I think it highly likely that alchemy did arise in India sometime before the appearance of systematized Tantric Buddhism in which it plays an important role. Yogic practices which are assumed into alchemy go back to the beginning of civilized life in the sub-continent. The seal from Mohenjo-Daro of the man in the lotus position, rapt in trance, with an erect penis, might well come from Woodroffe's *Serpent Power* or serve as a woodcut illustration for Ko Hung, the greatest of the Chinese alchemists. However, the most extensive work on this subject is still P. C. Ray's *A History of Hindu Chemistry,* published in two volumes in 1904 and 1925. Not only is it out of date but it is curiously exasperating in its ethnocentric conceit—as well as being quite unreliable as to dates. My objection to Indian writing in this field is the same as that of the Chinese critics of the T'ang Dynasty who concerned themselves with it. It is all so vague, full of shifting amorphous symbols, and impossible to date. So it is to Chinese alchemy I will turn to try to convey to you what a seventeenth-century Welsh mystic and poet and alchemist is talking about. Here we will be dealing with clear statements and definite dates and in all the body of alchemical literature such conveniences exist nowhere else.

The earliest sure date in Western alchemy is the treatise of Bolos of Mendes, the pseudo-Democritus, who wrote in the second century B.C. This survives only in Syriac, one of the clearer statements being, "The pledge has been imposed on us to expose nothing clearly to anyone." Next comes the collection of magical papyri in Leyden, with which are associated a number of tracts of what might be called proto-alchemy. Then come the miscellaneous Greek chemical writings contained in a manuscript collection in the library of St. Mark's. With few exceptions all of these deal exclusively with the adulteration of metals and the fabrication of false jewelry. However, they are couched in a special language of mystification. Furthermore, they and later documents like them are associated physically with the various tractates of the Hermetic literature. No one has ever given a satisfactory explanation of why these recipe books in the art of fraud should have been grouped by Byzantine and late Egyptian librarians and copyists with that corpus of Gnostic, Neo-Pythagorean and Neo-Platonic mysticism.

Flinders Petrie, to the scandal of his scholarly colleagues, dated the formation of the Hermetic tradition to Persian Egypt. There is, in fact, much to be said for this unorthodox opinion, but the works of "Hermes Trismegistus" begin to appear in European speculation in the late Middle Ages, and the originals are assumed to date from the first three centuries of the Christian Era. It is remarkable that, although medieval alchemists constantly refer to "Hermes," they show no knowledge of the mystical and philosophical tractates. However, I do believe that Gnosticism, and even the specific notions of Jewish Kabbalism, arose first in Persian and Hellenistic Egypt, when that country was a melting pot of speculations, cults and mysteries from all over the civilized world—including, at second or third hand, India and China.

The earliest appearance of alchemical, or rather proto-alchemical ideas in China are considerably earlier. The *Shan Hai Ching,* the *Classic of Mountains and Rivers,* in a passage which may date from the fifth century B.C. mentions six *wu,* shamans, who carry the corpse of the man-eating dragon Cha-Yu and have in their hands the death-banishing drugs which drive him away. Si Huang Ti, the Ch'in emperor, sends an expedition out to sea to search for the mystical isles where beautiful *wu* girls guarded the medicines of immortality. The greatest of Chinese historians, Ssu-ma Chien (B.C. 145–79), tells anecdotes of the quest of emperors for the elixir of life in the Ch'in Dynasty (B.C. 221–207), and a long story of the Han emperor, Wu Ti (B.C. 140–87) and his many dealings with alchemists. Prompted by his chief alchemist Lao Shao Chun, this emperor established a regular budget for alchemical researches.

Many Han, and reputedly earlier, works of alchemy survived into T'ang times—the eighth century A.D.—and were subject to extensive commentary. However, in the Sung Dynasty, the tenth to thirteenth centuries, all these which revealed any of the sexual techniques for attaining trance and longevity were purged from the canon of Taoist texts and survived from then on only clandestinely and in Japan.

T'ang intercourse with Persia and Inner Asia led to a proliferation of popular alchemy. Ch'ang An, the capital, swarmed with alchemists and magicians, along with Nestorian monks and shamans from Siberia. Li Mi-li, a Persian alchemist, after a period at the T'ang court, crossed over to Japan and was a factor in the civilizing activities of the court at Nara. It is in Japan that the largest collection of early texts of explicitly sexual yogic-alchemical practices survives today, although there are certainly plenty of late and more popular treatises of this sort to be found now in China.

During the T'ang period Buddhist monks visiting India were on the lookout for alchemists, and the famous traveller Hsuanch'ao, under instructions of the Chinese court, sought out the leading Indian alchemist and persuaded him to visit China. I give all these facts simply to show that there was a great deal of alchemy coming and going, beginning sometime prior to the third century before Christ.

Chinese lists of metals and inorganic substances with typical alchemical parallels or synonyms and correlations with parts of the body and the constellations date back to at least the fifth century, possibly to Tso Yuan in the fourth century B.C., and include quite sophisticated substances—arsenic, sulfide, sulfur, arsenious acid, mercuric sulfide, mercury, sal ammoniac, alum, diamonds, lodestones and other metals and their compounds. Mineral acids are described by the earliest Chinese travellers to India. Paraphrases of no crucial importance of passages from the Indian alchemist and Tantric philosopher Nagajuna (second century A.D.) occur in the writings of the founder of Neo-Taoist science and of fully developed spiritual alchemy, Ko Hung of the fourth century.

The illustrations of which Carl Jung makes so much in his "Secret of the Golden Flower" are in fact illustrations for Ko's *Pao P'u Tzu*. They were lifted from a nineteenth-century edition of his work and used by a syncretistic slum sect, of the type of our Holiness churches, Jehovah's Witnesses or the I Ams, without any understanding of their original significance. The most important illustration of all does not appear in Jung's book—it is a nude figure of a man in a position of meditation. In his body, corresponding in place to the major autonomic nervous system plexuses, are the various instruments of alchemy—retort, furnace and so on. This one illustration answers all the disputed questions, once for all.

By the early Sung period Chinese alchemy was very highly developed on both fronts. Yogic practices, that is, autonomic nervous-system gymnastics, sexual techniques and methods of achieving several kinds of trance, were as advanced as any to be found in India. "Several kinds of trance" needs explanation. It is only in recent years when neurological research has turned its attention to yoga that we have come to realize that, although these practices include auto-hypnosis, they are primarily concerned with the production of states, which, although entranced, are psychologically and even neurologically speaking exactly the opposite of the hypnotic state. At the same time alchemy by the twelfth century was busy with chemical phenomena that European science would not begin to explore until the end of the eighteenth century. Not only had they developed a crude but comprehensive chemistry of the common acids, bases, metallic salts, sulfur, invented gunpowder and greek fire, burning glasses, artificial pearls, discovered the use of coal and petroleum (Peking man used coal), but they had occupied themselves quite intelligently with various mysteries and intriguing phenomena, luminescence, magnetism, production of a vacuum and so on. Exactly as in Europe most of this literature is at least quasi-Hermetic with mysterious and misleading terms for sulfur, magnitite, mercury and the rest.

As Neo-Taoism matured it produced hundreds of alchemical tracts and dozens of major expositions, an output which was to come to an end only in recent times. Even the great Sung Dynasty Neo-Confucian philosopher Chu Hsi wrote a short treatise on, and more or less against alchemy. After the eighth century Tantric Buddhism became common in China, and brought with it from India essentially the same esoteric practices divorced however from any connexion with transmutation of metals and given a Buddhist philosophical basis. The frontispiece to Woodroffe's *Serpent Power* represents, in Tantric terms, the same method of yogic trance as do the illustrations to the *Pao P'u Tzu*.

Not only were the sexual techniques of alchemy assumed to develop internal processes which paralleled operations leading to the production of gold, the philosopher's stone or the growth of precious metals, cinnabar and sulfur in the wombs of the uprising mountains. This idea can be found in Proclus in the West and continues to dominate medieval ideas until the translation of Avicenna's *Treatise Against Alchemy*. The heirosgamos literally fecundates the earth. At the same time it achieves salvation for the soul.

Meditation; mental exercise which reduces the mind to a single point of awareness; breathing gymnastics which are a form of sustained hyperventilation; concentration of the mind on the major autonomic plexuses of the body, beginning with the lumbar or pubic plexus and rising to the head; orgasm without ejaculation—which by pressure of the heel on the perineal region is diverted into the bladder—all this by oneself or with a woman in the sexual act: is the entire literature of alchemy just a code communicating the secrets of this method of achieving trance and illumination?

No. Mary Anne Atwood, whose *A Suggestive Inquiry into the Hermetic Mystery* introduced alchemy into modern occultism in 1850, apparently thought this was the essence of the matter—but there is more to it than that. It is inconceivable that so immense a body of literature in so many languages over so long a period should be no more than an infinitely complicated rebus or cryptogram for a relatively simple discipline of the nervous system which can be revealed in a sentence and explained in a few pages.

Thomas Vaughan and his wife, his *soror mystica,* wrapped in entranced embrace at the Pinner of Wakefield, were, it is true, blundering into a region of revelation which they little understood and which, it would seem, eventually destroyed both of them. They were doing what Chinese adepts had done at least four hundred years before Christ and what others may have done in the Indus Valley three thousand years before. But they were also, and concomitantly, performing a chemical experiment, and they believed that neither could be successful without the other.

The doctrine of the interaction, and in most cases of the transcendental identity, of the macrocosm and the microcosm is as old as alchemy. It is alchemy. By manipulating oneself one achieves illumination. By simultaneous and parallel manipulation of physical reality, one achieves the philosopher's stone, or potable gold, or whatever may be the chemical end in view. (The final achievement of the Great Work is always thought of as the term of an enormously long and difficult process—both chemically and, to coin a word, yogically.) But both processes are thought of as equally real. It is curious that the "objective" chemical operation has been proven to be illusory, while the psychological, or neurological one is as operable today as ever.

It may be objected that I have not explained in literal detail exactly what Thomas Vaughan and his wife were up to. The reason should be obvious. It killed them. Tantric and yogic works are full of warnings of the dangers of unguided autonomic nervous-system experiments. The neophyte is told again and again that he can learn only by submitting himself to the personal guidance of a teacher—guru. If not, he is warned that he will certainly come to a bad end. Furthermore, all texts all over the world of this type of mysticism point out that the pre-condition and essential foundation for all such practices is right living, the fulfillment of the commonplace injunctions of Buddhist, Christian or Chinese morality. Without this foundation the would-be adept is, as the experience of millenniums has shown, inevitably doomed.

I am well aware that following hard on the heels of Carl Jung have come a horde of apostles of irresponsible do-it-yourself ecstasy. Alchemy, Gnosticism, Tantrism are today part of a world characterized also by hallucinogenic drugs, folk songs, peace marches and black stockings. The great trouble with these people is that they confuse transcendence with sensationalism. Thomas Vaughan was a wise, disciplined and careful man, yet vision was too much for him. His work may be an inspiration but it is certainly also a warning.

1967

2.
Moll Flanders

Down the years there have been many people whose judgment was worthy of consideration who have believed that Defoe was the master of the most admirable prose in English since the translators of the Bible. It is not fine writing in the sense that Gibbon's *Decline and Fall of the Roman Empire* is fine writing, and it is at the opposite stylistic pole to the Roman rhetoric of Sam Johnson or the lush flowered prose of Sir Thomas Browne or Thomas De Quincey. It is open to question if it is an exemplary style for any but born writers. As Walter Scott pointed out long ago it "is the last that should be attempted by a writer of inferior genius; for though it be possible to disguise mediocrity by fine writing, it appears in all its naked inanity when it assumes the garb of simplicity." Defoe was the first and he remained the greatest of the founders of the plain style which has become the standard English of the twentieth century. We think of it as being like speech, and as a matter of fact, to judge from our quite adequate evidence, prose like this created modern cultivated speech. Addison and Steele and Swift wrote plainly and directly. Defoe thought that way. He was a plain, direct man. The only criticism that has ever been levelled against him was that the homely personality he so obviously possessed dealt with all other personalities in terms of its own unmixed motives.

We seem to see Defoe's characters through the crystal-clear medium of his style with perfect verisimilitude, as real as if we saw them in a mirror which was so flawless that it was invisible. *Moll Flanders* is considered the most authentic portrait of a prostitute in English literature. It has been called "the truest realism in English literature," or on a more sensational level "red-blooded realism," the tale of a hot, earthy wench. As an example of realism it is supposed to be "like life," to give the impression of truth, the conviction of being based on real facts. It is widely supposed to be one of the more exciting erotic classics.

The first statement is true; the others are singularly mistaken. *Moll Flanders* is an authentic portrait of a prostitute but it is not a neutrally objective one. Indeed, it is a relentless evaluation, a judgment. This judgment is pronounced ironically entirely in the terms of the specific kind of realism Defoe chose to employ. The story is not only based on facts; it consists of almost nothing else. Defoe employs every device of verisimilitude of a certain kind—the book is full of things, material things.

Marcel Proust and James Joyce considered themselves "realistic" writers. Their major works purport to be truthful portrayals of different aspects of the interior life. *Finnegans Wake* would be inconceivable without a specific scientific theory of mental facts. Henry James imagined his novels to deal realistically with the real, hidden motives of his characters. So, obviously, does any contemporary novelist whose work has been influenced by psychoanalysis.

Like *Robinson Crusoe, Roxana, The Journal of the Plague Year* and Defoe's other fictions, *Moll Flanders* is a narrative of considerable materially factual complication, but not complexity, and of remarkably unmixed motives. The modern novel and the analyst's couch have conditioned us to expect from both art and life very mixed motives indeed. Complex psychology is almost universal in modern literature. It even lurks beneath the surface of the simplistic style of Ernest Hemingway, Raymond Chandler,

Dashiell Hammett. This has not always been true. Aristotle seems to have thought that complex, equivocal and ambiguous motivation corrupted or destroyed a work of art rather than improved it. Ben Jonson's theory of humours comes close to advocating the rationing of one motive to each character and the creating of artistic tension by the complicated interaction of limited maneuver—like a chess problem. One of the greatest works of fiction in the Western world is concerned with protagonists who are even simpler than those of Defoe—the villain and villainess of *Les Liaisons Dangereuses* are simply evil and the utter simplicity is bone freezing. *Don Quixote, The Tale of Genji, The Dream of the Red Chamber,* the *Satyricon,* these are the world's major works of prose fiction. In their external relations to other people and to things, their characters may be complicated or not; their responses and finally their motives are as simple as can be. Unity of character, simplicity of motive, complication of circumstance: these are the ingredients of what we call classicism in dramatic fiction.

Simpler than life? Of course. Any work of art is simpler than life. Is life like Dostoievsky or Henry James or Zola? Ben Jonson's theatre of humours is an artistic convention; Henry James' theory of vapours is equally conventional, so is Zola's Naturalism. Art imitates life—life imitates art and in doing so can be very misleading. Acting out is an ancient vice. People spring up all over the place like the teeth of Cadmus's dragon to try on the costumes of the characters in any successful novel. My mother's friends strove desperately amongst the tea things to fulfill the promises of Madame des Mauves and the lady of *Portrait of a Lady.* In San Francisco recently bearded barefoot monsters sprang from the sidewalks like alfalfa, sown on the air by one foolish novel. In the heyday of its popularity any number of literate whores may have modeled themselves in fancy, a little out of focus to be sure, on Waldo Frank's *Rahab.*

Moll Flanders gives the overwhelming and indelible impression that it is modeled on a whore in fact. Its authenticity is not due to the accumulation of elaborately researched detail. It has none of the sensory richness of background and local color we find in Zola's *Nana* although it says essentially the same thing about the profession of whoring. Defoe's is a classical realism. He con-

structs an archetype of carefully selected "abstracted" characteristics. These characteristics are in turn built up in the narrative by
material facts. *Moll Flanders* is a portrait of the kind known as
a Character, popular in classical times—the *Characters* of Theo-
phrastus, and popular again with the neo-classic taste of Defoe's
day—the *Caractères* of Jean de La Bruyère. These are behavioristic portraits from which all details have been shorn away
that do not reinforce the clarity of the purely typical. The method
is that of informative, discursive description. Zola's *Nana* is
such a character, too, but she is individuated by the detail and
complication of her background. Things and events in *Nana* are
presented with sensory richness but the woman herself is shown
with only the most meager interior life, just enough to make her
story convincing to the modern taste. Moll Flanders has no
interior life at all and the material facts with which her character
is constructed do not increase her individuality. They are chosen
as facets of her typicality.

There have been whores with hearts of gold, it is true. I have
even known some. But without exception they have been situational prostitutes, Negroes in America, working-class girls in
starving Europe immediately after the second war. Down the
ages, I am confident, there have been a considerable number of
golden-hearted hangmen but a novel about such a person would
verge on fantasy. Most voluntary prostitutes are lazy, greedy,
willful, lovelost and treacherous. They are incapable of con-
ceiving of the sexual relationship in any other than exploitative
terms. Men are either johns or pimps. Moll Flanders has several
sterling qualities, not least of which is fortitude. In the course
of time she even, for a whore, learns a certain amount of
prudence. To the end her virtues remain the Stoic ones un-
tainted by any glimmer of a higher ethic, and like the Stoic
master whom she did not know, Seneca, her outstanding virtue
is greed.

Defoe wrote two novels about whores. Today we would class
Roxana as a call girl; Moll Flanders as a common prostitute.
Both heroines are greedy. Roxana's greed is complicated. Furthermore it shades imperceptibly into covetousness, a far more
deadly evil. Moll's does not; it is simply greed. Moll is sane and,
in her way, honest. Roxana is hypocritical and if she is not self-

deluded at least she always tries hard to delude herself. Moll
Flanders is sane indeed and her sanity brings her to a good end.
Roxana is very nice and very nasty and her niceness and her
nastiness bring her to a wretched end—at least so she says as
she hurriedly finishes her narrative. I don't imagine that Defoe
thought the moral of the two books was that Stoic amorality is
more likely to pay off than Christian hypocrisy. He probably
thought that was self-evident. I do think he was interested in
Moll Flanders in portraying the ethics of a certain kind of survival against certain kinds of odds. I think he considered it a
common and typical success story of his day and I think he told
it in such a way that the reader would be forced to his own
conclusions.

Moll moves through a narrower world than one of ordinary
material objects; her life takes place almost exclusively amongst
commodities. For her the essential relationship in life between
human beings and objects and between men and women is price.
Whether it is a pearl necklace, a watch or a plantation in
Virginia, we never know what these things look like. We only
know that they'll fetch a good price. For Moll good men are
men who give her money and who have the "class" that goes
with money. Bad men are men who don't. She has husbands
and children. They come and go and she reckons them like a
bookkeeper as good or bad. Two children she gets off her hands
at a neat profit. After some men she is left in the red. Out of
others she is able to realize something, modest or handsome as
the case may be. Deaths, marriages, disasters, love affairs are
only brief, schematic notations on the left-hand side of a ledger.
What counts entirely for Moll are the figures on the right and
the totals at the bottom.

I do not mean by this that Moll Flanders was not a passionate
woman. She is, of course, the archetype of the lusty wench in
English literature. It is not that she did not enjoy herself in bed.
It is that every orgasm was measured out—so much and no
more for the price paid. This might seem a difficult biological
feat but in whoring it is of the essence. Not for nothing is the
commercialized sex act known in several languages as a trick—
truc, Kniff, trucco.

This concept gives a peculiar character to the entire book.

When we come to the end with Moll, old, comfortable and probably fat, and look back over a long life that came so often so near to total disaster, we think, "Well, old girl, you sure pulled a fast one." Her life story is the tale of a sharp bargain, a crooked deal with the devil, in which the bargainer was obstinate enough, unbreakable enough, had the guts and stamina to hang on until her adversary had paid in full.

People commonly speak of *Moll Flanders* as teeming with lusty life. It is certainly an accurate picture told in the first person of a life and of a lust but these are of such a character as to result in a narrative that is curiously abstract. It is not just, as many critics have said, that everything is stripped away from the narrative but pure action. There are plenty of descriptive adjectives in Moll's account of her adventures but they are all descriptions of a certain kind. Here is a passage taken absolutely at random which could be duplicated on any page of the book:

"I had made an acquaintance with a very sober, good sort of a woman, who was a widow too, like me, but in *better circumstances*. Her husband had been a captain of a merchant ship, and having had the misfortune to be cast away coming home on a voyage from the West Indies, which would have been *very profitable* if he had come safe, was so *reduced by the loss*, that though he had saved his life then, it broke his heart, and killed him afterwards; and his widow, being pursued by the *creditors*, was forced to take shelter in the *Mint*."

The italics are mine. If you go through the novel and underline in red every sum of money and every phrase referring to money or to business transactions you will discover that you have performed an automatic act of revelatory literary criticism. You will have uncovered the operation of an extraordinary irony. It is an irony designed to create tension. The tension arises, like the tension of humor, from radical incongruity, the incongruity of sex and price. The tension may discharge in laughter but it certainly discharges in judgment. Defoe, after all, was writing a novel. There wasn't really any Moll Flanders. She is a character in his book. He permits her to record her life only on the cash register, and in so doing judges her without mercy.

We should not forget that like most of Defoe's novels this is a first-person narrative, and not just a novelistic first person. It is not a story told by an omniscient "I." The facts are limited to what a real person could actually know and then drastically narrowed by the limitation of character which that person is assumed to possess. *Robinson Crusoe, The Journal of the Plague Year, Moll Flanders, Roxana,* in every case Defoe is careful to mimic the exact accents of a real person telling what actually happened. His use of the device verges on hoax. It is this elaborate authentication of utterance more than anything else that makes the woman come alive. Moll Flanders writes about herself, we are convinced, exactly the way Moll Flanders would have written it. People are obsessive about themselves in fact. The greedy will describe their adventures in the Battle of Waterloo in terms of profit and loss. The lewd will manage to find sex in the same unlikely place. Only novelists describe battles as have Stendhal, Tolstoy or Stephen Crane.

Is *Robinson Crusoe* a realistic story? Indeed not; it is something quite different, a false document. It is convincing as a first-person narrative of a man alone against nature. It is convincing because of its extraordinary purity. All one has to do is to compare the story of Alexander Selkirk, the prototype of Robinson Crusoe. He was anything but a man of singleness of purpose and seems to have enjoyed a remarkably tempestuous subjective life. He was summoned before the kirk for indecent behavior and ran away to sea. He was put ashore on Juan Hernandez Island at his own request after a quarrel with his captain and then tried to get back but was refused. He came home to quarrel with his family and to live in a cave which he dug in the backyard. He eloped with a young girl and immediately abandoned her and lived out his days in riot amongst loose women, beset with mild delusions and occasional hallucinations. The true Alexander Selkirk realistically described would make an excellent hero for a contemporary novel. Defoe is interested in another kind of realism, the careful construction of an absolutely convincing archetype. So too with Moll Flanders. The archetype is so powerfully developed that we can sense the living woman underneath. It is this sense of vital presence peculiar to Defoe's characters which is not subject to analysis but which gives them their unique life.

If we were to accept this story as all there was to the life of a real woman we should have to call her insane, a monomaniac. Underneath the limitations of Defoe's archetypical whore, the woman who never forgets for a moment that she is sitting on a fortune, we can feel the living body of the hot, complex woman. How? Why? This is the unanswerable question to which all literary criticism comes. Because Defoe was a great writer. I suppose he knew such women thoroughly and sympathetically and so as he wrote kept before his mind always the actual woman, forcing the living flesh into the mold of his irony. If this were not true the book would be a sermon, both self-righteous and obvious.

Critics have interpreted *Moll Flanders* as a kind of fiction-alization of Tawney's criticism of capitalist morality or as an anticipation of Marx's prophetic rhetoric in the *Communist Manifesto*—the cash nexus passage. It is true that all values are reduced to price and all morality to the profitable. Love is replaced by mutually profitable contractual relationships which are worked out in actuarial detail even when they are illegal. Money is not something with which to buy sex and other sensual gratifications; on the contrary, sex is something to be bartered with shewdness for as much money as it will bring.

Defoe was not stupid. He was perfectly conscious of the parallel he was drawing between the morality of the complete whore and that of the new middle class which was rising around him, yet he remains aware of Moll Flanders, a woman of flesh and blood, and we in turn are aware of her. She comes to life in our minds as clearly as Chaucer's wife of Bath but unaided by Chaucer's loving sensuousness of delineation.

Robinson Crusoe misled many people. *Moll Flanders* is a false document, too, but it never misled anybody. I think this is because Moll is less acceptable as at once human being and achetype. The moral is harshly drawn, while we, even if it is untrue, prefer to cling to the belief that there's a little bit of good in every bad little girl. Were it not for this common human failing the business of whoring would be much less profitable. A few men prefer to go to the bed of commercial love with their eyes open but they are very, very few indeed. We want a civilized man alone at grips with obdurate nature to be like

Robinson Crusoe—there is more than a bit of Prospero in him—whereas we prefer our whores like the Lady of the Camelias or Violetta of *La Traviata,* or at least Fanny Hill.

"A middle-sized spare man of about forty years old, of a brown complexion, and dark brown colored hair, but wears a wig; a hooked nose, a sharp chin, grey eyes, and a large mole near his mouth." So the law described Defoe when it hunted him out for giving a scandalous impersonation of a High Churchman in *A Short Way with Dissenters.* He sounds foxy and he was surely a master of plausibility. For many years he was a secret agent in the ranks of the Jacobites. He was very far from a colorful one. He went patiently about his business of keeping in repair his spurious verisimilitude. He was exactly the opposite of an *agent provocateur* or cloak-and- dagger man. He shared none of the gaudy glamor of other literary secret agents of the seventeenth and eighteenth centuries. The antics of Marlowe, the Jesuits at the Caroline courts, the bawdy English playwright and spy, Mrs. Aphra Behn, St. Germaine, the man who pretended to have lived forever, were not for him. He acted perfectly the role of a cautious, temperate, Jacobite editor for years and was only unmasked toward the end of his life by events beyond his control.

For a literary man he seems to have been an extraordinarily successful businessman and promoter. We can judge this only from the difficulties he got into, but they are a measure of his talents. Anyone who could fail at the age of thirty-two, for what was then the enormous sum of 17,000 pounds, and eventually pay off his creditors and through the course of his life do things like this again and again is a man of no small commercial talent as well as being what his time would have called a most plausible projector. In addition Defoe is usually referred to as the first professional journalist of the modern type. This is not exactly true. He did not live exclusively by writing but at least he has always merited the attribution. Actually it seems to me he was much more the man of affairs who uses literature for his own purposes. The comparison that springs first to my mind is not Clarendon, Sir William Temple or Jonathan Swift, to whom, I suppose such a description could be applied, but the, at first glance, somewhat unlikely banker, economist, sociologist, founder of modern financial journalism and uniquely temperate literary critic, Walter Bagehot.

Businessmen who succeed in literature or literary men who succeed in business commonly possess virtues found less frequently amongst literary men who succeed only in literature. Courage, prudence, fortitude, equanimity, steadiness of temper and diversity of interests are some of them. Bagehot himself summed up these virtues in magnanimity, and he spoke too of the prose of the literary man of affairs as usually being distinguished by what he called animated moderation and above all else by cogency. Cogency is not just persuasiveness, it is convincingness, the result of a kind of forceful literary prudence. It is a style which comes to a writer used to surviving in a larger arena than that of literature. One of the merits of a cogent style is that it practically demands imitation. Once seen it naturally urges itself upon all who would do likewise with language.

Like Defoe, Bagehot founded no literary movements, but he is one of the main founders of the modern expository style, whether in serious journalism, scientific treatise, exploration or any other variety of sober non-fiction. Out of Bagehot and his ilk are born great sleeping masterpieces of modern prose like the article "Polar Regions" by Hugh Robert Mill and Fridtjof Nansen in the eleventh edition of the *Encyclopedia Britannica,* an example of clarity and cogency that has seldom been surpassed, but has been equalled far more often than most literary people imagine who are unfamiliar with the world of workaday expository writing. Bagehot wrote the way any Mid-Victorian cultivated gentleman wished he could talk. In the course of time a large number of Late Victorian cultivated gentlemen managed to do so. Likewise with Defoe. As we read him today he seems to us to write just like anybody and everybody else. This is what we mean when we say he is the inventor of modern English prose. To his contemporaries his style must have been a most startling revelation of the power hidden in the commonplace. Writers like this are absolutely essential to the life of the language. Without them it sickens and dies, eaten to death by orchids, plucked to pieces by ducks and gnawed into dust by termites.

1962

3.
Franz Kafka's *The Trial*

The first thing you notice, consciously or not, when you read
an author is his style. If you are sufficiently experienced and
perceptive, the initial judgment of that first impact usually
proves the correct one. What is most impressive about Kafka,
after the first page or two, is a transparent honesty, a simple
ingenuousness, an instinctive avoidance of literary artifices. He
is as direct as a good detective story or a classic Chinese novel.
So it is that his narratives, as they grow ever more extraordinary,
grow ever more convincingly real. There are hardly ever any
figures of speech, metaphors or even similies, there is no artistic
intrusion, or visible distortion. The author seems to have ab-
sented himself and left only the characters, and the reader
quickly and imperceptibly fuses with the leading character. The
experience of a Kafka fiction is as unitary as experience itself—
in fact usually more so. It is this hidden construction of the
conviction of integral experience that is the art of Kafka—the
artifice that destroys artifice.

Now this is not just a matter of style—as style never is just a matter of style, but the outward sign and garb of an inner spiritual state. Style is the vesture of the individual moral life that makes man what he is. The story may sink deeper and deeper into fantasy, outrageous incongruity, nightmare, but all is given to the reader with a cool imperturbability, in the most direct presentational immediacy. As unreality leaks into, breaks through and finally overwhelms reality, the prose of Kafka's German or the Muirs' superlative English goes quietly on saying simply, "This is the real reality. This is the way it is."

He tells it like it is, as contemporary American speech has it. And that is the whole point of Kafka. Poe, Nerval, other predecessors to whom Kafka is often compared make no such claim. No one imagines that *The Pit and the Pendulum* or *The Fall of the House of Usher* are true to life in even the most remote allegorical sense. *The Pilgrim's Progress* may be true to life even beyond allegory as a complex, integrated symbol of the history of the soul, whether Christian, pagan or atheist, but symbol it remains. *The Trial*, like *Robinson Crusoe*, is not presented as fiction, as art or artifice, but as simple fact.

The narratives of Defoe are presented not as fictions but as pseudo-documents. *Crusoe, Roxanna, Moll Flanders*, the narrator of *The Plague Year* purport to be telling their stories exactly as they happened. Taken altogether Defoe's work forms a devastating criticism of a predatory society, united only by the cash nexus, in the years of its youth. Kafka describes the same society in its final years when it is being kept alive on the continent of Europe by massive infusions of dollars and bullets. It is a world of nightmare actualized. Kafka's heroes were presumably sleeping peacefully and woke into nightmare to discover they had been arrested by the lictors of anomie or had turned into cockroaches. They never question the actuality of what is happening to them. They take it for granted that they have arrived in the world of dreams come true, more real than it was before they fell asleep.

Kafka's plots are mirror images of the folklore of central Europe, of the tales collected by the Grimm brothers—counter-*Märchen*, journeys without a goal, quests that find nothing, trials of the soul that end always in senseless failure. Historical optimists like the Marxist Grygory Lukacz, or apologists for conventional Christianity or, of course, for the great Social Lie which holds together the dominant social order, are outraged by his pessimism. "Life," cries Lukacz at the height of Stalinist terror, "is not like that. Life is real, life is earnest and the grave is not its goal. The utopia of socialist humanism is just around the corner invisible to petty bourgeois cosmopolitan decadents in Prague." Spokesmen for the other great organization of historical optimism, that is, most American critics, may go so far as to admit Kafka as a purveyor of tonic bitters bracing but only an infinitesimal aspect of a steady diet. On the other hand he has been readily assimilated to the peculiar ethics of the existentialism of despair. He himself admitted the great influence of the Danish theologian Søren Kierkegaard who constructed an ontology, a philosophy of being, from the despairing cry of Tertullian, "I believe because it is impossible." The only thing that history has so far proven to be impossible in the plots of Kafka is that men can turn into cockroaches in their sleep. All the rest time has proven to be literally true. Men are tortured to death with ingenious devices in concentration camps. Men do spend their lives in spectral cities where nothing ever goes right, struggling to appeal to an invisible but horrible comedian called Authority. Men are awakened by policemen from an extra-legal court and tried and condemned for Nothing by a judge, jury and advocates of squalid absurdity. We should never forget that, perhaps mercifully for him, Kafka was dead before what must have seemed even to him to be fantasy all came true.

Perhaps that is wrong. Did it seem to be fantasy? The details perhaps he may have thought of as symbols which he had to manage with the greatest care to make them seem objective facts in a quietly told naturalistic narrative. But the basic fact that man is a folklore hero whose journey can never get anywhere and whose prizes turn out to be practical jokes—this conclusion is obviously true. There may be a transcendent solution, an answer beyond reality, but there is none in the context.

Paul Goodman once wrote of Kafka's prayer—it is a prayer in a completely secular universe from which anthropocentric man has vanished. Today, only forty years later, we accept this more easily than people did in the years from 1900 to 1929. There are more universes than stars in our universe visible in the 200-inch telescope, most of them billions of light years away. Man unquestionably does not do what Socrates said he must do in full possession of his faculties and all the information, infallibly choose the greater over the lesser good. There are plenty of people who choose positive evil. Many of them are in positions of the greatest power. Virtue does not triumph. It is more likely to end in prison or a gas oven. Innocence is not an armor; the innocent above all others are infinitely vulnerable to a vindictiveness that avenges Nothing.

So *The Trial* to us at this date seems a perfectly natural account of something that has happened all the time all around us for over a generation. Nor does it seem any more incoherent than the natural succession of such events. It is true that it was left unfinished and that Kafka ordered Max Brod to destroy it along with the rest of his unpublished work. Brod disobeyed him and arranged the chapters as he had remembered them from Kafka's readings of the work in progress. Later, specialists in Kafka have come up with different orders of the chapters and have insisted that their proposed sequences made tremendous difference in Kafka's meaning. This isn't true. The dispute over this question is only one aspect of the ambiguity of *The Trial*. *The Trial* is about ambiguity as a principle, or lack of it, of Being itself. Whatever order of events Kafka might have decided upon if he had lived to publish the novel, the fact is that what happens to K is not order but disorder, the radical frivolity that is the meaning of meaning. There is no point in trying to ferret out what it is that K is guilty of by tracing Kafka's ideas to St. Augustine or von Hartmann. What K is guilty of is Nothing. There is no point in trying to read into the chapter "In the Cathedral" a theology of penitence and reconciliation derived from Kierkegaard. The spiritual counsels of the priest are as frivolous as everything else in the story. They are a sort of crescendo of frivolity. The priest is only the spokesman for the infinite triviality that rules existence. His last words are, "I belong to the Court so why should I make any claims upon you? The Court makes no claims upon you. It receives you when you come and it relinquishes you when you go."

So much for Religion. Love is equally ambiguous and inconsequential. Women appear incongruously, behave inexplicably, and disappear unaccountably, and K's relationship to them is the most ambiguous thing in the relationship. Is this unnatural? So do lovers, wives, mistresses, daughters in anyone's life. The coming and going of love and lovers is as frivolous as the blooming and fading of flowers and so the world's lyric poetry has said since the beginning of literature on the banks of the Euphrates and the Nile. What does it mean when someone who is perhaps Fräulein Bürstner appears briefly and walks ahead of K and his robot executioners under the street lights on the march to death? Nothing. She comes and goes unaccountably, and it is impossible to tell who she is. But it was impossible to tell who Fräulein Bürstner was in the first place, where she came from, or where she went or even what she meant to K. So with death. At the last moment the execution becomes a suicide. Perhaps if K had sprung up and denounced the imbecility of the universe which had trapped him it would have disappeared. Then where would he have been? He woke up at the beginning in the hands of the Authority of namelessness. Where would he have been if he woke at the end from that?

There is no point in criticizing Kafka for a partial view of reality. No one is under an imperative to write everything at once, much less to answer all the unanswerable questions. What *The Trial* insists upon is that within the context of rationalism or humanitarianism the questions cannot be answered. The light of the Enlightenment is only the dusky light of the Court where evil clowns swarm in their own dust, or the flickering of the street lamps on the march to death amongst the rubbish. There may be transcendent meanings that glorify that life, there may be joy that arises from being itself. Perhaps joy can be called the source of being. This is not how Kafka sees the world. If we choose to take his fictions as arguments rather than poems the arguments must be answered before we ourselves can construct any poems of life.

We should never forget that as we launch into hymns of praise like those in *Faust* or *Thus Spake Zarathustra*, two obvious sources for Kafka, that we do so from positions of special privilege like those enjoyed by Goethe and Nietzsche. Whatever its merits Günther Schuller's opera *The Visitation* is most appropriately derived from Kafka's *The Trial*. Schuller's hero is a black American, the inhabitant of a world in which the adventures of K are a commonplace. Kafka never wrote a symbolic pseudo-naturalistic narrative which would deal with the waste of value in the world of fact as experienced by an Indonesian baby dying of starvation on the mud floor of a grass hut. The Greeks demanded of philosophy that it "account for all the phenomena." No philosophy of life can ignore the phenomena presented in *The Trial*.

1956

4.

Frank Norris and the Classic Past

Until recently what the contemporary reader found most difficult about fiction like *McTeague* was the remoteness of the idiom of a too-recent past. I think the time has come when the prose, the symbolism, dialogue formulas and moral earnestness of Frank Norris have ceased to be old-fashioned and have come to adjust themselves to the classic past. This is perhaps the most outstanding characteristic of taste in time even though few critics are aware of it. Nobody would call the Impressionists old-fashioned; everyone would agree that the surrealists, the proletarians, and the American Scene Painters were very old-fashioned indeed. Sherwood Anderson sounds funny to people under fifty. Hemingway's dialogue, which once seemed excruciatingly realistic, appears as stilted as Elizabethan blank verse. In my young days I probably thought Frank Norris's prose odd and clumsy, his construction obvious. Coming back to *McTeague* after so many years, I am amazed to discover that the writing is easy and natural, the moral earnestness refreshing, and the construction masterful.

Recently a young girl of my acquaintance asked me, "Did you ever read a novel called *Belladonna* by Robert Hichens?" I said, "Yes, it was a favorite of my mother's, along with Mrs. Voynich, George Egerton and others of that kidney." "Well," said she, "I found an old copy with Gibson Girl illustrations and an embossed cover on a hotel dresser where the Gideon Bible should have been, and sat up all night reading it. I never heard of Robert Hichens but he could certainly turn out a better job of work than most contemporary American novelists." I could visualize the book clearly in what must have been a Stone and Kimball binding, the stately, tragic people in the illustrations, Pauline Fredericks in the movie, Mrs. Fiske in the play and I allowed as how she was certainly right. I think we can look forward to a period in which the late Victorian and Edwardian novels come back into their own, especially the social and naturalist ones, the "problem novels," as they called them. A man like Frank Norris had a workmanlike conscientiousness that it would be difficult to match nowadays.

When he made *Greed*, Eric von Stroheim is said to have filmed *McTeague* page by page and never missed a paragraph. We'll never know because the uncut *Greed*, greatest of all movies, is lost forever, but well he might. From the moment McTeague awakes from his Sunday nap the book marches on, page by page with a relentless photographic veracity.

This does not mean that Norris was a photographic naturalist, just an American imitator of Zola. As Matthew Josephson pointed out years ago, Zola's own naturalism was a selective process, at least as artful as a cubist painter's and was, like the work of any other great artist, a symbolic criticism of value. In this sense, Norris is certainly a disciple of Zola. His photographic naturalism depends for its effects on selection and juxtaposition as arbitrary as von Stroheim's movie of his novel, or, for that matter, as the montage of Eisenstein.

How clear and vital it is, though, this steady stream of people and objects, actions and weathers, from eighty years ago. It's a wonderful nostalgia Frank Norris shares with other writers of a bygone urban life. Today we read Sherlock Holmes, partly for Conan Doyle's whimsical irony, but at least as much for the precious portrayal of London at the end of the century. So, too,

Wells' hero in *Tono Bungay*, wandering through his troubled adolescence along the crowded gas-lit London streets.

I can remember when McTeague's Polk Street was still little changed from his day, still lit with gas, still bustling with a big city neighborhood community life, modest, shoddy and now so out of date. I have watched it go, town by town, in my own lifetime, around the world. San Francisco was like that, old downtown Manhattan where Starr Faithful lived was like that; then it survived in Liverpool or Paris, then Bordeaux or Aix-en-Provence; finally it lingered in towns like Figeac in the Auvergne and now it is gone forever. But there it is, clearer than bugs in amber, in the pages of *McTeague*. For those who are too sophisticated to be moved by his hero's tragedy, Norris's meticulous stage setting alone should make the book worthwhile.

As for the tragedy of McTeague, Norris wrote better than he knew, or at least better than he explained himself. This is hardly uncommon. Flaubert identified himself completely with Emma Bovary and thought he was writing the tale of a small-town heroine of sentiment. As we know from his correspondence, the irony got into the book, one of the most ironic novels ever written, when he went back over it to brush up the rhythms and the syntax. So with Norris. He thought he was writing a deterministic novel, the story of a man moved irresistibly by heredity and environment. You would think from his account that he had written a lightly fictionalized tract against free will. May be, but the tragedy of McTeague is the tragedy of an irresistible force, the force of McTeague's will, hubris that brought low the kings and queens of pre-historic Greece with their ivory shoulders and golden faces—and so of course the novel is truly tragic, as timeless as any tragedy and it rises above the notions of Social Darwinism and naturalism that bothered the brain of Frank Norris in his time—when he was not creating.

Naturalism and Social Darwinism—these can be just ideological notions or they can be reflections of a certain kind of human reality. Frank Norris's characters are bright and clear; it is not just that he defines them sharply, we feel that as fictional personalities they are drawn from a world of unusually distinct individuals. What gives them individuality is all outward, char-

acteristics of physiognomy, dress and behavior. They have little
interior life unlike the characters in romantic novels of lowlife.
Norris does not envisage them as frustrated for this reason. Their
tragedies are all as external and behavioristic as they are themselves. Norris was not the first nor would he be the last California
writer to see his fellow citizens this way.

Edmund Wilson years ago wrote a series of essays on the
California writers of the Thirties, Steinbeck, Saroyan, Hans Otto
Storm and others, called *The Boys in the Back Room*. He pointed
out that they all had one thing in common. Their people were
sensate. Every year two or three books of sociological journalism
appear saying the same thing about the real, not fictional, inhabitants of California. I don't know why it's so easy to take this
view of human nature in California. Most men everywhere are
far from richly endowed with the capacities for complex and
profound interior life. If anything I should imagine that the
comparative prosperity and leisure enjoyed by Californians would
make it easier for a considerable section of the population to
indulge itself in its subjectivities. I know for a fact that in the
stately homes in Los Gatos and Saratoga, California, where John
Steinbeck lived for so many years, people carried on much like
the characters in Henry James, only more so. They may have
been his neighbors, but Steinbeck ignored them and chose to
write about idle Mexicans, cannery workers and harvest hands,
whose lives were motivated by the forces which operate in the
ecology of the tidepool, a study in which he himself was a gifted
scientific amateur. So too Norris, a California aristocrat if there
ever was one, and a ranking member of a social group whose
interpersonal relations were at least as cobwebby as those por-
trayed in the last novels of Henry James.

Norris did not choose to write realistically about his friends
and associates but about the people out there, beyond his own
involvement, whom he could reduce to the discipline of a system
of artistic abstraction. So too the great masters of the tradition
in which he worked, Balzac and Zola. We think of them as
working closer to reality than the authors of *Ivanhoe* or *Daphnis
and Chloë*. As a matter of fact, this is a conventional, learned
response; we do not think of Naturalism as systematic artistic
distortion because it is, or was until recently, one of our own
popular distortions. After all the opposite case holds also—for

half a century most people thought life was like the novels of Scott or the poems of Byron. Even today most writers from south of the Mason-Dixon Line still think so.

There is, of course, an interiority to the people of *McTeague* but it functions deep below the surface of Norris's objectivism. It is what moves us and what makes the novel valuable but we arrive at it as a deduction from our own feelings. Norris judges and evaluates but he does this in terms of objective symbols, the crazy servant girl's ancestral gold plate, the Sieppe's greyhound running in his treadmill, McTeague's great gilded tooth, Trina's lottery ticket—the passport to doom that brings on all the trouble, the dead man's handcuff that snaps shut on McTeague at the very end.

These symbols form a structure of their own in the narrative. Many critics have considered them obvious and heavy-handed. I don't agree. It is difficult to see how they could be improved upon. They are intensely dramatic but they are not melodramatic, that is, they do not give a false weight to the story, attribute values to it that it cannot bear. Furthermore Norris could claim the very best precedents. *Madame Bovary* or *The Red and the Black* are chockful of just such symbols which stand as pivots of evaluation around which the narrative moves. Again, Norris's symbols are if anything less obvious than those of anti-naturalist writers like Kafka.

The tragedy of McTeague is not sentimental because it is McTeague's tragedy; it is not Frank Norris's elaborately disguised. A romantic tragedy of lowlife always suffers from the reverse of—"there, but for the grace of God"—"poor guy, if he had had a chance he would have been just like me and my friends." Norris does not hint at thwarted possibilities of sensitivity and intelligence in McTeague. Quite the opposite. Until the notice comes forbidding him to practice dentistry he is over-extended. He has more opportunities than his limited humanity can take advantage of.

Clearly defined persons in verifiable relations to one another moving visibly toward objective doom, careful attention to the architecture of the narrative, refusal of the narrator to surreptitiously involve himself in his characters—this, I suppose, is what distinguishes classic from romantic tragedy. Norris in *McTeague* is not Sophocles but he certainly produced a minor classic novel. He would never do it again. Good as they are, his other novels suffer from tendentiousness. He could never quite recapture in writing of the great and evil the even-handed magnanimity which seemed to come to him so easily and naturally telling the story of these trivial people.

It is amusing to learn that Norris was, in a sense, involved in the story of McTeague. When he was about twenty, his father remarried and he was forced to face the fact he was no longer heir to a large fortune. In the next few years, working in two widely separated fits of intense creation, he wrote *McTeague*. Most of Norris's fiction is concerned with the same subject, a person possessed of great power, either of personality or of circumstance, or both, suddenly, and usually fortuitously, loses control, at first of his environment, then of others, and finally of himself. In McTeague this paradigm is fleshed out in the simplest and starkest terms. So simple and stark are they that it is possible to misunderstand them completely. Von Stroheim called his movie *Greed*, a title that may have been wished on him by the studio. There really isn't any greed in the book. Zerkow is not greedy, he is psychotic, and Trina progressively becomes so. McTeague himself simply fails and becomes alcoholic. In every case these people are unable to retain that tiny amount of power necessary to live successfully even on their poor level.

Frank Norris is not only a California writer but a San Francisco one. Not only are his people sensate; they are not Protestants. As the words are defined by the New England conscience there is not a trace of moral conflict in the book. And although *McTeague* is the story of interlocking failures to gain or keep control, it bears no resemblance whatsoever to Melville's handling of the same theme. Melville could write a fish story and make it as ethically turgid and as rhetorically opaque as the densest pages of Kierkegaard. A century later when Hemingway comes to tell the same fish story in a capsuled illustrated weekly version, Calvin's doom and Luther's blind leap still motivate the protagonists. Frank Norris knew as little about the existential dilemma as Aristotle and cared less.

This is San Francisco speaking, a city mercifully spared the westward radiation of the great light from Plymouth Rock.

McTeague is a tragedy but it is a tragedy of *la vie Mediterranée*. Its people have no intrinsic differences with Marius, Fanny and Cesar. Aristotle's *Poetics* has required thorough-going and far-fetched interpretation before it could serve as a guide to Romantic tragedy. Those critics who have dismissed it out of hand as a plot manual for western and detective story writers are perfectly right. Most novels are romantic products and their tragedies do not result from the conflicts arising from individual contradictory applications of the *Nichomachean Ethics*. Frank Norris's novels will never be numbered amongst the hundred best books, but Aristotle would have recognized their protagonists; Kierkegaard would have passed by on the other side of the road, wagging his head.

I side with the Greek. I must confess that I don't like novels very much. I think they're a class of literature for women and men under thirty. My taste runs to Stendhal or Simenon, *The Tale of Genji* or Sherlock Holmes. It's a long time since I got worked up over the over-educated conversation of the Karamazov brothers. I read Melville only when paid. After many long years I re-read *McTeague* with pleasure and absorption. There is both an hypertrophy of the Protestant-Romantic-Existentialist novel in our time and a revolt against it. There is only one trouble with the revolt. Most of its practitioners could do with the craftsmanship of Frank Norris. It is not the craftsmanship of Ford Madox Ford or of William Carlos Williams. It isn't even the craftsmanship of Simenon. Perhaps it is carpentry, perhaps some of the carpentry is obvious, but carpentry it is and sound enough to withstand the years as an impressive structure. I think of it as very like the wooden bay-window houses and apartments of San Francisco which were built in its day, with millwork acanthus leaves over the ten-foot windows and volutes holding up the cornices and plaster cupids on the ceilings and marble or Italian-tile fireplaces. When I was young and intellectual and first came to San Francisco I thought they were comic but somehow I've always lived in such a place and live in one now. It's not an Italian villa but its builders had the same thing in mind.

1964

5.

D. H. Lawrence: The Other Face of the Coin

At the height of the San Francisco Renaissance—the first focus of the Post-War Two rejection of the war-making State, the exploitative economy of both capitalism and Bolshevism, and the system of lies which those in power pretend is the Judaeo-Christian ethic—back in those gaudy and giddy days there was a middle-aged anarchist woman who was always getting up in meetings and saying, "Comrades, why don't we reprint Kropotkin's *Appeal to Youth* and distribute it upon the campus at the University of California and San Francisco State College?" She was quite convinced that that one simple act would bring the revolution a generation nearer.

Lawrence is one of those people like Emma Goldman, Isadora Duncan, Henry Miller whom the aged persist in assuming appeal to youth. Youth have never heard of Emma Goldman or Isadora Duncan. Henry Miller makes them giggle. Lawrence, I am afraid, exasperates them. So many revolutions have been won in our century and found not worth the winning. As Paul Mattick once remarked, Hitler fulfilled the entire emergency program of the Communist Manifesto and in addition made May Day a legal holiday. Few people are prepared to face the fact that the concentration camp (not the extermination camp) represented juridically, theoretically, on paper, the most progressive penological notions. Of all the revolutions which have come home to roost, the Sexual Revolution has turned out to be the most unwieldy cuckoo of all.

It was D. H. Lawrence's great misfortune that he permitted himself to be swept up in a fugitive cause and to become the prophet and polemicist of a religion which could not, by very definition, outlive the generation which gave birth to it. What we call Victorian morality was remarkably short-lived and more honored in the breach than in the observance. Prior to the appearance of the Prince Consort, British life was the wonder of Europe for its sluttishness. Debauchery was institutionalized in the highest and the lowest places. When Lawrence started his attack on Victorian morality, Edward VII had already lived in lechery and died in ignominy. Lawrence, himself a provincial, was unaware he had been eaten by the bear, that he was beating in a door which had long since been removed from its hinges and that his novels only reflected the curious customs of Lady Ottoline Morrell's circle or the reserved banques of the Café Royale. Throughout his career he tried valiantly to etherialize what was in fact foolishness. His courage was a function of his naïveté. It is this incongruity and the ill-temper which it engendered in Lawrence and which corrupts much of what he writes that exasperates those readers who have come to maturity long after the Sexual Revolution was over.

During his residence in Taos Lawrence carried on an affair with a very beautiful and passionate woman, tubercular like himself, which for complicated, clandestine subterfuges could not be surpassed in all the annals of the small-town ministry. Nevertheless, at parties at Mabel Dodge's when everybody was full of sugarmoon and dancing around half or all naked and whooping and hooting and making like Geronimo, if anybody told an off-color joke Lawrence would turn beet red and then snow white and leave the room, speechless with rage. It is this incongruity which corrupted him as a man, as a prophet and as a stylist.

He suffered another corruption too, a literal one. If one of the major factors in the tragedy of Sinclair Lewis was pustular acne, tuberculosis was equally a factor in that of Lawrence. He was a sick man. Not only that but neither he nor his wife nor his friends would face the simple medical facts of the disease. They all acted like peasants who believe that if you refuse to admit the existence of disease, it will go away. As Lawrence lay coughing out his lungs, his family and friends persisted in saying to each other, "Well, you know, Bert always *was* bronchial." Lawrence's irritability, his revulsion for society, his sexuality, all reflect morning faintness, 4 P.M. fever and night sweats.

I'm not saying this just to be nasty. These are facts that must be coped with in a literary diagnosis of Lawrence as well as in a medical. Koch's *Bacillus* did not invalidate Lawrence as an artist any more than spirochetes invalidated Baudelaire or Nietzsche. The men were destroyed by the microörganisms. This took time to do and the ravages are manifest in their work. The poets and the philosopher survived. But they cannot be evaluated without taking those ravages into account. It is simply ignorant to talk about the philosophical significance of Nietzsche's delusions when his brain was being eaten up.

A very great deal survives in Lawrence. He is certainly one of the major poets of the twentieth century, along with Guillaume Apollinaire and William Carlos Williams. He is one of the leaders in the rejection of rhetoric and Symbolism and the return of poetry to colloquial honesty and presentational immediacy. This was one of the remarkable *bouleversements* in the history of the human sensibility. It put to rest once and for all many of the major esthetic quarrels that have dogged literature since Euripides and Sophocles, the conflict of classicism and romanticism, form and content, architecture and emotion, and fulfilled countless programs of the sort promulgated in the preface to *Lyrical Ballads* or in the Imagist Manifesto.

However, the critic whose apparatus prevents him from realizing this is going to have trouble dealing with Lawrence and is hardly the sort of person qualified to introduce his *Collected Poems*. Vivian de Sola Pinto is as whimsical a choice for such a task as Diana Trilling was for the *Viking Portable Lawrence*.

He engages in amorphous argument with a minor American academic critic of the now-forgotten Reactionary Generation, Professor R. P. Blackmur. These people were left in the ditch of the high road of literary history thirty years ago in America. Alas, alas, for England—over there they have just discovered Professor Yvor Winters in all his rigor. The rigor mortis of The Movement has moved inexorably as the glaciers from Red Brick to Oxbridge and Camford, as those venerable institutions have sunk to the same dead level of mediocrity. Under the leadership of those aging imitators of John Galsworthy, the AYM's, British writers have forgotten the very existence of the Common Market of the international intellectual community. Mr. de Sola Pinto is worried because D. H. Lawrence writes free verse and he bravely attempts to defend his new-fangledness against the traditionalist strictures of Professor Blackmur. He is under the impression that the colloquial clumsiness of his rhymed verse is not deliberate. His preface as an introduction to Lawrence for people who have never read him is completely misleading. It resembles nothing so much as an argument overheard on the sunny piazza of a Confederate Old Soldiers' Home. Nothing is to be gained by discussing Lawrence in terms of the militant provincialism and anachronism of The Movement. What we need here is a Channel tunnel.

For a stylistic introduction to Lawrence's poetry, I can think of nothing better than to reprint verbatim the students' analyses of his early poem, "Piano," from Ivor Richards' *Practical Criticism*. Lawrence was not only a consummate artist but an exquisite sensibility. He was able to weigh and measure that sensibility with amazing exactitude until fever distracted his poise; and it is only this lack of balance that injures his later poems.

Several of his poems in *Birds, Beasts and Flowers* and his death poem, "Blue Gentians," are the perfect expression of what in England was called the Imagist esthetic. They are quite the equal of anything by Apollinaire, Reverdy or William Carlos Williams. The only English poem of the period that compares with them is Ford Madox Ford's "L'Oubli, Temps de Sécheresse." Lawrence may have been sick, but poetry like this will always be a life-giving metaphor for literature, a mithridate for the young poet. For the layman it will always be a permanently memorable experience, more real than real. That, after all, is all Lawrence wanted.

There is another aspect of Lawrence that needs to be faced which is usually dodged by everyone except the more tendentious Marxist critics. Like Yeats, Stefan George, T. S. Eliot, Valéry, Unamuno, Ezra Pound, von Hoffmansthal, Lawrence was a dedicated spokesman for what Joseph Freeman thirty years ago called the fascist unconscious. Note the "f" is in lower case. Lawrence did not live to see the horrors of Nazism, but the Nibelungen *Geist* that haunted Frieda's relatives aroused in him only amused contempt, as did the more trivial popinjay antics of Mussolini's minions. Nevertheless Lawrence was anti-humane, anti-humanist and anti-humanitarian, like most of the leading poets of the international community of the first half of the twentieth century. Mistral — Marinetti — Maiakofsky — Genet — a progress from the ridiculous to the infamous. Unfortunately, Lawrence is caught in the middle of this tradition along with the greatest of his contemporaries. It is true that the exponents of humanism were frauds. In Europe they were proved so by the First War. In America, where by an historical accident the hereditary guardians of humanism were given the chance to act personally in committee their very selves, they were proven malevolent frauds by the Sacco-Vanzetti case. But this does not mean that humanism is a fraud. Nor does it excuse an anti-humane way of life. Lawrence once remarked that the beastliness of man to man increased in proportion to growth in membership in the S.P.C.A. and the perfection of painless dentistry. This is probably true, but it does not excuse Ernest Hemingway's attendance at bull fights.

This question is usually dismissed as one of the out-of-date concerns of the Thirties. It is not and some day it is going to be necessary to revaluate book by book and almost sentence by sentence the moral meaning of the leading poets of the first half of the twentieth century. Since Lawrence occupies so exposed a position in this context, he would make an excellent subject for the first chapter. The polemics of the Thirties were very far from settling the matter since both sides of the controversy were in fact militant anti-humanists, whatever they called themselves.

In America one sect of them did in fact call themselves Humanists —as of course did Zhdhanov in the last bloody hours of Stalin.

Nor is there much to say about *The Paintings of D. H. Lawrence.* I have the original book. It has become completely unobtainable and fabulously expensive. It is good to have a copy of the new edition, with more and better reproductions, that is, if you are a Lawrentian. Like most famous people, Lawrence was indulged and self-indulged. Like Henry Miller, he was persuaded that he was a painter. Painting is hard work and the business of professionals. Lawrence was not as skilled an amateur as Winston Churchill or Dwight Eisenhower—much less Estlin Cummings. He painted for relaxation, not least the relaxation of sexual tensions. His paintings are rather silly, just like the verses he wrote for such purposes. Some of them, with red naked males with Abyssinian faces and mountainous women with Brunhildian bottoms, are diagnostic *Krankenkunst,* slightly crazy fantasies of himself and Frieda. The whole book is one of those embarrassing historically important documents so vital to the history of literature but so expendable by good taste.

Finally to return to the *Collected Poems,* as a final *editio princeps* it leaves nothing to be desired. *Juvenilia* and *variora* and *dismembra rejecta,* all are here, edited, collated and printed with loving care. It is hard to see how, barring the discovery of a trunkful of unknown manuscripts, this edition will ever be superseded.

1964

6.

Ford Madox Ford

Ford loved mystification, and if he can look down from some transcendent garden in Provence and survey his whole career including his posthumous reputation, he must be very pleased with himself. There are several factors in this complicated story that have to be understood before you can make an intelligent evaluation of his reputation as distinguished from a judgment of his literary merit.

First, he was an incorrigible romancer about himself. His enemies considered him a psychopathic liar, but it's just that he found spontaneous fiction vastly entertaining, both to himself and others, and the handiest principal character was usually himself. He was full of tales about his intimate knowledge of the pre-Raphaelites and "my aunt, Christina Rossetti." Ford's mother was the daughter of Ford Madox Brown and half-sister of the wife of William Rossetti. In fact the time gap was just a little too large to have permitted such knowledge to even the most precocious infant. Ford Madox Brown was his grandfather, but his family connections with the Rossettis were rather tenuous.

This never inhibited Ford, who could hold a room full of people spellbound for an evening with the most intimate details of the pre-Raphaelite moral underground as witnessed by the infant Ford, as sophisticated as La Rochefoucauld though but in skirts. You visualized him, less than a yard in length but sporting a vast, yellow moustache and a glaucous eye, a rattle and a nursing bottle. His picture of Swinburne sitting on the floor, his scarlet locks enclosed in the celadon green velvet thighs of the Sid— Rossetti's first wife, Agnes Siddell—seated on a settle in a mullioned bay reading the Marquis de Sade in her nervous, consumptive voice and sticking the poet betimes with her embroidery needle while blonde baby Fordie looked on is a hilarious tableau no artist could paint, not even Dante Gabriel Rossetti. The fact that some intervening years made it impossible was of no moment, least of all to Ford's friends.

His stories of James, Conrad, Frank Harris, Stephen Crane, Wells, Shaw, Bennett, Belloc, were as imaginative as Frank Harris at his most outrageous. But they had the virtue of being patently false and absolutely accurate, a gift Harris, who could not make the simplest truth believable, lacked.

Americans cannot understand the peculiar boycott of Ford, H. G. Wells and D. H. Lawrence by London literary circles of the first quarter of the century even though the reason is patent upon simple inspection. All three men lived openly out of wedlock with women who were their social equals. In addition, although Ford liked to call himself a Tory or, at other times, an anarchist, depending on which would have the most stimulating effect on the company, they were all republicans. This is how to forever cease to be a clubable man.

It's all right to keep a tart in Twickenham, or, nowadays, even to invite her to partake in romps in which the whole family shares at weekends at stately homes. It is quite all right to be Prime Minister of England and a leading theologian to boot and have as mistresses three of the most aristocratic and beautiful women in England, whom one never escorts but one of whom is always in the adjacent bedroom in that stately-homed weekend. Quiet little gay pubs like the Running Footman cater for generations to titled queers only. Leading figures in government can be seen coming and going through the nail-studded portals of the exclusive flagellation brothels conspicuously located on Piccadilly Circus. The one thing that is never permitted to this day is the flagrant practice of decent free love with partners whom everybody knows socially.

Ford managed to spin around his relationships cobwebs of mystification that were masterpieces even for him. Whatever the relationships, they got him ostracized and he found it more pleasant to live abroad. Establishment-provoked sarcasm helps to explain the special temper with which Ford approached both the art of fiction and the art of life. His very syntax is saturated with irony and so too the casual encounters of his life. Hemingway, as is well known, virulently hated everybody who had ever done anything for him in his youth. It is hard to believe that even he, with his elephant-gun sensibility, never realized that he was being made a fool of by Ford in the story he tells in *A Moveable Feast*.

Ford's talent for confabulation and benign sarcasm has led to him being doubted when he told the truth, especially when the truth is more astonishing than his many fictions. There is certainly no question of his great influence on Conrad. The novels in which his name shares the title page are quite sufficient evidence. Under his tutelage Conrad's novels acquired a profundity of motivation and a complexity of architecture which changed him from a deep Kipling to a peer of Flaubert and Turgeniev. What the Englishman Ford did was to cut Conrad loose from the tradition of late Victorian fiction and link him onto the long train of continental fiction with its acute and constant awareness of the crisis of man, the revolution of the human sensibility and the religion of the integrity of the esthetic conscience. Not only that, he took a writer twice removed from his native language—the early Conrad wrote as though he had learned French in Poland and then English in France—and helped him to become one of the three or four subtle English stylists of the first quarter of the century.

There are other aspects of Ford's extraordinary life—his career as one of the most creative editors of all time, the strange trip to Germany, the changing of his name from Ford Madox Hueffer to Ford Madox Ford, for instance—which I don't wish to go into. They have been discussed exhaustively in any number

of books. More books than I can number, for hard as it may
be to believe, Fordie, like Léon-Paul Fargue whom he greatly
resembled, called the last of the bohemians, has become the
darling of academia. Hardly a year goes by that an overblown
doctor's thesis on Ford's novels emanating from a cornbelt college is not uttered in print.

Like those of Wells and Lawrence, Ford's best novels are
concerned with the struggle to achieve, and the tragic failure of,
sacramental marriage. *The Good Soldier* is probably the best of
all the novels on this subject which so tortured the Edwardians.
Parade's End, as the four Teitjen's novels are now called, is
about the same subject. It has the additional merit of being the
best "anti-war novel" provoked by the First World War in any
language. The reason I suppose is that the two moral tragedies
are presented as aspects of one another. In *Parade's End* a
vision, as vast and as minute as that of Dante, emerges of the
First World War as the gigantic, proliferating hell of the lovelost
—known to itself as Western European culture.

All sorts of people have written books about Ford—geniuses,
pipsqueaks and personal friends. None of them talks very much
if at all about his poetry and nobody has given proper consideration to his last poems. Perhaps this is due to the fact that
they are very difficult to obtain. They are the final section of the
final edition of his *Collected Poems* published by Oxford in 1936.
He calls this section "Buckshee" and explains that this is a British
Army word which signifies something unexpected, unearned—
gratifying. They are possibly the most remarkable love poems of
middle-aged love in the language. Ford grown old, although he
wasn't really all that old, in his *mas* on a hill in Provence,
looking out over that old, worn-out sea, with his young wife
painting under the fig tree, is haunted by marriage come so late
that it comes as a ghostly presence. It is typical of Ford that
when poets like Pound and Eliot were writing self-conscious
philosophical reveries full of indigestible learning, and strictly
avoiding the slightest hint of self-revelation, and never under any
circumstances using the first-person singular pronoun, and so
shamelessly revealing themselves as naïve, unformed and hopelessly vulnerable, Ford should have sat himself down amongst
the fruits and vegetables withering in the heat and written his

philosophic epic about what was before his eyes and about himself, so simply in his bedroom slippers, and so achieved a profundity and an integrity and an invulnerability to the abuse of
fate which is not to be found in the *Cantos* or *The Waste Land.*

It is not only Ford's objectivism that counts, although certainly "Buckshee," along with a few poems of D. H. Lawrence's
Birds, Beats and Flowers, is the high point of British Imagism.
A lifetime's training, daily practice of his scales, had given Ford
the ability to relax and improvise the most poignant and searching music. F. S. Flint, Harold Monro, D. H. Lawrence, Herbert
Read, are the only other successful English practitioners of what
the French call, since Vielé-Griffin, *vers libre,* a very different
thing from American free verse, which they all wrote as well.
Flint's poetry is very touching, especially his last poem, where
he bids farewell to literature forever. He is still the best translator of the Heroic Age of French modernism, but he is by no
means as skillful a poet as the other three.

Harold Monro is a very skillful poet indeed, and a Little
Master of profound intimacy. Fashion has moved so far from
him that it has never been possible to revive any interest in his
poetry, although his influence upon Lawrence, Ford and Herbert
Read is obvious and pronounced. Lawrence is once again fashionable and everybody is familiar with the subtle modulations
of "Bat" or "The Lion of St. Mark" and the intimacy of "Piano"
and "Hymn to Priapus." Ford is less muted than Monro and
less strident than Lawrence. The rhythms of "L'Oubli, Temps
de Sécheresse" twist and untwist, and rhyme and assonance chime
and counterchime, quietly, subtly, and yet with a gripping intensity that is a perfect expression of the sadness of love found
late.

Ford liked to point out that Dostoievsky was guilty of the
worst possible taste in making his characters discuss explicitly
the profundity of the very novel in which they were taking part.
Ford's Ivan and Alyosha would talk only about the quality of
the cherry jam and thereby reveal gulfs unknown to that gam-
bling and cadging Russian, gulfs known only to gentlemen. And
so with "Buckshee." It is a tragic story, tragic in the sense that all
life is fundamentally tragic, of love fulfilled. He doesn't talk

about it, yet Ford conveys its reality with the most innocent candor.

Down the years I have read "Buckshee" to many audiences. A tape of my reading was a perennial favorite on KPFA — WBAI — KPFK radios until one day it got erased by accident. I have read it to music—a kind of quiet Pacific Jazz with echoes of Satie's "Gymnopedie # I." It has never failed to stimulate very considerable interest, for it is certainly the finest ignored poem sequence in modern English, and people always ask where they can obtain it, and poets go to the library and copy it out. It is now finally back in print.

1968

7.

Tenth Street on the Grand Tour

During the past winter two shows of American painting organized by the Museum of Modern Art have been travelling about Europe. One, "The New American Painting," opens in New York on May 28, 1959, and runs through the summer. It is a representative selection, some four or five pictures each, of William Baziotes, James Brooks, Sam Francis, Arshile Gorky, Adolph Gottlieb, Philip Guston, Grace Hartigan, Franz Kline, Willem De Kooning, Robert Motherwell, Barnett Newman, Jackson Pollock, Mark Rothko, Theodoros Stamos, Clyfford Still, Bradley Walker Tomlin and Jack Tworkov.

In Europe at the same time was a large—some 29 (or 33?) pictures—one-man show of Jackson Pollock. In Basel, Berlin and Paris the two exhibitions were shown together. In Amsterdam and London the New American Painting followed the Pollock show. In three cities—Milan, Madrid, and Brussels—the Pollock exhibition was not shown at all.

This is the first chance most Europeans have had to see this aspect of American painting. Most other shows have taken in the whole range of contemporary and not so contemporary styles, from Grant Wood to Clyfford Still, and so have been, to strangers certainly, confusing rather than informative. Most informed people in America would consider this selection, give or take a few names, truly representative of the most important recent tendencies in our painting. And certainly it is amongst these painters that the first American "movement" to exert a powerful, world-wide influence was generated.

How did Europe react? On the visible official surface, that is, how did the critics react? Beneath the surface, what was the real reaction? How did the artists, the people one knows—how did the people the show was for respond? By and large, as might be expected, the two levels had little in common.

Newspaper art critics prepare themselves for their careers by memorizing a collection of acceptable stereotypes. This works just fine, year after year after year. Who will dispute that Cézanne is powerful, Van Gogh is forceful, Picasso is inventive, Vermeer is lucid, Tintoretto is noble? By judicious extrapolation you can keep pretty well up to date—three paragraphs of Cézanne, one paragraph of Van Gogh, one paragraph of Ryder, apply to Marsden Hartley and rub well. Once in a great while something comes along that can't be handled by stereotyped response and then all breaks down in confusion. It is just a simple fact that most journalists over the world are quite incapable of looking at pictures, and seeing paint and canvas and not preconceptions.

The press reception of "The New American Painting" and the big Pollock retrospective show by most European newspaper critics was, by and large, a parade of busted clichés and demoralized preconceptions. The majority didn't, apparently, bother to go to the show (or shows, since sometimes the two collections were shown together, sometimes separately). They just went to the newspaper morgue and had the librarian fish out the press notices of Buffalo Bill's first European tour, and went to work with scissors and paste. Even those who did go somehow got hold of the wrong catalog and were under the impression the pictures were painted by Wyatt Earp and Al Capone and Bix Beiderbeck. This is a generalization. It isn't altogether true, but it is certainly the first impression you'd get from reading the ten-dollar airmail stack of clippings sent to me by the Museum of Modern Art. Two nights spent struggling through artistical journalese in six languages and you're in complete agreement with George Washington—"America has nothing to gain from European entanglements."

There were exceptions and there was a definite pattern in the exceptions. Those countries which are too small to even dream of competing with America politically and economically were, to judge from their press, most receptive. Not only were most of the Swiss, Belgians and Dutch receptive, some of them were very astute. A Belgian said wryly that Sam Francis should be the most popular because he is so perfectly in the French taste. A Swiss said that Grace Hartigan would be liked because critics can pretend to like her "abstractly" while really approving of her because she is mildly "figurative." A Dutchman said that it would be a mistake to think of De Kooning as a missionary of European Expressionism in uncultured America just because he once lived in the Netherlands. Another said flatly that we must never forget that it is America that first appreciated the masters of modern art, and that painters like Kandinsky, Picabia, Klee had a great influence on American painting before they were known outside of small circles in their own countries. Again, a Dutchman: "These painters have been criticized because they make a great deal of money. Is it a fault in the Americans that they pay their artists well, that most modern European painting is now in America, and that the Americans are slowly buying up all the so-called Art Treasures of Europe? Is this a fault? If it is, all we have to do to overcome it is go and do likewise." This may not be art criticism of the highest order, but it is certainly an astute observation.

Vulgarity is international. We expect the lower British gutter press to make bad jokes, run solemn features under the byline of newspaper "psychiatrists" and generally behave in a rowdy (what they would call "American") manner. Still, it's a bit of a shock to find an apparently civilized man in Lausanne saying, "One turns away from this violence, fraud and depravity to stand in reverence before the *Angélus* of Millet." Honest, the man said that.

On the other hand, thinking back over the long struggle that modern art of every variety has had in Great Britain, it is more surprising to discover that the best-tempered and most judicious reviews were in the better English papers. However, these very reviews did reveal one thing. By chance of location, the Tate, a most perfect and perfectly valid comparison, lay right to hand, but nobody used it. Housed in the same building as the great abstract Turners, the show never once elicited the comment that Turner was the artist who, of all British painters, was an ancestor of this show. The old imaginary gulf between *"moderne"* and *"passéiste"* art still seems to act as an effective barrier in England.

If this was true in London, it was far more true everywhere else. With the exception of a few scholarly art historians, mostly German or German-trained, everybody accepted these pictures as either utter novelties, subversive of all tradition whatsoever, or as just amateur provincial imitations of their own painting of years gone by—École de Paris, or Expressionism, or Futurism, depending on the nationality of the critic.

The French, as might be expected, were by far the worst. It is an embarrassing task to review the French press on any subject involving America. In France the words "United States" do not mean a country—they mean an extremely disagreeable reaction pattern common to almost all Frenchmen, a purely subjective phenomenon. The vulgar press was just vulgar, like the British, but it is always a little startling to see the ravings of the *American Weekly* of the nineteen-twenties about lunatic modernist painting, or, still worse, the *pompiers* of American charlatans financed by the Guggenheim billions, translated into the French language. Most of the criticism was entirely political, and had nothing to do with any kind of painting. Even civilized papers like *L'Express* and *Combat* had their men bone up by going to a Western movie and reading some of the more inflammatory recent statements of American generals. They may have read the catalogs, too, but there is little evidence they entered the galleries. They agreed that these Americans, like all other Americans, were dangerous and ignorant barbarians, redskins, in fact. On the other hand, the critics of the "official" Left were singularly open-minded and judicious. One of the most intelligent reviews was in Aragon's *Les Lettres Françaises.*

The reason may be that it is Be Kind to Americans Week in the Kremlin, but still it must be admitted that here was a man who had considerable intelligence and insight when he was permitted to exercise it. The review ended, "Fine. But this is only a beginning which has itself already come to an end. What next?" Since this is exactly what the boys themselves are saying along Tenth Street, it is hard to quarrel with it. The best French reviews by far were in *Le Monde* and *France Observateur,* representing the moderate Right and the Independent Left, respectively. Both critics pointed out that although the paintings were truly American, their sources were in the whole European tradition, but most especially, amongst modern painters, in Expressionism, Klee, Matisse and the organic surrealism of André Masson and the whimsical forms of Miro. The critic for *France Observateur* made the specific comment that these American painters were amongst the founders of a new international style and ended his article: "Jean Cassou in their behalf speaks of waterfalls and fields. In Soulages it is the forest. Truly all these works discover a new Nature. Abstract painting? No. Natural painting."

The French, however, even the best intentioned of them, like the English, did insist on always talking as though these painters were quite novel, with no roots in the older past. No one mentioned Guston's connections with Monet and Turner. No one noticed the influence of Tintoretto or Delacroix. This sort of comparison appeared only in the culture area of German art history, except for Italy, where of course painting like this is almost as old and well established—academic, if you will—as in the States. It is my opinion that *Le Monde, France Observateur,* and *Les Lettres Françaises* represented real opinions of the bulk of the educated visitors to the shows, Left, Right and Left-Center. Almost all other criticism was simply a workout of the given paper's editorial policy vis-à-vis the State Department, Standard Oil, Coca-Cola, and rock 'n roll. "The subversive and dangerous plot of a barbarous and immature people." Indeed!

So much for the press. What did all this expensive wordage in six different languages mean? Practically nothing. It simply reflected what a hundred or so newspaper men and/or their editors felt about America and sometimes about some paintings.

But, as is well known, newspaper men are picture-blind unless the pictures are taken with flashbulbs. The artists and the people who look at pictures, how did they respond?

The *France Observateur* man was right. Most artists are quite well aware that one of the major contemporary international styles started in America with some of these painters. In 1949 I exhibited a small showing of pastels in this idiom in Paris. Plenty of French painters came, but with few exceptions they all obviously thought the pictures were frauds, not bad, but actual jokes on the public. It was quite apparent on their faces and in their kind remarks. Ten years later, during the time the shows were in Paris, there was an abstract show in Aix-en-Provence, where we were living, and the oldest painter there, Engel-Pak, a man about Picasso's age, was very obviously influenced by Rothko. That same month a friend of mine who works on Cahiers de Sud and the newspaper *Le Provençal* came back from a journalistic stint in Central Africa with three "abstract expressionist" paintings done by a young black student at a Brazzaville *lycée*—a painter who had never been out of Africa. Except for their slightly tropical color sense, they might well have been done in the California School of Fine Arts.

Older painters like André Masson are proud of their influence on this American painting. Masson has been accused of boasting, but he is perfectly right. In 1929 my first wife and I were both conscientious compass-and-ruler painters and the appearance of the first Massons with their spontaneous, organic line had a tremendous effect on us and on all our contemporaries. Masson himself, of course, started out as one of the most rigorous cubists—(and a painter of birds, like Morris Graves!). So he knows how hard the break was. Most older painters and most older serious critics, like Waldemar George, are still monogamously wedded to the cubist tradition and find it very difficult to see anything else. If a picture doesn't look like Poussin and Raphael, it just isn't there, or worse, it is totally re-seen, not just reinterpreted, in terms of early twentieth-century classical, architectural painting.

Nobody except journalists talked about Primitive Energy and Fantastic Vitality. The people you knew seemed all to have actually looked at the paintings. In fact, a considerable number of them travelled to Bâle to see the show the first week it opened in Europe. Pollock, whose thirty-three large paintings were hung apart from the rest, towered in prestige. Most European painters have seen a Pollock or two and a lot of reproductions. His own statements, and the sometimes unfortunate praise he has received, had prepared people for a combination James Dean, Davy Crockett and Jack Kerouac. Pollock they discovered, in his completely achieved later paintings, to be a very quiet, very lyrical sensibility, one of the least violent painters who ever lived. It is remarkable how quickly intelligent people faced with the record of his accomplishment (with, incidentally, plenty of storm and stress visible in the early paintings on the way to the final goal) made an immediate adjustment and took the paintings on their merits, not on their propaganda. It was a little like dropping in to hear Eddie Condon and discovering you are listening to Charles Mingus, but almost everybody managed the readjustment. I think, in fact, that this was the biggest achievement of the show or shows. They demonstrated once and for all, to people who are not picture-blind, that these painters are precisely the opposite of what their newspaper critics—and for that matter, sometimes their own anti-verbal selves—say they are. I for one don't think it is wise to fill catalogs with "statements" by painters. No painter, not even Bougeareau, or da Vinci, or Marcel Duchamp, has ever been able to say what he was about. It just gives ammunition to the worst idiots of the press.

Pollock, De Kooning, Hartigan, Guston, Rothko, Gorky—all these painters have some obvious link with "the European Tradition," if not with the specifically cubist-Classical one, as Kline has with China and Japan. Everybody with any sense managed to *see* them. But Clyfford Still, who didn't bother to furnish a "statement" (the catalog quoted some remarks from long ago) or even a photograph of himself—Still was another matter. People came up to his vast pictures very quietly, and toppled over into them without a murmur and came out with nothing to say. It was all very still. It was really wonderful to relive the first years of his reception in California, where now, alas, the Still Style has become a mass-produced academic cliché.

I should say that we can expect a lot of echoes of his painting to crop up in Europe in the next year.

Everybody knows that from Barcelona to Warsaw, maybe even Moscow, in spite of all the billions spent by the American government to lose friends and influence people, the most powerful American influences are modern jazz and these very painters. "Everybody knows" that these paintings were the beginnings of a new way of seeing things; as the man said, a new natural painting of Nature. Huge pictures into which you can walk like Alice, marshalled on wall after wall—and so quiet.

It was the sense of achievement which impressed many European painters. To quote from a letter from Edwina and Barney Rubenstein, two painters in the same general tradition, from Boston (the home, as somebody in Switzerland pointed out in attacking the show, of "the great American school of Bitter Realism") but now permanently resident near us in Aix-en-Provence:

"The sour note was struck by a not-too-young French painter who remarked that while it was good to see what had been done during a powerful creative period, one felt that it was as much finished as Paris, in exactly the same sense. Not that no more painting could or would be done, merely that the thing had 'set,' the mold was formed with its own concurrent corruptions and repetitions, its own academy and hierarchy. He could not understand how all this stuff got to be hanging on the walls of a museum, catalogued and labelled Great Art for all the world to see. What we see here on the wall, is it still happening, or have we been invited to a funeral?"

Since these are exactly my own sentiments, and those of the people with whom I talked about the show in Aix, and of similar Catalan painter friends in Barcelona, and of people I talked to in London and here in Italy, and of everybody in North Beach, and of everybody I ever talked to about it in the Five Spot, I would say that, discounting the expected nonsense in the press, Tenth Street had been well and intelligently assimilated by Europe.

1959

8.
The Mirror
of Magic

The literature of magic is extremely controversial. The very definition of the word is subject to endless dispute. *The Mirror of Magic* by Kurt Seligman, and *Magic* by Hutton Webster, are two books which ignore this situation, which means ignoring quite a bit. Professor Webster is well aware of the controversy, and his book is definitely a part of it, but he simply presents his material and allows it to speak for itself. Kurt Seligman's book should have been called *The Mirror of the Occult*. It is a popular picture book, with chapters on Gnosticism, alchemy, Kabbalah, Rosicrucianism, Freemasonry, various other matters which are not magic in any accepted sense.

Although controversial and critical handling of the material probably has no place in a popular, bookstore table sort of book, there are many places where Seligman seems to be unaware of the literature of the subject. (His bibliography, though fairly extensive, is extremely spotty and erratic.) For instance, A. E. Waite points out the patent flaws in every "authenticated" story of transmutation of baser metal into gold, and the Nicholas Flammel myth has long since been exploded. No one has ever been able to demonstrate that the Rosicrucian Brotherhood ever existed, nor, on the other hand, that Descartes, Bacon, dozens of other Renaissance illuminati did not belong to it. The equation of Gnosticism with Manichaeanism is shocking but forgivable. It has recently become a fashionable error. Denis de Rougemont wrote a most influential book on love and Western man which is built entirely on this misconception. Martin D'Arcy, S. J., in his recent digest of fashionable reading, *The Mind and Heart of Love*, does the same thing. He, at least, had a course in patristics and should know better. Gnosticism is a system of emanational monism; Manichaeanism is sharply dualistic. One was ritualistic and probably often antinomian, the other was extremely puritanical—and so on. Seligman lumps together all the interpretations of witchcraft. It is possible that, at different times and places, it was descended from Roman or folk witchcraft, was a survival of pagan religion, was Christian heresy, but these are three distinct things, and it would be better if this had been made clearer. Statements like "Plotinus' view of the world was fundamentally magical" are just due to philosophical unsophistication. Better say Aristotle, whose *dynamis*, in earlier Greek, meant exactly occult power—mana. The Lévy-Bruhl heresy, that "natives" think somehow fundamentally differently, with less distinction of subject and object, from white Europeans, is uttterly discredited. This silly idea, which could only occur to French anthopologists who had never been further afield than the terrasse of a Montparnasse café, is repeated as gospel by Seligman. After all, he has lived in the U.S. for some time, and with his interests, must have gone out of his way to avoid the work of Boas and his followers who laid this chauvinistic myth to sleep long ago. The Nietzschean division of Greek thought and art into Apollonian and Dionysian is fruitful if not overworked. But there is no sharp line separating the mystery religions from the Olympian pantheon and the civic cults. The worship of Apollo was orgiastic and "mysterious" too in many places, all over the Greek world.

However, *The Mirror of Magic* is worth having. It is excellently illustrated with some scarce and beautiful, and sometimes extraordinarily profound pictures. The jacket introduces Seligman as a well-known surrealist painter. One does not look for judiciousness *chez Breton*, but, except for errors of special scholarship such as I have mentioned, he writes with great circumspection in a field beset with thousands of booby traps. There is nothing about the Holy Grail being a Gnostic Mass, none of the cracked mythology of Freemasonry, no echoes of the jabberwocky of Eliphas Levi and his friends who made up occult traditions to suit themselves. Even the question of spiritual alchemy is handled with great caution. Some of the material seems to have been inserted because Seligman had some nice pictures he wanted reproduced, for example the chapter on the Jansenist cures at St. Médard, which has nothing to do with magic, but which is accompanied by a handsome engraving. The final editions of A. E. Waite's books on alchemy, magic, Rosicrucianism, Holy Grail, Freemasonry, Kabbalah, Tarot cards, are better, but Seligman does not suffer from Waite's occult crochet of pretending to be disproving what he is actually trying to prove, and has not written in Waite's godawful High Church prose, full of clinking thuribles and swishing acolytes. Then too, Waite is unobtainable and in many volumes. I should say that this is about as good a one-volume compendium of the non-Oriental occult prior to the twentieth century as can be found, and it certainly has plenty of pretty pictures.

Hutton Webster's book is totally different. It is an elaborately documented anthropological study of the magic of pre-literate peoples. Magic is fairly defined as "the recognition of an occult power, impersonal, or only vaguely personal, mystically dangerous and not lightly to be approached, but capable of being channeled, controlled and directed by man. As a practice, magic is the utilization of this power for public or private ends, which are good or bad, orthodox or heterodox, licit or illicit, according to the estimate placed upon them by a particular society at a particular time. Magical rites are classified as divinatory, productive or adversive in character." This is about as good a definition as has ever been given. Hutton is a strict interpretationist. He even calls Frazer "an adherent of the animistic hypothesis"! There is nothing of the Lévy-Bruhl fallacy. However, there are many signs of an even worse bias, that magic is somehow more degraded activity than the science of civilized man.

He says, "Magic must rank among the greatest of man's delusions. In the presence of the unknown and disconcerting the
magician does not investigate critically, but is content with any
explanation which appeals to his imagination. He builds an airy
fabric of fancy and discovers in the external world sequences
of cause and effect which are non-existent. He thinks that he
understands them, and, self-reliant and imperturbably, would
turn them to his own benefit. Thus an element of the capricious
and incalculable enters into all his activities. Considered in the
large, magical beliefs had operated to discourage intellectual
acquisitiveness, to nourish vain hopes that can never be realized,
and to substitute unreal for real achievement in the natural
world. Between the methods of magic and of science, how impressive a contrast. The choice of the one or the other has long
confronted humanity." I have quoted at length because, oddly
enough, this could all be applied so aptly to those busy little
fellows of the Manhattan Project with the change of a few words
—mathematics for imagination in the second sentence, moral
for external in the next, scientific for magical throughout, responsibility for intellectual acquisitiveness, and moral or spiritual
for natural in the third sentence from the end.

Webster does give a brief tribute to the psychologically help-
ful aspects of magic, but these are conceived entirely in terms
of placebos, giving confidence in difficulty and aiding in preserving the social cohesion of native custom. He shows no awareness
of the integrative power of socially acceptable and largely "verifiable" paranoias. There is a chapter on the making of a
magician, but again, there is little on the significance of the
phenomena of trance and possession, nothing on the nature of
paranoid belief, nothing on the function of the insane in society.

Neither book touches on modern occultism and magic. The
school of ingenious charlatans descended from Eliphas Levi are
really very engaging, and it is a pity that Seligman ignores them.
Sar Peladan, for instance, called himself Bar Merdoach, and
claimed to be an avatar of the Babylonian god. He also had a
most fetching theory that the major plays of Shakespeare were
cryptic portrayals of the rituals and teachings of the "Universal
Mystery Religion." There is nothing on the magic and occultism
of civilized China and India and Japan. This is a pity, because

there are to be found the answers to a lot of much mooted questions. Thus, the very existence of "spiritual alchemy" is hotly debated, that is, whether the chemical language of many alchemical treatises was not a sort of code for the description of mystical states and the techniques for arriving at them. Any acquaintance with Indian or Chinese alchemy would solve this problem immediately. For instance, any edition of Pao P'u Tzu (the fourth-century founder of the mixture of alchemy, magic, mysticism, superstition and popular cults which goes by the name of modern Taoism) contains illustrations of the human figure in the well-known yogi postures, and with the alchemical retort, furnace bellows and other apparatus drawn in the place of the major autonomic networks. The translation of yoga, neurological gymnastics, into alchemical terms is explained in careful detail. The illustrations in the Jung-Wilhelm "Secret of the Golden Flower" are taken from a pamphlet circulated by a debased, synchretistic slum religion which resembles in its social role of a combination of the I Ams, the Trotskyites, the Jehovah's Witnesses and the raw food addicts. Originally they were part of the sequence of illustrations for Pao P'u Tzu, and were misunderstood by the Golden Flower Secret Society. It is remarkable how much Jung was able to make of them, considering the material he had to work with. Unfortunately, the specifically alchemical illustrations were not used and Jung is apparently unaware how close he came to substantiation of his own theories of the psychological significance of alchemy. Again, although Plotinus certainly had anything but a magical conception of life, modern Indian Tantrism, and to a lesser degree, Lamaistic and Shingon Buddhism do so have. The Indian literature is immense, greatly detailed, and sometimes very sophisticated. Much of it is readily available in the writings of Sir John Woodroffe and the publications of his Tantric Text Society. Curiously enough, the substance of such a philosophy is far removed from what in the West we know as idealism, spiritualism, mysticism. It resembles most, in the words of Sir Charles Eliot, in *Hinduism and Buddhism*, the deserted mansions of Herbert Spencer.

Neither book makes any attempt to reveal any mysteries, to divulge any secrets. As far as Seligman is concerned, this is a definite lack and gives the book an air of unreality characteristic of most literature of this kind. What is occult in the occult, mysterious in the mystery religions is really pretty obvious. It is erotic mysticism of one sort or another. If one reads Pao P'u Tzu (briefed by Father Weiger), Pseudo-Flammel (briefed in Waite), Christian Rosycross (in Waite), Thomas Vaughan, in order, it is not difficult to see what is going on. The methods of achieving the trance state, especially the manipulation of breathing and sexual techniques, and the stages and nature of the trance are actually the "occult" subject of discussion. This, following the "law" of the correspondence of the macrocosm and microcosm, is, in turn, developed into a cosmology and cosmogony and physics.

This brings me to the significance of magic for poetry, for the arts in general. Mr. Seligman seems to have the idea that it is important, certainly his associates amongst the Poissons Solubles never tire of talking about it, and it is a widespread if vaguely held notion amongst modern artists generally.

There are two aspects of magic—its philosophy and its symbolical world, the picture it draws. The aim of magic is no different from that of science, the coercion of nature. Science believes that results can be achieved by the manipulation of a manifold of physical forces which obeys certain mathematical laws, in other words, its ultimate principle of coherence is logical-rational. Magic assumes a world of usable forces, too, but they are thought of in terms of their emotional weight, the principle of cohesion is aesthetic, in the technical sense. Fundamental to both are the concepts of uniformity and necessity. If the conditions are all fulfilled, the spell has been said properly, the gestures and drawings are correct, the results must follow. The disposition of the practitioner and the demons or deities, if any, or the impersonal power, Shakti, mana, orenda, te, makes no difference—to the results sought. Magic, however, recognizes that very grave consequences may ensue to the inadequately prepared or immoral magician. Mr. Oppenheimer and his pals, on the other hand, have been taught by the logical positivists that science is "value neuter."

In this sense, magic is a more respectable philosophy of nature than science. Nature, obviously, when tinkered with, does not give value-neuter results. Science, like magic, is a responsible activity. The atomic scientists are just as guilty of murder as if they had gone through the streets of Hiroshima and Nagasaki and stabbed to death that many women and children with their own hands. The moral effects of raising the devil are well known and demonstrable. Similarly, the unprepared and irresponsible practice of "Spiritual Alchemy," any of the more advanced forms of nervous system gymnastics, is fraught with the gravest peril. It killed Thomas Vaughan. The Indians and Chinese say that the being—the "child" of the alchemists—the achievement of extrapersonalization—will, if the trance has been entered upon unworthily, turn into a demon and destroy the practitioner. Nevertheless, magic separates itself sharply from religion, except "occult," gnostic religion, by believing that the ultimate spiritual good is a kind of knowledge, and that it can be achieved by manipulation.

The idea that good can come from monkeying with the machinery is an extremely common aesthetic heresy. Because the existence of irrational proportions (notably the Golden Section) can be demonstrated in the relationships of the guide lines of most artistic masterpieces, many have fancied that similar masterpieces need only a rule and compass and the "secret" for their construction. It is not the Golden Section that made the Parthenon beautiful, it was Phidias. Similarly, poets have believed that it is possible to discover a master recipe for poetry. In the case of Poe, this delusion is pathetic. Poe is like the magician, ill-informed, self-deluded, and full of charlatan dodges when pinned down. However, the Cambridge set of a generation ago, I. A. Richards, William Empson and their friends, believed that they were really scientific, and were dealing only with demonstrable causes and effects. Their naïve heresy, dead now several years in its homeland, but still all the rage in U.S. academic circles, has been responsible for some of the most dreadful verse ever written and has all but emasculated contemporary poetry. The sort of stuff you see in the *Partisan* and *Kenyon Reviews* is magic—manipulation of an imaginary, impersonal, value-neuter force. R. P. Blackmur and Elizabeth Bishop differ very little from a poet they both doubtless find distressing, Maxwell Bodenheim. All three believe that poetry is impersonal invention, artifice. Today, nobody except other English Assistants reads "straight" American poetry, and small wonder. It has become a craft of sterile gadgetting, perpetual-motion machines that don't move at all.

In the symbolical world of magic and the occult of value, are the surrealists right, are there perspectives more deeply penetrating here than can be found in the orthodox, scientific world? Yes and no. Doubtless an artist should know all the possible resources of his craft if he finds it convenient so to do. The poet should know quite a bit about how the human mind works, just as he should know about linguistics and phonology. Also, no artist can function in the realm of the purely rational, he must have some source of contact with the lower centers, even if it is, as in Valéry or Mondriaan, the delusion of utter rationality. The forebrain is not enough, even a forebrain with accessories from Cambridge.

Into the gap between technology and environment, a black and fearsome chasm, man pours himself. Ultimately this means his unconscious, the way his lower nervous centers work when the forebrain cannot control matters. It is because all men are pretty much alike in the region of the navel that this unconscious is collective. The bricks with which men construct a causeway into the unmanageable never change in substance, however much they may in pattern and shape. The human mind functions, when it functions from its base, in terms of a limited number of great archetypes. By this I do not mean to evoke the doctrine of any particular modern psychologist. The symbolic dictionaries of the schools of psychoanalysis do not depart very far from the dream books of the ancient Greeks or the paperbacked ones that are sold in cheap bookshops, or from the symbols of the Tarot cards or the figures of mythology. The divergence may be wide, but it is divergence in a circumscribed area, along a limited pattern of lines. Anyone who sets out to operate on the human mind will obviously be better off for knowing and being in vital contact with his material. Especially is this true of anyone who plans to attack such vital spots as are the specialty of poetry. This does not mean, again, that this knowledge, any more than any other, is an infallible tool, a charm book from which results must necessarily flow. This was the heresy of the surrealists. They used the unconscious as a sort of Bisquick, a patent flour from which masterpieces could be cooked without trouble. That is just the trouble with the unconscious, it is collective; down there we are all alike, we have heard it all before. So, unless you are a rich, vapid and idle woman without anything down there yourself, surrealism is deadly dull. Nothing happens.

Finally, artistic expression is grounded in the person, the irreducible source of responsibility and communication. Out of the dynamic necessities of this self, for communion, for responsibility, flows the living speech that is poetry. Everything else is cookery.

1948

9.

William Golding: Unoriginal Sin

About the last writer in the world it would ever occur to me to read is William Golding, so before I start this little essay I want to make it very clear indeed precisely where I stand. Many years ago my friend Dwight Macdonald wrote a book about Henry Wallace and everybody said, "Poor Dwight, he takes it all so seriously—it just goes to show that he's jealous—he wishes he was Henry Wallace." Later he wrote a devastating essay on James Gould Cozzens and everybody said Dwight wished he was James Gould Cozzens. He wrote another about the Hundred Best Books more devastating still. His friends couldn't make a mock of him by accusing him of wanting to be everybody from Gilgamesh to Marcel Proust. That would have been an estimable albeit inflated covetousness. So they just said he wished he was Mortimer Adler. It didn't seem to occur to anybody that editors paid him money for doing these jobs.

I haven't any desire at all to be William Golding, much as I would enjoy spending my declining years pacing the lawns of Salisbury Cathedral Close while reading my Sarum Breviary, or seeking a glimpse of the protonothary curlew in the copses while the most gracious spire in Europe regarded me across the water meadows. It would be nice but I wouldn't want to write novels to do it, least of all such novels.

When Edward Weeks called up and asked me if I would do a comprehensive piece on all the books of William Golding for the *Atlantic*, a spontaneous yes popped out of me across the country before I realized what I was getting into. After all, Gertrude Stein spent most of her life trying to get into the *Atlantic* and they didn't take her until she was older than I am now. Years ago I turned down their invitation to do a somewhat similar job, and if I say no a second time I'll probably never be asked again. Besides, there's the pay to be considered. So it's just prestige and money. I do not inhabit a universe of discourse in which the turbulence of controversy about William Golding is likely to arise. Like Salinger, Golding is one of those authors school teachers say all the young read. It's easy to see how this works out. They say to their classes as they assign *Catcher in the Rye* or *Lord of the Flies,* "You have to read this book. All young people think it's terrific. It expresses The Alienation of Modern Youth." So they did with my daughter. "How do you like *Catcher in the Rye*?" "Not much," she said. Later, "How do you like *Lord of the Flies*?" "I can't read it." Maybe she was just raised right.

Who does read William Golding and why? Since taking on this job I have asked around pretty extensively. I think his reputation is based on the strong physical response and moral identification he arouses in that class which worries all our social analysts—the great horde of the newly arrived of the new professions, the affluent parvenus of cybernation, the upwardly mobile. He expresses their rootlessness, their complete lack of connection with either social or literary tradition, their amoralism—what used to be called Social Darwinism—their always haunting sense of being unfree, perhaps their most distinguishing characteristic, and itself the primary expression of their lack of that unfashionable theological virtue, hope, their lack of all sense of style. This is the definition of a parvenu. Every time society passes through a critical point in its technological evolution, such people become a problem. The traffic management of taste breaks down, and the permanent issues of life and literature become confused and obscured. Right now, of course, with the population explosion and automation both happening at once, Neanderthals with slide-rules are all over the place. William Golding does not only write about them in scarcely veiled allegory, he writes for them. His message is not unlike that of Jack London—a now forgotten (except in Russia and the nations of rising expectations) American author who spoke for the Nietzschean parvenus of the boom times before the world depression of 1912–14. Golding's prose is almost as bad. In some ways it is worse because it lacks specificity. In London there is a degree of sensual immediacy and passionate rhetoric unknown to Golding. The *homo homini lupus* conclusion is there in italics, q.e.d., at the bottom of every page, but in the older writer, it seems to be based upon facts of a rather adventurous experience. In Golding experience is replaced by a kind of truculent rhetoric. The lack of concrete sensual apperceptions, the lack of interesting events in the lives of the twenty-thousand-a-year technical and professional intelligentsia in the garden suburbs and the high-rise condominiums lies at the root of their nausea, their inescapable boredom and contempt of life and of each other, their truculent rhetoric.

The reason of course is that they are uneducated. Education is the imparting of a life style, whether it be that of a German Socialist tool and die-maker, the proverbial sturdy English yeoman, a Chinese mandarin or the former inhabitants of Brattle Street. Each has his special spiritual etiquette which can always be relied upon to cope and which comes to him through a social umbilicus. If the navel string is snapped before gestation begins, such endowments obviously cannot be transmitted. In a special sense of the word, it is taste with which we cope. If we cope, we are heroes, even when we go under, as eventually we all do. There are no tragedies in lives without style. William Golding's thesis is that there is no such thing and that the pretense of it always ends in a shambles. I think he intends his novels to be terrible warnings. Behind them I suspect he agrees with me, but alas, he himself lacks the style necessary to an Old Testament prophet. He leaves me unmoved, but to his audience he oversells his case. They agree with characters in the novels, but not with any implicit lesson to be drawn from their behavior, because they find themselves therein, just as the gray-flannel junior executive who has never known anything but *taedium vitae* finds his own fantasy's shadow in the picaresque adventures of the dope and switchblade school.

Each novel is the story of the impossibility of coping, not of failure. Agamemnon failed. Prometheus on his rock coped. A deaf and blind man run over by a driverless car, which has broken away on a hillside, has not failed. Since life is not in fact like this, Golding's novels are rigged. All thesis novels are rigged. In the great ones the drama escapes from the cage of the rigging or is acted out on it as on a skeleton stage set. Golding's thesis requires more rigging than most and it must by definition be escape-proof and collapsing.

Such self-destroying machines are perfectly conceivable, but they must be made of carefully tooled gears and pinions and put together with great style. I do not believe they are that, but it is arguable that the first great books of this *métier* are Céline's *Journey to the End of the Night* and *Death on the Installment Plan*. There is a world of difference in style and skill between Céline and Golding. Céline is full of unforgettable minute particulars of time, person, place and thing. Golding is uniformly disoriented and ambiguous for time, person, place and thing.

The Lord of the Flies is simply a carelessly documented book. Its opposite number, *Swiss Family Robinson*, is ridiculously impossible, with flora, fauna and geology from the ends of the earth, all dumped on one tiny island, but we forgive the improbability because the boa constrictor really seems to eat the mule and if polar bears had eaten breadfruit we would have believed it. *The Lord of the Flies* functions in a minimal ecology, but even so, and indefinite as it is, it is wrong. It's the wrong rock for such an island and the wrong vegetation. The boys never come alive as real boys. They are simply the projected annoyances of a disgruntled English schoolmaster. At the end of the book, you are not convinced of the obliterative effects of original sin; you just feel that Mr. Golding should get a better job. Certainly this is not a picture of the juvenile delinquency that has swept over the world from Jakarta to Reykjavik. Hell's Angels, hooligans, Mods and Rockers, tricheurs—these people are after more reality, not less, and their explosions result from frustrations coming from outside, deliberately inhibiting their quest for a wider reality. They do not come from within what sociological cant calls their peer groups.

If *The Lord of the Flies* is an unsuccessful attempt to deny *Swiss Family Robinson*, *Pincher Martin* is an even less successful denial of *Robinson Crusoe*. Since it is all an hallucination, it eludes comparison with Defoe's flawless orchestration of specificities. That's just the point. If reality had been allowed to intrude, the thesis would have fallen to the ground. I do not accept Jean-Paul Sartre's philosophy but he had sense enough to know that a one-man *No Exit* is, as it were, a denial of terms. Besides, Golding's book is simply annoying. I object to having to read 185 pages of a worn-out gimmick.

Free Fall should be the best of Golding's novels. The people are more vividly drawn, motives are more complex. There are dramatic rather than melodramatic tensions. The thesis again is Golding's obsession, original sin, but in this case the story is of the struggle to transcend it. Yet again it is all hallucinatory. Furthermore, since the characters seem at first not presented purely as vehicles of the thesis, it is possible to judge them as people. So judging, it is apparent that there's something nasty about all of Golding's people; not evil, just nasty. One of the things wrong with them is a kind of special muzziness that he is able to give to all of his characterizations—or unable not to give. They are uncleanly seen. If you are going to undertake this journey, you should never forget that the clarity of Dante's vision is never impeached by the confusions of either the damned or the undamned.

The Inheritors shares with the other novels their imprecision of documentation. Modern paleontology simply does not support Golding's picture of Neanderthal man nor of his relation to Cro-Magnon man. To judge by his remarkable brain pan capacity, he may well have been smarter than us. Certainly he was in many ways more specialized and so, I suppose, what we used to call further evolved. We know nothing about the relations between Cro-Magnon and Neanderthal man. There is no evidence that the second race exterminated the first. More likely Neanderthal man was over-evolved, specialized for the peculiar conditions of the late Pleistocene, and died of disease and with hundreds of other Pleistocene species. The cave bear was not exterminated by the grizzly, nor the ground sloth by the bison. Nor do we know enough about Cro-Magnon man to justify Golding's picture of him. I know the sources of Golding's characterization. It is very moving when the Sorcerer of the cave of Les Trois Frères suddenly makes his appearance but the evidence does not in fact warrant such deductions. I know that it has become fashionable to write books called *The Religion of the Cave Man* but they are all as imaginative as any fiction.

Of course, there's nothing wrong with invention, extrapolation and anachronism in a novel about Neanderthals, if it can just be made convincing. The Neanderthals don't have to have been really like that—nobody ever really lived who was like the characters of Henry James either. It's the end in view and the means employed that count. I think the end is false and the means are imprecise. The Neanderthals were not a race of Adams and Eves with red wool nor the Cro-Magnons moral monsters, the issue of the sons of God that mated with the children of men. It's not just that Golding projects the present into the past. Wells, London and many others have done that, writing of the same subject. It's that he projects a compound of personal problems which are essentially trivial into the birth of humanity.

The Spire is the most exasperating of all these books. Here the anachronism is breathtaking. This is not the Middle Ages, and it is certainly not Salisbury Cathedral. It is certainly William Golding. *The Bad Rover Boys on a Desert Island, The Bad Rover Boys at the End of the Ice Age* acquire a sequel—*The Bad Rover Boys in the Age of Faith Build a Cathedral*. Again, Mr. Golding judges human beings, past or present, far or near, the way a British school master who doesn't like teaching in a provincial town regards his charges. This is a symbolic tale of the upwardly mobile with a vengeance. The thesis is they are snotty-nosed little boys. Maybe they are; they seem to enjoy being told they are.

What depressed me most was that Mr. Golding doesn't even like that pretty church, perhaps because it is so perfect an expression of style. He shouldn't only get another job; he should move. Maybe he has. He's sold enough books to live on the Riviera where it's stylish.

1965

10.

Poetry in the Sixties

American poetry spent the last war and the years immediately after it in the doldrums. War is supposed to be just dandy for poets, especially if, like Rupert Brooke and Wilfred Owen, it kills them. As a matter of fact, both wars produced poetic revolutions in Great Britain, but neither made much difference in American poetry. Perhaps it's sunspots, the number of cyclonic storms or the volume of cosmic rays, the stock market, but some cyclonic phenomena seem to determine troughs and crests of American poetry regardless. 1940 to 1950 was a trough. Few new people appeared; Randall Jarrell, Peter Viereck, Karl Shapiro, Theodore Roethke, John Ciardi, Elizabeth Bishop and Jean Garrigue made reputations early in these years. However, they belong in the context of the last years between two wars. With the exception of John Ciardi, all are at home in the Reactionary Generation, that strange alliance of penitent Marxists and Southern Cavaliers whose organs of literary intimidation were the now forgotten quarterlies, the *Kenyon* and *Partisan Reviews*.

The poets before the war antagonistic to this tradition had

far larger audiences and greater influence—Richard Eberhart, Muriel Rukeyser and Kenneth Patchen. Most of the old poetic establishment and their new recruits wrote little poetry during the war. In their comfortable roomettes on the propaganda gravy train they were too busy turning out redundant packages of unusable morale builders to have time for poetry, notoriously an expression of conscience. Although some conscientiously approved of the war against Hitler, one of the easier wars to conscientiously approve of, extraordinarily enough no "pro-war" poetry of the slightest importance was written. Randall Jarrell was in the Air Corps, Karl Shapiro in the Army, Richard Eberhart a commander in the Navy, Muriel Rukeyser worked for the government. Kenneth Patchen was crippled; otherwise, he would have been a conscientious objector. Yet all said the same things. If poetry is a symbolic criticism of value, the poets found only intensely negative values in those years. Richard Eberhart left the preparatory school where he taught to join the Navy. His pupil, Robert Lowell, left for prison as a conscientious objector. Lowell's poetry extended and fulfilled Eberhart's. The constant, underlying substance of their poetry is a Protestant mysticism, shorn of overt faith, concentrating on the existential dilemma of man as mortal and contingent over against unknowable, eternal omnipotence. This is a life attitude the war was to make universally popular. *Le monde concentrationaire* was Existentialist, from Paris prostitutes to German theologians. Perhaps our only naturally Existentialist writer, Lowell didn't get it out of a fashionable book, and because he has always approached "the anguish of the abyss" of the Existentialists as totally realized spiritual experience rather than as doctrine, much less literary fad, his poetry has an extraordinarily gripping power of form. Behind Robert Lowell lay thirty years of academic imitations of seventeenth-century English metaphysicals. Nothing could be less like these exercises than Robert Lowell's poetry for the simple reason that he actually thinks and feels like Donne himself. The more apparent literary influences of Blake and Lawrence he shares with Eberhart. There is Melville, and more important, the blood of the *Mayflower* passengers that flows in his veins.

Younger than Lowell are Richard Wilbur and W. S. Merwin. For a modern poet Richard Wilbur is singularly untroubled.

Modern anguish and terror never overwhelmed his wit's capacities to deal with them. The basis of wit narrowed as he has grown older. Now he is seldom more than deft and polished. Merwin is a more ambitious poet. However colloquial and domestic, the poem always has mythic scope, less subjective, more, not social, but anthropological than Robert Lowell, but like him in Melville's tradition of overturned Puritanism. Merwin shares a literal resemblance to Melville in his intense feeling for the specific, under the storm of language. Little contemporary poetry is as dramatic as his full of different people in different relationships to each other, not a common habit of serious American poetry, which tends to be elegiac and subjective even when this is denied, as by Frost or T. S. Eliot. Merwin, like the older poet of the *Partisan Review* set, Delmore Schwartz, or the post-war French poet Claude Vigée, both disciples of André Gide, may not consider himself such, but his concern is the same—the integrity of the acutely conscious conscience. The difference is he works in an architecture of interpersonal tension—a cast of characters, like Thomas Hardy or Browning. Each of Merwin's books has been a step from that academic fashion of imitation baroque, which he handled with great skill, toward ever-greater modesty and immediacy of utterance. Then comes a succession of poets who have evolved like Merwin—W. D. Snodgrass, James Wright, Robert Bly, Louis Simpson and their school, who might be called the new conservatives, but they're not very conservative. They all teach. Most publish in *The Sixties* edited by Robert Bly; most started in the Middle West. Today a younger contingent, inheritors of this group, might be called "The Reformed Neo-Academics." Most impressive are Anne Sexton, Tim Reynolds, Adrienne Rich, Thom Gunn and A. R. Ammons. Coming up behind them are William Knott (Saint Geraud) and Robert Kelly. Their characteristics are acid wit, a relaxed use of conventional form and a return to intimate speech in the first person that the misleading snobbery of T. S. Eliot had made unfashionable for thirty years. Tim Reynolds is the best on the border of this group, and shares attitudes and techniques with the two groups that I want to discuss next.

After years of destructive intestinal fighting, Black Mountain College, the dishevelled progressive school in the Southern mountains, had been reduced to poverty, a handful of students and a tiny covey of teachers. Charles Olson survived, a disciple of William Carlos Williams and Ezra Pound, an extremely infectious teacher. In a few years he gathered a definite school. I don't think any of them read French, certainly not for pleasure, and like almost all American poets, had heard of no one later than Jules Laforgue. Basing themselves on the few Americans of the international avant-garde of the older generation, Louis Zukofsky, the early Walter Lowenfels, Parker Tyler, Gertrude Stein, Walter Conrad Arensberg, Mina Loy, and myself when young, they found their way out of narrow provincialism and pseudo-British insularity, the enforced orthodoxy of the Reactionary Generation and their quarterlies. Olson's outstanding disciple who for a while surpassed his master was Robert Creeley. Unknown to himself, he learned to write in the transitional style from symbolism to anti-symbolism or "literary cubism." His verse resembled Mallarmé's "Petit air" or "Un Autre Eventail," those cryptic anagrams of exacerbated sensibility. For several years Creeley, in North Carolina, Majorca and Aix-en-Provence, established in *The Black Mountain Review,* on as firm foundations as might be, a new poetry once again international in speech, capable of standing comparison with post-war Polish, Catalan, German or Yugoslav poetry, better than contemporary French poetry—which has run steeply downhill for years, no mean achievement.

Black Mountain's best younger poets are Jonathan Williams, Ronald Johnson, Wendell Berry, Edward Dorn, Gilbert Sorrentino, not all of whom fit comfortably into this classification. With the Black Mountain group is associated an independent writer, probably America's best post-war poet, Denise Levertov. As a young girl in England she was the most promising of British New Romantics, who have run down even steeper hills than the French into practical oblivion. For a while in America she was influenced by the Southern Cavaliers, but soon developed her own pure, intimate, classic style. She too resembles Mallarmé or Pierre Reverdy, except that she is easily understood. She remains completely a poet of married love, motherhood, daughterhood and the problems of a transfigured domesticity, practically unique in the long tradition of woman poetry in

raising these elements to the effective universality of great literature. We have never had anybody like her. Comparison with
Edna Millay or Marianne Moore, Eunice Teitjens or Amy
Lowell is ridiculous. Only Coventry Patmore, but as a male, had
tried to do what she does and he did not do it nearly as well. The
universal respect in which she is held by Academics, Beats and
Black Mountains has led her to be identified with one or the
other by careless critics and anthologists. She is in fact classically
independent.

During and after the war there grew up in San Francisco poets
with no connections with the dominant cliques and tendencies of
American poetry but with anarchists and pacifists, and New
Romantics of London, the youngest French surrealists and the
past of Classic Modernism, especially with poets like Mallarmé,
Reverdy and Desnos. When Denise Levertov was a land girl in
Essex, more people read her in San Francisco than had heard
about her in the British Empire. France's poetic underground
resistance of new writers in *éditions de minuit* and Pierre Seghers'
Poèsie reached San Francisco by various channels of G.I. mail
and were read as excitedly as in Paris. Cadou, Follain, Frenaud,
Guillevic, Daumal, Rousselot, Emmanuel, Char, were read in
San Francisco when only maverick French teachers had heard
of them east of the Sierras. As in France, but quite spontaneously
and independently, there was a tremendous outburst of oral
presentation of poetry for similar reasons. The Nazis did their
best to exterminate those who published significant poetry in
Paris. So too the American quarterlies prevented anything that
did not meet their specifications.

In the west were a number of conscientious objectors' camps
where young men who had bullheadedly gone on believing what
their Sunday School superintendents had suddenly stopped teaching, were hammering out, with no guidance whatever from a generation which had deserted them, new and truly contemporary
philosophies of life. They came down to San Francisco on their
leaves, mingling with local exponents of irreconcilable libertarianism and unfashionably international modernism. In the
war years and for five years thereafter until it was deliberately
destroyed by an invasion of ideologists and apparatchiki from
New York City, San Francisco had an anarchist-pacifist move-

ment with regular meetings, larger than all the factions of Socialists and Bolsheviks combined. These meetings alternated discussions aimed to give the historic libertarian tradition contemporary relevance, with larger meetings for readings of poetry of
a kind unheard in America since the demoralization of the Great
Depression enabled a combination of Bolsheviks and parvenus
to smash native American modernism.

This was the beginning of the San Francisco Poetry Center,
long since captured by the most sterile academia and now known
locally as the Anti-Poetry Center. Those years of tremendous
excitement produced a number of tremendously exciting poets—
Robert Duncan, William Everson (Brother Antoninus), Philip
Lamantia, Jack Spicer, amongst others. They made poetry a
social force in San Francisco and started the renaissance of oral
poetry that now threatens to degenerate into an Academic Or-
pheum Circuit for mediocrities.

Ten years after the San Francisco Poetry Renaissance had
thoroughly consolidated itself and its spokesmen were famous
in London, Paris, Warsaw and Barcelona, if not in New York
and Cambridge, Mass., two prize students of those eminently
cultivated men, heroes of that well known song, "I love a New
Yorker," Jacques Barzun and Lionel Trilling, showed up in
San Francisco. They had flunked the Columbia football team,
got lost in Minetta Brook and surfaced in San Francisco Bay,
like the nymph Arethusa. Their names were Jack Kerouac and
Allen Ginsberg, both extremely conventional writers with an
inflexible Madison Avenue orientation. The liberating San Francisco atmosphere, free of all vestige of market pressures, exploded them, or maybe just gave them an incurable case of the
bends. They took up and vulgarized any number of San Francisco customs—poetry and jazz for one, which they almost
immediately succeeded in destroying.

However much Allen Ginsberg may be Henry-Luce-as-poet
—the perfect media image of the *révolté* from whom society has
nothing to fear, the allowed clown—he nevertheless is a remarkable poet. The person in the past whom he most resembles
is Vachel Lindsay, another shopkeeper's idea of a poet, equally
noisy and equally sincere. As an effective denunciation of a
totally hypocritical society, Ginsberg's *Howl* did its job well,

especially with the many thousand young people who bought it. Its literary merit can be measured by the running and barking fits it still gives older academicians long after it's forgotten in campus coffee shops. Whatever its faults, and they are not actually very serious, it is a great vatic poem in the tradition of Hosea. In spite of all the uproar in the yellow press of ten continents, there is only one other Beat poet—Gregory Corso. He is a naïve writer, a natural wild man, a combination of Alfred Jarry, *le douanier* Rousseau and Essenin. The world is not kind to naïve writers and few survive. The wonderful Negro instinctive Dadaist, Eluard Luchelle McDaniel, never able to publish, except in San Francisco, was killed in Spain. Like the painter Rousseau, Corso is a skilled artist with his own totally eccentric scheme of values.

Gary Snyder, Philip Whalen and Lawrence Ferlinghetti arrived in San Francisco about the same time as Kerouac and Ginsberg. They are grouped with the Beats, but their association is purely fortuitous. Ferlinghetti, whose poems are intensely American, is of French ancestry and has spent many years in France. He belongs squarely in the tradition of the great *café chantant* poets, Charles Cros, Aristide Bruant, Jehan Rictus, Francis Carco, Robert Desnos, Pierre MacOrlan, Jacques Prevert, Raymond Queneau, Georges Brassens. I name all these over because it is to the everlasting shame of American culture that we have produced nobody like this, except Ferlinghetti. Until the Beats killed the gig, he and I enjoyed a couple of years of jazz poetry and managed to perform in all the leading jazz rooms of the country. Independently Kenneth Patchen did so too, but in a radically different style. The movement is still astonishingly popular in Europe. In New York it was overwhelmed by bearded, barefoot hobo-poetasters willing to perform for a glass of white port or a half-smoked roach, who knew nothing about jazz or poetry.

I recently polled a wide representation of colleagues of all ages and conditions of poetude for another article on the best poets under thirty-five. Abou ben Adam was Gary Snyder, one of the most remarkable young men ever to show up in American literature. A Buddhologist, a professed monk, not a Zennik, he reads Chinese, Japanese and Sanskrit, a discovery that frightened the wits out of Jack Kerouac. He also reads several other languages and has absorbed influence from all the vital poets of the twentieth century, transmuted them into an idiom which resembles Pound's *Cantos,* William Carlos Williams' *Paterson,* Mallarmé's *Un coup de des,* but which is inescapably Gary Snyder. I think he, more than any other contemporary poet, has lived a life of unlimited eventfulness. He has done all sorts of things which have no connection with literature, whereas most poets today have moved from studying courses in creative writing to teaching them, with summer vacations in the Maine woods, the Café Flore or the Via Vittoria Veneto. He is genuinely engaged in the things other people give money to, like Peace or racial equality, and genuinely disengaged from the things they put down in sociology seminars at $20,000 a year. His motto is, "Don't own anything you can't leave out in the rain." Snyder comes a short literary generation after Denise Levertov and Robert Creeley and I think they are our three leading post-war poets.

Philip Whalen is a similar writer, sharing with Snyder youth in the Northwest, Reed College, a similar philosophy of life, and the influence of the dauntless adventurousness and gaiety of the Northwest intellectual climate that was the creation of the I.W.W. intellectuals and the very intellectual I.W.W.'s who were not intellectuals. Whalen also shares with Ferlinghetti an acute ear for the rhythms of speech and jazz. He is a retiring individual, modest to a fault, and deserves to be far better known.

A little group of poets known as the New York School whose leaders are Kenneth Koch, John Ashbery, Frank O'Hara and Barbara Guest were closely associated with the Tenth Street Club of Abstract Expressionists. I must be some kind of defective or deviant because they do not move me. They seem to me to be impersonal, uninvolved to the point of superficiality, and witty in a kind of post-*New Yorker* cartoon way, and Frenchy without having digested the blood and iron of the heartbreak of Europe, the source of all the greatest poetry since Baudelaire. Except for Barbara Guest, who seems to me a low-pressure Denise Levertov and whose poetry is very good indeed, but which would be greatly improved by the excitement of dramatic and verbal tension.

For a number of years LeRoi Jones was the most significant

Negro poet to come up since Jean Toomer. His first two books contain poetry which is moving, penetrating and independent of race, except as a given factor of the poet's situation. In recent years he has succumbed to the temptation to become a professional Race Man of the most irresponsible sort. Coming as he does from middle-class suburbia, his attitude is indistinguishable from Senator Eastland's image of the Negro, and differs only in that he approves enthusiastically of this artifact. His loss to literature is more serious than any literary casualty of the Second War, a particularly tragic loss to the tradition of Daddy Grace, essentially a White Man's Negro, a kind of Tom Uncleism, a hot commodity for white masochists.

An ever-growing number of young Negro writers are still learning to free themselves from all kinds of stereotypes they have acquired like parasites from both races. Welton Smith and G. C. Oden are very different poets indeed. Welton Smith is a modernist with a philosophy which might be called Highly Sceptical Negritude. Gloria Oden, a more conventional poet, was thoroughly assimilated and widely published long before she let any editor know she was a Negro. I am inclined to think after Welton Smith's "Malcolm X" poem in a recent issue of San Francisco's *Black Dialogue* that he is one of the most promising young poets in America. The best anthology of recent Negro verse is Rosey Pool's *Beyond the Blues,* and the best new poet in it, to my taste, was Julia Field. Young Negro writers today are undergoing a period of terrific storm and stress and transvaluation of values. I believe the significant advances in American literature in the next decade will be made by these people, but today they are just beginning.

1965

11.

New Sex?
New Church?

The assumption is that there is an ongoing revolution in the sexual habits of the human species, and an ongoing revolution in ritual belief and morals, or at least ethics in the Roman Catholic Church, and that these two movements will have to find adjustment to each other. It is wise not to assume too much. Fairly reliable surveys of various social strata, concentrating mostly on people under thirty-five, have discovered that actual sexual practice amongst the present generation has not changed as much as might appear. The key work is "appear." Sexual relations of all kind are simply more open, less hypocritical. I have often been asked, "What is the essence of the Social Lie?" and have come to answer, "I suppose the statement, 'Your father never masturbated in his life!' and other remarks like it." Two generations ago maturity used to consist of the discovery that your parents probably enjoyed sexual intercourse as much as you do. The realization occurs much earlier now, but it is still a great help in growing up. The literature of the world in all civilized languages presents a picture of human sexuality vastly different from the middle-class Social Lie of the past hundred years and recently there has been quite a fad for the underground literature of the rutting and kinky Victorians. The same class of people come and go in the drawing rooms of Jane Austin or Anthony Trollope as do in the pages of *Fanny Hill* or *The Pearl*. It's safe to assume that the facts lay somewhere midway between them, that is, at about the point revealed in the various Kinsey reports. Readily available contraception, especially the pill and inter-uterine devices, have of course had a liberating effect, but they have probably increased the quantity of sexual intercourse, and, to a lesser degree, of pre-marital and extra-marital sex, rather than changed the character of the relationships. If anything there has probably been in the last ten years a slow drift toward more conventional, so-called normal sex for obvious reasons; "abnormal" sex is a form of birth control.

It is true that there is a growing subculture of group sex, orgies, communes that function as extended families, and the almost total disappearance of civil marriage amongst some young people. All of these people are lumped together by the straight world as hippies, although there are several quite antagonistic groups in this general category. Over against this little world of communal life and rather simple and honest sex relations is the "swinger" subculture of the straight world itself. The alternative society, those who have disaffiliated from the dominant culture, do NOT get together in one another's split-level homes, watch blue movies, smoke grass and then play musical pudenda all over the floor.

As persecution of the homosexual has decreased homosexuality has simply become more visible. It is doubtful if it has increased at all. Certainly in bohemia and in the alternative society its decline has been nothing less than astonishing. Not some, but I suppose most, of my friends among artists, writers, actors, musicians of my own generation have been homosexuals. In the present generation even in fields like ballet and various kinds of designing, from stage sets to fabrics, where there is not a tightly organized—by older people—commercial monopoly, there are today few young male homosexuals. Female homosexuality of course has always been hypocritically tolerated by the straight world.

There is one factor which it would be wise not to ignore and which may be responsible for a considerable increase in the number of people who become homosexual, or at least adopt homosexuality after adolescence. This is the profound perversion of "normal sexuality" by the commercial society, the continuous barrage of the mass culture which above all other things strives to reduce sex to a commodity, as the *Communist Manifesto* says, reduces all human relationships to the cash nexus. The huge outdoor advertising billboard with an obviously newly married couple at opposite ends, their stylish clothes dishevelled with excitement, each gripping the telephone and separated by an immense undulant caption, "Darling, I just bought the new Ford!" while both of them are patently in a state of orgasm, has probably ultimately produced more homosexuals than all the gay bars in San Francisco or New York. Until the recent reform California divorce laws were notoriously written by criminal lawyers for movie actresses. I once went into a bar around the corner from my place in San Francisco to get a pack of cigarettes. It had formerly been a jazz club but it had just turned into a gay bar. It was fifty feet wide and fifty feet deep and it was so packed with junior executive types that I don't know to this day if it contains tables or not. I said to the bartender who was a friend of mine, "My God, where do all these square-looking queens come from?" He said, "Over half of them are paying alimony and child support to at least two women." He may have been exaggerating a little, but there's no doubt but what the straight, square marriage in America is very sick. The desire to escape from it into a more normal life undoubtedly is responsible for recruits to all the sexual subcultures.

Of course, the old-time happy marriage still exists. There is still a sizable minority of people who have either the devotion or the lack of imagination to find happiness in a life-long marriage of lovers as envisaged by the teachings (by celibates) of the Church. Atheists, Protestants, Jews, Catholics, a lot of people entering marriage, are going to stay with it for life and end up as Baucises and Philemons. The reason, ironically, is the same as that which permits the sexual revolutionaries, the swingers, the alimony bums, and the very bourgeois homophile organizations—money. There's nothing to buck up a marriage in its early years like modest affluence. Anyone who has ever been a counselor of the distraught, whether priest, or psychoanalyst, or lay therapist, knows that contrary to popular mythology, more marriages break up for economic reasons than for lack of sexual satisfaction. A happy marriage is a spiritual vocation, like being a revolutionary, and a lot more people can afford it today. *A chacun son gout.*

Where does the Church stand in all this? In the first place, at this precise moment the Church is in the grip of a baby counter reformation. In 1970 the policies of the Vatican resemble those of the White House or the Sacramento Governor's Mansion. This is the real reason why thousands upon thousands, from bishops to parishioners, are flooding out of the Church all over the world. People are voting with their feet against what they consider the betrayal of *aggiornamento,* the promise of Pope John and the Second Vatican Council. That passed away; this will too. The Roman Catholic Church will either abandon a very large number of absurd dogmas and moral commandments or a schismatic church of new Catholics will take form in the next few years and reduce the Papal Church to a small sect in possession of a vast financial empire. There are common bumper-stickers and buttons which say, "Up against the Wall with Pope Paul" and there's no doubt but what that revered gentleman has painted himself into a corner. The Church has overcome infinitely worse popes than he. What is likely to happen?

First, compulsory celibacy of the clergy will go in the near future. No other Church that calls itself Catholic practices it, nor did the Roman Church until well into the Middle Ages, nor do the Uniate Churches of the Orthodox Rite in communion with the Vatican—and this means millions of people, nor do thousands of Roman Catholic clergy safely secreted in the backwoods of backward countries. A married clergy, it is presumed, will make more understanding confessors.

Second, the prohibition of birth control will go. It already has and everybody knows it but a minority of the Roman Curia.

Third, the impossibilist ethic preached from the pulpit will go, already is going amongst theologians. The purpose of the impossibilist ethic is compromise. The impossibilist exaggeration of Jesus' gospel of love led to compromise as soon as the apos-

tolic tradition died down, and made Christianity the world's
bloodiest and angriest religion. That was the purpose of its moral
hypertrophy. Constantine's successors could have used Franklin
Roosevelt's pet phrase, "We planned it that way." Unbeknownst
to the lay Catholic there exists an immense literature of casuis-
try, properly so called, the careful weighing of every conceivable
moral problem, and direction for the subtlest decisions in the
confessional. The most perverse and outrageous sexual capers
are commonplace to thousands of skilled confessors. One of the
most popular American religious orders has had for fifty years,
at least, a specific but never openly admitted concern for the
cure of souls of homosexuals. The gay world has always been
aware of this, even if many of the members of the order themselves are not. A few years ago an organization calling itself
"The Church and the Homosexual" was formed in San Francisco by a group of Roman, Anglican and Protestant clergy, all
of them very straight. Their first dance was raided by the police
and men in drag and clergymen's wives were bundled in the same
paddy wagon together. The police apologized, and the organization has spread across the country, and there are many others
like them in England, the Netherlands, France, Germany especially. Here and there in the underground Church, so called,
ministers, priests and even rabbis are already blessing marriages
of people of the same sex. Fifty years ago when I was a boy,
two priests of the Old Catholic and the Liberal Catholic sects
were already doing this in Chicago and New York. It will come.

Fourth, the doctrine of the Church is that marriage is the one
sacrament that layman perform together. The Church acknowl-
edges the marriage and the priest blesses it. This is disputed, but
since Vatican II it has become the prevailing doctrine. Baldly
stated this means that the sexual act itself is the "matter" of the
sacrament. Just as the Church sacramentalizes the other great
facts of life, birth, death, sexual maturity, vocation, eating and
drinking, so it sacramentalizes sexual intercourse; that is, it says
that this is one of those moments when the life of the human
being rises into transcendence and comes in contact with infinity, eternity and all the other absolutes. If the sexual relation,
whether it be communal, homosexual, polygamous, polyandrous
or whatever, genuinely possesses the potential for transcendence

and is not destructive of the individual or group concerned, there is no reason why logically the Church should not eventually come to bless it. Contrary to Gentile, non-Mormon opinion, the usual Mormon polygamous marriage was unusually happy and apparently blessed. We forget that thousands and thousands of young women crossed the Atlantic and the plains and deserts to partake in it. And certainly the prohibition of polygamy in certain African societies has had gravely destructive effects and led to widespread "immorality"—socio-pathological behavior. We're back where we were with the seventeenth and eighteenth-century Jesuits in Peking with the rites controversy. Who knows? Who knows even if the group sex and orgies of the counter culture will last the immanent collapse of the dominant Western civilization?

Already there has grown up, especially amongst intellectuals, and certain so-called hippies and flower children, a kind of Tantric Catholicism, Gnostic in character, with special emphasis upon the spiritual illumination to be achieved in a Yogic control of the sexual act itself. The average parish priest may not know it, but there is considerable evidence that this sort of thing was common amongst the early monks of the desert, in early Celtic monasticism and was what was occult in much of occultism, most especially spiritual alchemy. If a mystic and his *soror mystica* present themselves for the sacraments and do not choose to say anything about their practices I don't see what the clergy can do about it. As time goes on there may well grow up within the Church an underground Tantric Catholicism. I for one think such ideas incomparably more wholesome than the romantic nonsense derived from television and the movies that seems to fill the heads of all too many of the priests and nuns who are renouncing their vows and getting married today. Me, if I was going to marry a nun, would greatly prefer a *soror mystica* to a soap-opera heroine.

1970

12.

Faith in an Age of Faithlessness

Today there is going on the greatest reorganization of values in Christianity since at least the Protestant Reformation. Actually, this revaluation goes deeper. It is unparalleled since apostolic times. Accompanying it is a widespread failure of belief in the Church, in its discipline and dogma, in the Christian doctrines of the incarnation and atonement, in the concept of deity which is peculiar to Christianity, Judaism, and Islam. This has happened suddenly and within the Church itself. It is not the Gentiles who find it all a stumbling block and confusion, but the Chosen People themselves. The revaluation of values is shaking thousands out of the Church altogether.

Men outside the Church have little conception of the depth of questioning, not just amongst the laity but amongst priests and nuns, monks, theologians, and bishops. A few of the clergy and religious who renounce their vows and marry get into newspapers, but this is only a superficial symptom, sensational and easily comprehended by the non-religious public, of far more fundamental questioning, doubt, and rejection. We are witnessing a wave of disbelief, greater than those which accompanied the growth of modern scientific materialism in the nineteenth century, and of rationalism in the eighteenth. Furthermore, the people concerned are precisely those to whom we would not have expected this to happen—trained theologians and dedicated religious who were given ready answers to every conceivable doubt. It would seem that the world view of Christianity is no more implausible now than it was in the days of Mill, Spencer, Haeckel, or on a popular level, Thomas Paine and Robert Ingersoll. They have all been answered. Suddenly the answers have become irrelevant.

What are the reasons for contemporary loss of faith? Once we have found them, perhaps we can redefine both faith and its foundations. How can a man of the latter end of the twentieth century, thoroughly familiar with modern science, literature, and the arts, be a Catholic?

The world view of science has changed, not just since the days of Newton or Darwin, but of Einstein. We live in an illimitable universe in which, visible in the largest telescopes, sub-universes other than ours, galactic nebulae, are more numerous than the stars in our own nebula. We can measure phenomena coming from six billion light years away. Whether this universe is infinite and eternal, contracting and expanding, steady-state or exploding, room in it for a moral cosmogony which is man-centered on this solar system, or even this little universe, seems ridiculous and trivial. Buddhism, on the other hand, begins with a compound infinity of infinities and goes straight to the empirically validated religious act, unqualified and unqualifiable.

We can etherialize the myth of creation and redemption in the Old and New Testaments but however much we do so, we are haunted by a hankering sense of its implausibility, its lack of sufficient reason. It simply doesn't seem to be an efficient way to go about things. Of course, there are plenty of absolutely conclusive neo-scholastic arguments in its favor. They don't seem to be relevant, however logic-tight. Their very logical efficiency seems to invalidate them. This has nothing to do with the dilemmas that trouble liberal theologians. The easiest thing in the world to believe is a mystery. It is easier to believe that Our Lord came through the maidenhead of the Blessed Virgin like light through glass than it is to believe in the efficacy of the incarnation and atonement under their historical circumstances. Of course, it is even more difficult to believe, walking about St. Peter's and the gilded, painted halls of the Vatican, that these buildings house the always authentic voice of the creative principle of a universe of infinitudes. The skeptic can say, "If I had been the Deity, I wouldn't have had any trouble figuring out a more effective way to go about it."

For all the efforts of Pope John, Vatican II, and the agitators of *aggiornamento*, the Church is still part of what St. Paul called the world, the interlocking hierarchies of power which rule mankind, based upon the Social Lie, which have become not just evil, but an immediate threat to the survival of the human species. Black cardinals, blood in the draft-board files, short skirts for nuns, rock masses, situational ethics in the confessional, are not enough. In the world in which we live, any truly religious, much less Christ-like, action, must be utterly drastic. The Holy Father has flown to all sorts of places. Why hasn't he flown to Hanoi and from there to Washington? The Vatican is one of the largest capitalistic enterprises on earth. Why hasn't it been totally liquidated since Vatican II? As thousands of pulpit orators have pointed out, Christ advised the rich young man to sell all he had, give to the poor, take up his cross, and follow Him, not because riches were necessarily evil or the poor deserving, but because the Apocalypse was coming—the judgment, the fire and the Kingdom—and all excess baggage should be thrown away. Well, Apocalypse is here.

The great issues of faith and morals are remote from the lives of Catholics except sometimes in moments of crisis. The entire structure of Catholic practice as it is lived out in ordinary life is designed to both coerce and protect the individual by the sheer exertion of power—worldly power—and also designed to prevent anything resembling a spiritual crisis arising in the lives of the obedient. Dostoevsky's Grand Inquisitor was perfectly right. What sort of eschatology is this?

The Grand Inquisitor sounds very noble in the pages of *The Brothers Karamazov,* but in fact what is wrong with the Church in its day-to-day life is vulgarity, a vulgarity far more deeply rooted than a taste for pink and blue statuary. The Church is supposed to be the custodian of the gospels and the sacraments, a community of love into whose hands has been given the trusteeship of the infinite, the eternal, and the holy in the lives of men. The sacraments are the channels through which the holy enters life and sanctifies it in its most elementary functions— eating, drinking, sexual intercourse, birth, adolescence, vocation, sin and amendment, death—the great rites of passage common to all folk religions. So the ceremonies of the Church's seasons are rites of the year, the sanctification of time. Religion in this anthropological sense goes back to the Stone Age. Catholicism is supposed to have preserved it and glorified it. As folk religion suffuses the life of the individual and the community with transcendence, so Catholicism claims to be distinguished from all other organized religions in preserving the old folk religion and charging it in turn with still greater transcendence, the transcendence of the incarnation. Would a visitor from another planet inspecting the actual life of the Church as lived corporately and individually find this a plausible claim? Does it look like the incarnation, the at-one-ment, is manifested in the lives of men? Unless he were a being of truly Christian charity the interplanetary visitor would say that the evidence made the claim not implausible but absurd. The best the most devout of us can say living on this planet—in this Church—is that the Church is the body of Christ, but the body of Christ crucified, in which the promise of the incarnation resides: "Lo, I will be with you always, even unto the end of the world," means only that the holy will always be somehow accessible. It will never be utterly impossible to become a saint. But this can be said of any of the world religions or of purely secular life.

Certainly one thing transcendence is not, as it suffuses immanence, is vulgar. One of the principal signs of Grace is grace. Holiness is graciousness. The sanctified should be noble with the good taste and *courtoisie* of holy gentlemen, like the archangels who are the courtiers of heaven. Does the Church foster such personalities? It is terrified of them. When signs of the development of such a personality show themselves in parochial school, the child is suppressed, or if irrepressible, shunted as early as possible into the "religious life," an isolation ward for people infected with prayer.

Anyone who has conducted retreats for a wide variety of people knows that today with the great religious awakening going on outside organized religion, it is far easier to find a sense of the higher forms of prayer in the secular world than it is in the Church. Meditation, contemplation, communion, are motor and fuel for many thousands of lives never touched by any Church. Religion as experience, for most men and women, is accessible only at the price of total rejection of everything they have been taught to identify with religion. This is far more fundamental than the manifestly un-Christian behavior of the Church in its relations with the power of the world. No matter how decadent the particular cult, most Buddhists seem to share something of the love of the historic Buddha for all sentient creatures. Islam is saturated in every department of life with Mohammed's sense of utter contingency in the face of the Absolute. Orthodox Judaism sacramentalizes all the details of life with faith made manifest in rite.

Outside of convents, one of the very few corporate groups of Christians who consistently manifest the personality of Jesus Christ are the Quakers. The distinguishing characteristic of the Quakers is their belief that it is comparatively easy to be a Christian. Catholic devotional manuals would indicate that it would be practically impossible without the continuous supernatural aid of the sacrament of penance. Yet to the non-Christians of this world, the characteristic Christian virtues are righteous anger, sexual repression, bigotry, spiritual pride, and simple bad taste. It doesn't do to say that it was different in the Middle Ages and that these are bourgeois characteristics. Quakerism is a religion of merchants if ever there was one, and what we call, pejoratively, Puritanism, was far worse in the thirteenth century.

How many Christians ever face the charge that Christianity itself is immoral; not its hypocrisy; not its captivity by the social and sexual lies that hold together an exploitative society; but immoral when it is sincerely true to the Gospel? We are so used to calling the Gospel of St. John the Gospel of Love that we are horrified when the non-Christian points out that it is full of ill-temper, and that its account of the passion, sung in the most impressive ceremony of the Church, is a constant source of anti-Semitism in the world, and of hate in the hearts of its listeners. Such a charge may be true or false, but even the most sophisticated moral apologetic never faces any fundamental moral challenge but contents itself with "answering" Nietzsche or Marx.

What is happening today is the laborious, inchoate struggle to develop such an apologetic. Neo-Thomism had all the answers but we stand outside it and walk around it. Its effectiveness is that of a completely autonomous work of art. One reason I suppose is that Thomism is not really a Christian philosophy as such. It is only in Eastern Orthodoxy that the Church, building on the foundation of the patristic period, has tried to develop a philosophy which would be Christian in its essense. So even today Russian philosophers and theologians like Frank and Berdyaev, once we discover them, seem more relevant than even the most progressive in the West. There is something extraordinarily primitive about Rahner, Küng, Schillebeeckx, Congar, everyone but the Catholic circle influenced by the Paris Russians and by Martin Buber. They seem to be discovering their meanings as they go along. This should make them exciting reading, but it does not. Something seems to drag, impede progress, confuse the issues. Each of the non-essentials of the Catholic religion is let go with the greatest reluctance and then comes creeping back in disguise. It is ridiculous that in the latter end of the twentieth century the Church should be convulsed over doctrines and practices that are patently false or unnecessary. Even worse is reformation by ukase. Mass in Latin, communion in one kind, celibacy, right down to fish on Friday, should be freely optional, neither enforced nor forbidden. It is this authoritarian temper in *aggiornamento* itself that only provokes laughter in those who are invited to share in our infallible ecumenicity.

The specifically Roman aspects of Roman Catholicism provoke only hilarity in the theologically informed of other sects so that conversion tends to be an affair of the uninformed or the neurotically driven who above all else must find absolute authority demanding absolute submission.

The term "other sects" is deliberate. Arnold Toynbee is not the only man to have pointed out that the Roman Catholic

Church had its last chance to become a truly ecumenical world religion at the time of the rites controversy with the Jesuits in China, and threw it away to become just another Western European Christian sect. Sectarianism is not a specialty of Rome among the sacramental and episcopal churches. Orthodoxy is not just ethnocentric, but nationalistic, and Anglicanism for the most part is simply an etherialization of Britishness. True, there has evolved over the past 150 years a remarkably ecumenical concept of Catholicism within the Anglican Church, but it is a movement in the last analysis of individuals. There are probably proportionately just as many Roman Catholics of like mind. Until recently they have not been permitted to speak publicly.

Over and above all the objections to outrageous and anachronistic doctrine is one which is probably primary and primarily spiritual, although it might seem to be simply a matter of infrastructure. Roman Catholicism says that its very life blood flows in holy communion, yet its entire structure is fundamentally anti-communitarian. Power is not spiritual power flowing between communicants but physical power over men and things, in a religion of hypostatized administration. It is not true that this structure is feudal; it is post-feudal. The papacy is the first of the absolute monarchies. It invented the idea, which is the reason for its bitter struggles with its competitors like Philip Augustus and the Hohenstaufen. This anachronistic structure is still there, only ever so slightly modified. There are twentieth-century forms of authoritarianism, but the college of cardinals yielding before the demand for collegiality is like a replay of a minor reform in the tenth-century Byzantine court. All this struggle takes place at the top.

Basic are the simple questions: Who owns the churches? Who chooses the clergy? Who disposes of the entire apparatus of infrastructure and its hierarchy of administrators? Not certainly a vestry, a convocation, or a presbytery, not the communicants of communion. It is absurd to claim that this structure preserves doctrine and practice. The historic Jesus, the comradeship of the apostles, the *agape* of the apostolic community, is self-evidently more alive in the Society of Friends, whose methods of administration have provided a model for an entire tradition of secular libertarianism and anarchism. Today the secular society likewise is caught in a crisis of administration. The apparatus which governed the mechanical, industrial extractive economy is impossibly inadequate for a technological society. The difference is just a matter of five hundred years. The crisis in the Church is a whole historical epoch too late.

These are the items of the indictment of the Church, drawn up by the people who are voting with their feet, as well as religious people in the outside world. How can anybody admit all this and still be a Catholic? It isn't hard, but it certainly requires a special temper. Lord Acton, the most intellectually impressive Catholic of the nineteenth century, is the man who said both, "I have never been troubled by an intellectual doubt," and after Vatican I, when he was asked why he didn't become an Anglican, "Just because the Pope has changed his religion is no reason why I should change mine."

At this juncture one can only speak personally. I am a Catholic, simply, neither Orthodox, nor Roman, nor Anglican, because the Catholic Church has preserved the anthropological, the folk religion, that engendered and nourished Western civilization. These are our own rites of passage and of the year. The Church has sheltered, usually with great reluctance during their lifetimes, our mystics and our philosophical theologians, and it has also sheltered, as Baron von Hügel loved to point out, our millions upon millions of saintly common people, that Irish washerwoman dying of cancer with whom von Hügel went to early morning Mass, and her kind.

It enables and even fosters, within narrowly defined limits, communities of prayer, lives dedicated to meditation, contemplation, and communion, lives seeking that vision out of which all good works flow. Although as a corporation it defines faith as belief and excludes the disbeliever, it still can nourish faith as life in an age of faithlessness. Religion is something men do, not something they believe. Creeds and dogmas exist only to protect a kind of life, a kind of act. That act culminates in prayer. In Christianity its abiding point of reference is an historic Person, whose acts are most accessible through the communion of his followers. Yet it was Allen Ginsberg who said, "The Sacred Heart is enough." Finally vision becomes habitude and we realize, with St. John of the Cross, that visions are symptoms of the defect of vision, the defect of luxury. Today the Church can still provide an ambiance of illumination in which we move like fish in water.

Men stay in the Church because they know empirically that the sacraments provide the food and drink of a life of communion and illumination. All the rest is distraction. Simone Weil, who prowled like a hungry animal outside the doors of the Church, the visible Church of distraction, called it the Great Beast. It is the life that counts, and I for one refuse to be distracted from that life, although I may be sufficiently exasperated in the mundane world by the specific sectarian absurdities of the Church. That sacramental life is all one to me—Roman, Orthodox, Anglican, Old Catholic, Polish Catholic, Hussite, Swedish Lutheran. In Paris I go to Saint Severin; in New York to St. Luke's Trinity. I can find other traditions, other sacramentals. I do not agree with the recent fashionable Dominican and Benedictine writers on Buddhism, that Zen, which is all the Buddhism they know, is an inferior thing called "natural mysticism." Natural it may be, but it is far more profound than anything casually encountered in most parish churches or all but a few of religious orders. So likewise for the Vedantists or Quakers or Hasidim.

We are far from having a claim to sole possession of the Inner Light. We can only say that we have never permitted it to go out completely. When the light of contemplation goes out in a society, civilization perishes, usually in catastrophic ruin.

1969

The Far East

13.
On Japanese Literature

For many years the only Western anthologies of Japanese literature have been W. G. Aston, *A History of Japanese Literature,* published in 1899, and Michel Revon, *Anthologie de la Literature Japonaise,* about 1930. Both have been translated into practically all European languages of importance. Neither is reliable for modern times. Both could stand considerable improvement of their translations. There is still only one comprehensive study of Japanese poetry of all periods, Georges Bonneau, *Yoshino,* not yet completed, in French. This is an extraordinary situation, for not only is Japanese one of the world's most important literatures, it is one of the most engaging. It is not everyone who likes the Finnish *Kalevala,* or the *Shahnamah* of Firdausi, but few indeed can be so ethnocentric as to be repulsed by *The Tale of Genji* or the poetry of Hitomaro. One of the great troubles with the widespread appreciation of Japanese verse has been the vulgarity of most translators, especially those who have found it necessary to use rhyme. Japanese poetry is, like that of Mallarmé or Anyte of Tegea, a poetry of sensibility. In the hands of a literary oaf sensibility turns instantly into sentimentality just as subtle verse turns to doggerel. Japanese literature is unquestionably one of the world's great traditions. It contains the greatest work of prose fiction in any language, *The Tale of Genji,* dozens of poets the equal of Mallarmé, two of the best books of *pensées,* the *Hojoki* and the *Tsuredzuregesu,* one of the very greatest erotic novelists, Saikaku, a whole species of drama of sensibility, the Noh, unknown elsewhere, and one of the finest romantic dramatists, Chikamatsu.

Donald Keene has managed to gather all this, and much more, up in one volume of 450 pages without making a collection of snippets and fragments. In *Modern Japanese Literature* he really gets across the meaning and flavor of Japanese writing, in each example and as a whole. He even conveys something of a sense of its scope. He has selected translations, many of them his own, which are both accurate and in good taste. There are sizable chunks of the novels and "notebooks"—a favorite form in Japan —whole plays, and many pages of poetry, almost all of it poetry in English as well as Japanese. Certainly there is no better introduction to Japanese literature in any language except Japanese, and few better in that. *Modern Japanese Literature* is, as a job of editing, equally judicious, equally comprehensive, with the same high standards of translation. Unfortunately, Japan has produced no major writer, in any medium, in the last hundred years. By major I mean "like Horace or Baudelaire," not "like Eliot or Hemingway." Few of her writers have risen above the dead level of Western popular reputations. Again, the modern Japanese writer operates under certain disabilities. His tradition is one of sensibility. However great, *Genji* does seem a little hysterical in comparison with the vastly humane Chinese novel, *The Dream of the Red Chamber,* let alone *Don Quixote.* Classical Japanese literature has one very conspicuous lack—guts. It is not, cannot be, salty, or "of the earth, earthy." It lacks the broad humanity which has its roots in the large bowel and the gonads. I know that I will be told that the haiku writers of the Yeddo Period had this—especially Bashō and Issa. But you have to be Japanese to believe that Zola's *La Terre* can be condensed into 17 syllables. Now it is very easy, in literature as in life, to cross from sensibility to neurasthenia and sentimentality. This is the besetting sin of most modern Japanese literature derived from the native tradition. There are still others handicapping the forming of a new tradition derived from the West. Not least is a kind of utter misunderstanding, the sort of failure of intercultural communication we know for instance in Pope's Homer. For this reason Western influences tend to operate on the level of the least common denominator, the formula, the stereotype. Possibly this is the reason the Japanese are so good in the media of the mass culture where nothing but stereotype is expected—

photography, movies, commercial art, sex novels. All too often, unfortunately, ambitious imitations of Picasso or Max Ernst tend to look like commercial art too, and the imitations of Shelley or Éluard to sound like the lucubrations of the Lonely Housewife School of Poetry Club Imagism. Japan, incidentally, is one of the few countries where poetry clubs and outfits like P.E.N. are taken seriously. There is one thing about Western culture, you can't take it at its face value without making yourself ridiculous. I do not think there is any question but that the primary problem for Japan is not the assimilation of the West—it has been sufficiently assimilated, but the restatement of the native tradition in terms negotiable for the creation of a totally new cultural synthesis. Of course this is such easy advice to give from the sidelines, but it is nonetheless true. So the stories and poems with the deepest roots in Japanese soil are usually the best. On the other hand, there is too large a class of pseudo-archaistic writing, of which the popular retelling of the *Heike Monogatari* by Eiji Yoshikawa, which I reviewed recently, is an example—this is just conventional costume romance, not refounding of a tradition. That is the trouble, most Japanese literature of the past hundred years is conventional. If it is naturalistic, it is conventional naturalism. If it is surrealistic or proletarian, it is conventionally so. Most of it is just plain conventional, like a story picked at random from the pages of the *Atlantic* or the *Partisan Review,* of any year, from the days of Frank Stockton to those of Flannery O'Connor. I suppose the word for this is provincialism, and by and large Japanese culture today is still a provincial outlier of Paris and New York. Still, there is something else, a core of Japanese sense and sensibility which is almost always there, however thin, ultimately irreducible, and, at least sometimes, still the creative center of the work. What this means is that although Japan may be provincial now, she will not, barring international catastrophe, be so forever. In fact, it is my personal belief that it is in Japan, even more than in China or India, that a great new cultural synthesis is beginning to take form.

My only criticism of Donald Keene's second volume is that he does not give adequate representation to Japanese surrealism and other modernist idioms, and to the proletarian school of pre-war days. True, they are derivative, but that granted, they are very good, better than much of the conventional, in the ordinary sense, poetry and prose he does give. I would have printed some Katue Kitasono, a modernist poet very well known in the West, more of the exquisite traditional poetess Yosano Akiko, more the wry modern haiku, in fact more poetry generally. Inadequate or dated as it is, Bonneau's *Yoshino,* volume 10, *Lyrisme du Temps Present,* is much better, at least for the pre-war period. The best prose on the whole is traditional in feeling, Takaboku's *Romaji Diary,* Junchiro's *Thin Snow,* Fumiko's *Tokyo,* the famous shocker by Osamu, *Villon's Wife,* and the selection from Takiji's *Cannery Boat,* the best Japanese proletarian novel, often compared with Traven's *Death Ship* (which is the best of all).

I should say that the first volume was practically perfect, its selections could be changed but slightly and they could hardly be improved. The modern collection is more than adequate, but it is more easily disagreed with.

1956

14.
Scrolls and Sculpture
of Japan

The Harvard University Press has done quite a job on Langdon Warner's *Japanese Sculpture of the Tempyo Period,* and well it might have. Although it is a splendid book—or box of pictures— on Japanese sculpture, even more, it is a memorial, a characteristic personality of a type that is almost vanished—the classic

Cambridge, Mass., intellectual, the true Boston Brahmin. Nowadays Far Eastern Studies, especially around Cambridge, Mass., have become what they call a "discipline" and a rather harsh one at that, full of overspecialized predatory scholars, always on the prowl for whatever erring colleague they may devour. Langdon Warner belonged to a mellower and better day, when knowledge of Japanese culture was a Bostonian social accomplishment, like the ability to bring off a good succotash or chowder. This is the world of gentlemen and scholars—always gentlemen first—of *The Book of Tea* and Arthur Davidson Ficke's book on Japanese prints. There is nothing whatever wrong with this—Sir Charles Eliot (gentleman and British Ambassador to Japan) produced a history of Japanese Buddhism that Professor Elisiev's disciples have yet to overtake and surpass, for all their rigor. Warner was not Eliot, but he was a civilized man with a deep human love of Japan—its people, its culture, its landscape. Although he had many scholarly attainments and gathered loads of scholarly honors, he never ceased to be an amateur in the finest sense of the word, and he never ceased to be a popular lecturer, an extremely popular one.

The Harvard Press has transmitted all this to perfection. This is the sort of production once done by subscription—the list led by The Family and a pride of Dukes, when the Edwardian, *cette belle époque,* was in flower. The copy of an ancient Japanese brocade that covers the box, a very Japanese box, like the ones that used to house the super de luxe edition of *Kokka,* even the gorgeous heavy paper and the slightly brownish ink of the old-fashioned-looking collotypes—how redolent it is of those Back Bay homes—and Brattle Street homes, which owed their wealth to the opening of the Japan trade and their pedigrees to the *Mayflower* steerage list! Warner's text is like that too, so humane, so well bred—and what is most important, it is a perfect example of convergence, because it is well bred and humane in a Japanese way as well as in a Bostonian one. In this world of gentle enthusiasm and scarcely perceptible misinformation, you feel that a "rigorous" contemporary, even another highly civilized amateur like Donald Keene, let alone somebody like Reischauer, would be an intruder, vulgar, clumsy, too loud. Why quarrel with Langdon Warner's superficial description of the *Kegonkyo,* that mystifying vision of exploding universes of universes? Why disagree with his special interpretation of Shinto? Why quarrel with his lack of detailed, precise information? It wouldn't be well bred. I'm not being ironic, really it wouldn't. Berenson might have written this way if he hadn't been just a little too over-specialized, and so just a little vulgar. The accompanying booklet, posthumously put together, is really a collection of essays, and lovely essays they are, full of a warm human feeling for the once living Japanese sculptors who made these things, for the living priests and temple servants who served and still serve them, and for the common Japanese people who still pray to them. The pictures themselves are splendid. There is nothing artistic about them, they aren't bled, or taken from funny angles. As photographs they never compete with their subjects, they simply show Japanese sculpture in its earliest civilized —and some people think by far its best—period. They show most of what has survived, with details, rear-views, close ups, and no monkey-shines. So, so different from a recent book on Egypt which only needed a few naked girls holding telephones to look like a photography magazine.

Tempyo is the eighth Christian century, roughly—the T'ang Dynasty in China, what most people consider the highest point of the later Chinese civilization. So little T'ang sculpture survives, and almost no painting. In Japan, and in a book like this, if we can't get there we can see what it must have been like. This was before Far Eastern Buddhism became what might be called over-specialized in certain aspects of the religious sensibility, let alone before it became a mass of popular superstitions. There is nothing odd or eccentric about these statutes—they never seek a new shiver—only peace and dignity and magnanimity. I suppose they are gentlemanly in the same way but infinitely more profoundly—as Langdon Warner. No wonder he loved them so. And, although they are cult objects of a very late Mahayana Buddhism, they embody something of the magnanimity that shines through the earliest Hinayana texts—the personality of what we like to think of as the "Historic Buddha"—who was, we should never forget (and especially now when his name is being invoked by rascals), a great prince and a perfect gentleman, who believed and taught, as a gentleman should, that sympathy redeems the pathetic transitoriness of all enticing things and all desperate lives. Brancusi, I suppose, in the West, sought such qualities in his art, and the unpretentious sculptor of the Good God on the doorway at Amiens.

The first scroll painting in *Emakimono* is, at this present moment, one of the most influential works of art in the world. Doubtless, you don't know this, but it's true. I shan't name names but an awful lot of modern abstract Japanese painting, here in the States, in Paris and in Japan, owes almost all of its special character to the *Genji-Monogatari-Emaki*. The modern artists have not only studied it exhaustively, in some cases they have come very close to copying it. All you have to do is look carefully at any one of a dozen contemporary Japanese painters and then study these reproductions and it is obvious. This is fine, it is what the classics are for. Where would Mark Tobey be without Tintoretto, or Picasso without Raphael? Or, to update it a little, Guston without those waterlilies?

What is this painting and what is its special quality? Some time in the early part of the twelfth century Takayoshi Fujiwara, the court painter and himself a member of the imperial clan, supervised a group of artists in the production of probably ten or more scrolls illustrating the greatest of Japanese novels, *The Tale of Genji*. In the course of time all but four scrolls were lost, and the remaining ones were cut into nineteen separate pictures. Now the *Tale of Genji* is not only the greatest Japanese literary work, everyone competent to judge agrees that it is the greatest novel ever written in any language. Great as it is, it found an illustrator worthy of it. Now *Genji*, superficially a novel of erotic adventure, is certainly the most profound, philosophically speaking, work of fiction in all literature, and one of its minor, easily grasped points is the haunting permanence of impermanence. It is this sense of sad and splendid things that flee and are forever held in transcendental stillness that the *Genji-emaki* communicates with totally accomplished skill, and communicates entirely by plastic means. In a sense all emakimono are continuously unrolling glances at the floating world, out of the genre ones come the pictures of the floating world par excellence—ukiyoye—the Japanese color woodblock prints. But the *Genji* scrolls are something special—the colors are gentle, the lines softly fluent, the forms obtuse, forms hang and shift as in a quiet dress—and the color chords are certainly amongst the most *recherché* in all art. As in W. J. Turner's rather sentimental poem: "In time like glass/ the stars are set,/ and seeming fluttering butterflies." All stays and all passes in a supernatural stillness.

In this book there are thirteen large plates from the *Genji-emaki,* the most ever reproduced in the West, and they alone make the book worth the money. (I might mention that the whole surviving work is reproduced in facsimile in Japan and can be obtained through a good importer. I think the Boston Museum sells a facsimile of its own great scroll—the *Heiji-Monogatari-Emaki*—with its famous pictures of the burning of a palace.) The *Genji* scroll is one of the world's major masterpieces. No others quite come up to it, but the five scrolls reproduced in this book are certainly amongst the best, at least they are the best in color, surpassed only by the black-and-white landscape scrolls of Sesshu. There are examples of all the major types, religious history, humor, court rituals, landscape, and of the whole period, from the twelfth to the eighteenth century, when the horizontal handscroll was at its best.

Since by their very nature these paintings must be unframed, unlimited, completely fluent, they should have much to teach those modern American painters who seek in their work the same qualities. On the whole, I think they are better source material for our own development than even the best of the Baroque—the unlimited compositions of Tintoretto and Tiepolo. And they are so much more civilized than the latter-day ancestors of contemporary painting—and that is wholesome—we can use some over-civilization along Tenth Street and in St. Germain.

1960

15.

The Pillow Book of Sei Shōnagon

The Pillow Book of Sei Shōnagon is a great Japanese classic, certainly one of the hundred best books of Japanese literature. In translation it will certainly come to take its place as a world classic. It is a mystery. The mystery is the same as the mystery of the behavior of the dog in the night time in Sherlock Holmes. The dog did nothing in the night time.

There is no readily apparent reason why *The Pillow Book* should be read at all, much less be a classic. Sei Shōnagon was a contemporary of Lady Murasaki, the author of *The Tale of Genji,* indisputably one of the greatest novels ever written, if not the greatest. In those years, the latter third of the tenth century, the Heian court in Kyoto included a number of the most remarkable women writers who have ever lived anywhere. Sei Shōnagon is ranked second only to Murasaki Shikibu. Why?

The book is a collection of random notes of every sort. Little stories, anecdotes, reveries, lists of things pleasant, things unpleasant, splendid things, ill-bred behavior, birds, insects, priests, men, women, and dozens and dozens of poems by herself and others. The term "pillow book" is usually interpreted to mean that she kept the sheets of these jottings in the hollow of the wooden pillow still used by many Japanese women to hold up the head and protect the elaborate coiffure during sleep.

Toward the end of the collection, which is not arranged chronologically, Sei Shōnagon says that she started keeping the

pillow book because one of the nobles gave her some bundles of
very nice paper so she thought she had better use it up. This is
typical of her tone throughout. She was a very waspish lady. A
slight note of sarcasm runs through almost all her comments on
human beings or things involving people—except babies.

She writes of babies with the unreal sentimentality not of a
childless woman but of someone who doesn't know anything
about babies at all. She is comfortable and at ease with herself
and the world only when responding to the stereotyped little
crises of the sensibility that are the subject matter of so much
Japanese poetry and painting. Blossoming trees and rain-ob-
scured hills in the spring, reddening maples and the death songs
of crickets in the autumn, snow-laden pine boughs over a single
line of tracks in the winter, the midsummer moon over the hazy
moors.

Many of the notes are about pilgrimages to temples and visits
to shrines, and encounters with monks and abbots and the religious ceremonies of the court. They are with hardly an exception totally devoid of ethical content. It is not true that Japanese
religion, Buddhist or Shinto, is not ethical. *The Tale of Genji*
is very likely the most profoundly moral work of fiction ever
written and it is certainly religious. Sei Shōnagon may well have
seen Murasaki Shikibu coming and going every day for twenty
years but the world of the latter chapters of Murasaki's novel
was utterly inconceivable to her.

Lady Mary Wortley Montagu, Hester Stanhope, Madame de
Staël, Mary Church Terrell, the great women of the past have
almost all been a bit of the waspish bluestocking. If not, they have
been women of almost unbearably exasperated sensibility—that
sensibility exasperated by love—Louise Labé or Gaspara Stampa.
Sei Shōnagon is positively disagreeable a good deal of the time
and almost always, in her comments on those she considers her
social inferiors, insensitively cruel. Her sexual encounters seem
to have been nothing but exercises in one-upmanship, the clever
return of a flirtatious poem or remark with a complicated verse
full of double meanings, most of them uncomplimentary. Her
personality has become an archetype for the Japanese, as stand-
ardized as a Noh mask. Yet all this doesn't matter, or rather it
does matter, to make her great. She is endlessly fascinating, as

self-revealing as Boswell and as comprehensive as he in the picture she gives of a world as over-specialized and peculiar as London of the eighteenth-century coffee shop.

The Heian court in *The Tale of Genji* is a bridge of dreams into a metaphysical realm. *The Pillow Book* is a collection of innumerable tiny, biting realities, whose cumulative effect defines, not just one person, but an endlessly unraveling web of people. Murasaki may be truer but Sei Shōnagon is more real.

Ivan Morris, whose recent *World of the Shining Prince* was about *The Tale of Genji,* has become with this work one of the historic Orientalists. The second volume of exhaustively explanatory notes is as endlessly fascinating as the text itself, which in fact it greatly resembles. Every reference is traced, every pun is explained, every quotation or echo is translated and all the Japanese and Chinese poems are transliterated into Romaji—the Western alphabet—and the translations are uniformly excellent.

It is easy to say that there are plenty of Japanese scholarly editions full of notes and explanations and all Ivan Morris had to do was to translate them. But he has done far more than this. His scholarship is a living thing and he shares with Sei Shōnagon the virtue of not being a square, as are, alas, all too many modern Japanese authorities on the period. He sees through all the painted paper screens. That he is more sympathetic to the unbelievably artificial Heian court and to Sei Shōnagon herself only makes him that much better an editor. She wasn't.

This is certainly one of the outstanding works in the Columbia Oriental Classics program edited by Theodore De Bary, a program that has already taken a great step forward toward internationalizing our taste and forever making impossible an education based on One Hundred Best Books, limited exclusively to the narrow tradition of Western European orthodoxy.

1968

16.
The Prayer Mat of Flesh

Li Yü, author of *Jou Pu Tuan,* lived in the middle years of the seventeenth century, the troubled period of the fall of the Ming Dynasty and the Manchu conquest. Dispossessed from an official career by the change of dynasty, he became a professional writer, publisher, bookseller and dramatist, director, manager and owner of a travelling theatrical company. He is best known in the West as one of the editors of the famous manual of painting which we call *The Mustard Seed Garden,* a title derived from his own small estate above Nanking.

The *Jou Pu Tuan, the Prayer Mat of Flesh,* until it was translated by Franz Kuhn, was unknown in the West, and scarce enough in China. It is an erotic novel in the tradition of the *Chin P'ing Mei,* "Golden Lotus," or "Hsi Men and His Six Wives" as it has been called in English. It differs from this work in several particulars. First, it is much shorter, less complex, more compact. The older novel devotes much space to detailed description of physical reality—landscapes, food, clothing, shelter, all the abundant features of the circumstances of Chinese life in the Ming Dynasty. Li Yü shows his long experience as a playwright. He concentrates on character, psychology, motivation. His people and their motivations are presented largely in terms of their active relationships and dialogue. Each chapter of the novel is constructed like the act of a play, and chapter by chapter the characters interact, change and develop. "Golden Lotus" is a remorseless epic of decay and doom, and wages of lust. The *Jou Pu Tuan* is a tale of what we would call poetic

justice, ending in repentance. As such it compares rather more
with the greatest of all Chinese novels, *The Dream of the Red
Chamber*. It is, however, an ironic and popular telling of a
similar story, characterized by comic exaggeration and tongue-
in-cheek moralizing. Li Yü does share with his greatest Chinese
competitors their characteristic virtues, pure direct narrative,
even-tempered irony, and the sharpest microscopic and tele-
scopic vision.

The best Chinese fiction is like a clear lens, the narrative is so
transparent that nothing seems to intervene between you and
the characters in all their moral nudity. Once you have become
enveloped in the special idiom, you no longer seem to be reading,
it is all as though it were really happening somewhere, in another dimension on which you impinged, unseen and all-seeing.

The best erotica, for reasons I have never analyzed to my own
satisfaction, seems to be ironic. There is always present a subtle
undertone of self-mockery. The author shares it with his protagonists, and involves the reader as well. Perhaps it is our
instinctive self-consciousness as the privates become the public's.
Could it be the comic face of modesty? Anyway, it is as present
in Lawrence Durrell as in John Cleland. When it is lacking the
story becomes simply, naïvely funny. Henry Miller, for instance,
is totally unaware that he has emitted one of the funniest lines
in English as he opens his tale of the Cosmodemonological Tele-
graph Agency—"There was great sexual confusion in New York
that summer." With this kind of innocence, we must perforce
provide our own irony. Petronius, Chaucer, Mirabeau provide
it for us and it is the essence of their charm. In Rabelais the distortion of mockery is so vast that it becomes—Gargantuan. So
too in the hilarious parody of pornography written by Guillaume
Apollinaire, "Onze Mille Vierges," a uniformly incredible explosion of lechery, the willful violation of all proportion produces
great comedy. De Sade, I suppose, was the first of the sick
comics. His utterly impossible exaggerations are comic all right,
but it needs a strong stomach to laugh at the perils of Justine
and the wiles of Juliette.

Are we supposed to take de Sade seriously? Certainly he took
himself in deadly earnest—quite literally so. Are we supposed to
take Henry Miller's flatulent mysticism seriously? Does he? The

measure of the greatness of picaresque and erotic novels is their authors' degree of slyness. We read Li Yü to laugh in passing and at the end to speculate—to be amused and to muse.

We read him for his bedroom scenes. It would be silly hypocrisy to pretend otherwise. But what makes him re-readable, and what saves the succession of erotic episodes from tediousness, is the ironic wisdom and understanding of human folly with which Li Yü moves his characters from one encounter to another. In other words, we read him for entertainment, racy and comic, but in the last analysis, far from superficial entertainment. His wisdom does not lie in the moralistic *dénouement* with which the book ends, but with the all-prevading insight that is everywhere in it. His people stand revealed, not judged. To see them so simply is to understand them, and to laugh.

17.
The Tao of Painting

Mai-Mai Sze, with Zao Wou-Ti, is probably one of the two best living Chinese painters working in anything resembling contemporary Western idiom. Miss Sze is, in addition, a writer of great fluency, charm and intelligence. It is impossible to think of a person better fitted to edit, translate and comment on the classic Chinese artists' manual, *The Mustard Seed Garden*. In fact, her edition of *The Tao of Painting* is one of the happiest inspirations ever to strike Paul Mellon, the committee of the Bollingen Foundation and the editors of the publications program. Furthermore, it is singularly free of quotations from the great Swiss mahatma and there is not a single picture of a snake swallowing its tail. I am all for the elaborate Jung program of the Bollingen people, at its worst it still makes entertaining lenitive reading—but it must be admitted it has been getting a little excessive here of late. Miss Sze's introduction is a most judicious and even-handed exposition of the philosophical principles underlying, and the esthetics of, Chinese ink painting. Any resemblance to "The Secret of the Golden Flower" is purely fortuitous and due to the nature of the subject matter.

This is a book every American artist and art critic should buy and study—every night for several years. Nothing could be a better answer to the problems and dilemmas of modern abstract expressionism. Nothing could be a better antidote to the ennervating poisons which have debilitated modern painting. This is a lucid, profound and exhaustive explanation of what you think you are doing, but aren't what you would like to do, but can't. Furthermore, the larger second volume consists of more than two hundred detailed pictures, with complete explanation, of how it was done, long ago, by far better men than you. It is all there—a complete alphabet of expression—men, flowers, insects, rocks, water, mountains, artifacts, birds and animals. In important subjects the brush strokes of the major Sung masters are classified and analyzed. To those totally ignorant of Far Eastern art this may seem a flagrant, even absolute, contradiction of Miss Sze's introductory volume. Perhaps it does require a little explanation. In fact, perhaps that explanation touches on the very heart of the dilemma of modern American painting. Miss Sze, and everybody else who has ever written about Chinese painting, has dwelt at length on the special Chinese creative response, the rising of spontaneity out of passivity—the creative act which flashes out of inaction. There is, on the other hand, nothing whatever spontaneous about the memorizing of formulae for reproducing the aspects of nature —and a very limited armamentarium of aspects at that. Furthermore, all these little stereotypes are based on the brush strokes, on the actual details of construction, of the Chinese written character, and in the final painting, after they have been learned seriatem, they are assembled like so many minute bits of a puzzle, even a crossword puzzle, with certain traditionally divided areas occupied, and others left blank. The answer is obvious. The technique of painting has been reduced to a bare minimum necessary to provide a self-governing discipline which will *permit* spontaneity. You cannot transcend a medium until you have so mastered it that you are unaware of it. Chinese art is motivated by a kind of empirical mysticism, a non-religious (at least by Western terms) suffusion of the whole being of the artist with an abiding realization of the self and the other, passing beyond such categories as the ego and the world, let alone the soul and God. To support such insight the technology of expression must be sufficiently complex so that revelation does not lapse into platitude, and it must have sufficient technical interest to attract and satisfy the first superficial interests of the spectator. Beyond that it need not go. The elements of Chinese painting could be mastered by any gentleman who could "write a good hand," and were by most before modern times. The majority of the great painters of China, as well as most of her great poets, were men occupying positions analogous to those filled by Engine Charlie Wilson and even Joe MacCarthy. Ponder that for a while and you will readily grasp the difference between the American Way of Life and the traditional Chinese. To have something to say in the arts the Chinese believed one must come with determinative experience, of the world, not art—whether acquired through meditation or through the mastery of affairs; one must have come to profoundly rooted conclusions—wisdom; one must have the automatic facility of the chess prodigy or the master pianist. I am afraid that none of these qualities is very apparent at a Carnegie International or a Venice Biennale.

Over and above its pedagogic value, which is obviously limited, this is a book of great beauty to anybody. The pages of *The Mustard Seed Garden* have a simple charm which is approached only by certain eighteenth-century French masters of drawing, themselves of course greatly influenced by the Chinese, even by this very book. Miss Sze has chosen to illustrate her introduction with some of the most splendid examples of Chinese painting and they are perfectly reproduced. It is certainly one of the loveliest books ever put out by the Bollingen Foundation, and although $25 may seem expensive reading, with the actual book in hand it looks very cheap indeed. I would hate to guess what it cost to produce. Certainly it could not be sold at that price without the subvention of the Mellon millions.

1957

Religion

18.
Ecclesiastes

Ecclesiastes or *Qoheleth* is certainly the strangest book in the
Bible. It not only has no relationship to Judaism but no relation
to religion in the sense commonly accepted when the Bible was
formed or now. Its language is an odd Hebrew full of words
derived from Aramaic, several words which occur nowhere else,
Phoenician influences and two loan words from Persian: *pardes,*
"park," the origin of our "paradise," and *pitgam,* "decree,"
which serve to date it later than the spread of the Persian Empire in the sixth century B.C. It has been said often enough that
Ecclesiastes was influenced by Greek philosophy, by Heracleitus,
the Sophists, the Stoics, Skeptics and Epicureans, which of
course would date it, if they all influenced it at once, after the
conquests of Alexander. No hint of the intensely sectarian Judaism which prevailed in all this time, from the priestly "seizure
of power" in the days of Ezra and Nehemiah, down to the
Scribes, Pharisees, Zealots, Saduccees, Essenes and the Qumran
Sect at the beginning of the Christian era, not a vestige is to be
found in the whole text of *Qoheleth.*

Most of the Wisdom literature of the Bible shares this international and religiously ambiguous character, whatever its date.
The Hymn to Wisdom in Proverbs, the Book of Job, certain of
the Psalms, the Hymn to Wisdom in the Wisdom of Solomon
in the Apocrypha, as well as The Song of Songs and tales like
Esther, Ruth, Tobit, Jonah and Judith, that have been more or
less Judaized in their final form, are survivals of a Near Eastern
ecumenical literature shared by all the peoples of the Fertile

Crescent and created by what comes close to being an international community of intellectuals. The significant relationship between *Qoheleth* and Greek philosophy is the reverse of that commonly accepted. The early nature philosophies of Greece flourished in Ionia, now an integral part of Turkey, in Greek cities that were neighbors of Semitic towns whose ruins, like Ras Shamra where the Ugaritic texts were discovered, are now yielding up literary and religious documents which illuminate the whole dim field of human speculation on man's ultimate problems in the days before philosophy. The Egyptian Memphite Theology with its *Logos* doctrine and "great chain of being," and the collections of Sumerian and Egyptian skeptical aphorisms on the puzzle of existence go back to the very beginning of history. *Qoheleth* is almost certainly late, but books of this sort were being written soon after writing itself was invented. Men in the three great river valleys had discovered the existential dilemma, the absurdity of the human situation, before they discovered the use of bronze.

The basic character, the inescapable insights, of all this literature has led not just to the inclusion of the *Megilloth*—the "Scrolls"—the tales, speculations, and poems—in the canon of Scripture; the fact that they are revelations more fundamental than those of Moses and the Prophets has led to them being especially attractive to piety and mysticism, meditation and contemplative prayer amongst both Jews and Christians. Kaballists and Hasidim, the mystic theologians, Hugh and Richard of St. Victor and St. Bonaventura, the baroque mystics St. Theresa of Avila and St. John of the Cross, down to Teilhard de Chardin in our own day, all have turned to this literature because it opens channels into the deepest recesses of the interior life.

The Song of Songs is probably a collection of group marriage hymns sung at the ancestral Feast of Tabernacles—Succoth—when runnels of the new Water of Life were turned into the fields from the irrigation ditches and the young men and maidens together made love in the grape workers' huts in the fields, a period so long ago that the date has moved across the calendar. Yet The Song of Songs has been the favorite book of the most intense mystics, holy women walled up in the apses of medieval English churches and drunken Zaddiks in villages in the Polish

Carpathian forest. The Wisdom who danced before the face of the Almighty, before the beginning of days, has been hypostasized as the female szyzygy of Yahweh, the Shekinah. Much of Proverbs has been interpreted as a contention between Wisdom, the Divine Woman, and The Adulteress, the Scarlet Woman of the Apocalypse—Ishtar, Anat, Astarte—the "abomination behind the altar," the benign and maleficent aspects of the Ba'al who in the end won out over all the other ba'als of all the High Places of the Near East. This is an interpretation which leaps over orthodoxy from the Neolithic to the contemporary occult, Jewish, Christian or syncretistic.

So likewise Ecclesiastes. It probably owes its survival in the canon of Scripture to the connivance of the disciples to whom the author was the Qoheleth or Teacher above all others. His philosophy is a skepticism common to men who have grown weary of handling words as a business, the philosophy of scribes who see through their commissions, whether they press styluses into wet clay or dictate in sumptuous suites on Madison Avenue or in Washington. As so many people in similar positions before and after him, Qoheleth is always careful to avoid a direct offense to orthodoxy, and his editor appends an apologetic footnote designed to soften the blow of the relentless existentialism of the philosopher.

Qoheleth never challenges miracle, mystery or authority directly. Rite, dogma, taboo and superstition are bypassed by routes that are always uncomplicatedly moral. He never advises his hearers to eat pork or marry within the forbidden degrees. He never challenges the historicity of Moses. He only says that there is no evidence of a divine moral order in the affairs of men. What God may be doing he keeps to himself. As far as we know life is a puzzle bounded on all sides by oblivion. Its satisfactions are to be found immediately in existence itself and existence may well betray the seeker. The wicked triumph more often than not and there is no reward for good. In fact, the definition of good cancels the notion of reward as life cancels death. There is a basic and incorrigible folly that haunts the ways of men. God and eternity may be unknowable but the tendency of man to choose a trivial, immediate good over a great final good is indisputable. What future ages were to call original sin is the only provable theological dogma. Socrates was wrong. Man does not follow his reason if only he understands it. Unless one faces facts and learns to live with what cannot be changed and finds enjoyment in work, and in understanding of the simple facts of life, he will live and die in folly, and never have been fully a man.

"Face existence" might not have been the first and greatest of the commandments, but it is the first and greatest of realizations, and on it hang not only all the law and the prophets but all religion in the modern sense whatsoever, whether Paul, Augustine, Kierkegaard, Scheler or Sartre. This is where the religious experience begins. The vessel must be emptied before it can be filled. Western philosophers and theologians are verbally explicit, but this is the meaning of the emptying sought as the preliminary to religious growth in all the philosophical religions of the Far East, whether Buddhism or Hinduism. Zen is only a practical non-verbal technique for realizing the philosophy of the Void. St. Paul's word was *"kenosis"*—"emptying out."

Another consideration which undoubtedly aided the admirers of Qoheleth in forcing his book into the canon of Scripture is its superlative literary quality. As a piece of writing, it is one of the finest and most sustained things in the Bible. Its elevation compares with the great canticles, the Song of Deborah (Judges 5), the Song of Hezikiah (Isaiah 38), the Song of Moses (Exodus 15), the Magnificat and Benedictus in Luke, the Song of the Three Holy Children (The Apocrypha), the Song of Hannah (First Samuel 2), the Song of Isaiah (Isaiah 12), the Song of Habakkuk (Habakkuk 3). These are all moderately short and extremely intense lyrics, very fittingly sung on the different days of the week in the monastic office of Lauds. Ecclesiastes is an extended philosophic revery, a discursive questioning of the meaning of life which relies very little on the devices of poetry for its effect and yet this effect is that of a profound philosophic poem. It ends, however, with one of the finest poems properly so called in all the Bible—"Remember now the Creator in the days of thy youth . . . ," an elaborate metaphor of the decline and fall of the noble palace of the human body into decrepitude and then oblivion. The King James Version rises to no greater heights. Whatever Tudor ecclesiastic was responsible for its tremendous language was a very great artist indeed. It is true that as a translator he gives the text an unwarranted interpretation which greatly aids its adjustment to orthodox taste. The first line almost certainly read originally, "In the days of your youth remember your grave," a different pointing of the Hebrew, *boreka* for *bor'eka*, "your grave" for "your Creator." I suppose this is a kind of final irony, a subtle change in the last words of The Teacher, that he would greatly have appreciated, for it is this slight change which has insured that he would be heard amongst the Gentiles, in parts of the earth he never dreamed existed, for two thousand years.

1966

19.
St. Thomas More

It has certainly taken a long time but Christians are slowly coming to realize that their religion, even when considered only a system of social ethics, is utterly incompatible with modern civilization. Catholic *aggiornamento* must be understood as the onerous and complicated struggle of the Church to free itself from unholy alliances and to return to the evangelical person of Christ and start over. This has led to a new emphasis on the theology of the Apostolic Age and the early Fathers of the Church in Alexandria and Asia Minor. This was a period before Constantine when Christianity was still a subversive creed offering its own social ethic in complete opposition to Imperial Rome. There was a similar movement amongst the Humanists of the early sixteenth century, contemporary with the Renais-

sance and the Protestant Reformation. They attempted to develop a social philosophy based on the Gospels, the Acts of the
Apostles, Clement of Alexandria, John of Damascus and similar
thinkers. Its basic concept was the establishment of a community
of love encompassing all of society and having as its final end
the divinization of the world. These words are John Damascene's.
They are also Teilhard de Chardin's. They are also Karl
Rahner's. They are also St. Thomas More's. This is the basic
reason for the tremendous revival of interest in More today.
Yale University is issuing a critical edition of his complete works.
Accompanying it will be a popular edition of selected works in
translation. Edward Surtz, S.J., and J. H. Hexter are editors of
the *Utopia* in the complete works and the separate paperback
editions by both Surtz and Hexter respectively together consti-
tute the best text and the best introduction to it there have ever
been. One of the most extraordinary things about the *Utopia*
is the immense literature which has developed since the rise of
our civilization founded upon covetousness to explain the book
away. Pro-capitalist churchmen have dismissed the moneyless
communism of the *Utopia* as just another of More's witticisms,
and attempted to prove that his slashing criticisms of sixteenth-
century society were motivated by a scholastic defense of monasticism. Socialists, on the other hand, have dismissed his attempt
to construct a society in which covetousness, pride, sloth and
anger were inhibited to the greatest degree compatible with an
organic social flexibility. To them such ideas have been just the
reflection of the poverty of the pre-capitalist mode of production.
They have seen his communism and his emphasis upon education, creative work and technology as an attempt to escape from
this into a communist society with the unlimited satisfaction of
human appetites as its highest goal. Since they cancel each other
out, both arguments are obviously false.

J. H. Hexter and Father Surtz have been leaders in the movement in More studies which has insisted that St. Thomas More
meant what he said. Since they are themselves profound students
of More's sources in the pre-Constantinian past and amongst
the pre-Reformation and pre-Counter-Reformation Christian
Humanists who were his contemporaries and immediate predecessors, they are able to speak with completely cogent authority.

More's book, as Gibbon says of Boethius's *Consolation of Philosophy*, "a golden book worthy of the leisure of Cicero or Plato," and in fact surpassing either, has provided all languages with a common noun which means an idyllic society of social peace, justice and abundance inherently impossible of achievement. Marx and Engels constantly contrasted "Scientific Socialism," their own kind, with all others—"Utopian Socialisms." What they meant was that all other Socialist thinkers have undertaken schemes for the basic reconstruction of society for ultimately moral reasons, while their Socialism had accepted from classical economics an idea ultimately derived from Newtonian physics, that a society which released the maximum number of individual social evils would result in the greatest possible common good.

Whether Adam Smith, Ricardo, Benthem or Mill, classical political economy was a pseudo-science of human relationships emptied of moral content, and so today its descendants, whether Marxist Communism or Capitalist Democracy, are founded upon amoral assumptions. But there are no such things as amoral societies. A value-neuter philosophy or science of man is a contradiction in terms. Therefore a society guided by value-neuter principles and amoral in the assumptions which underly the action of its social mechanisms simply becomes ever-increasingly immoral until the acceleration of the destruction of human values drives its best minds from it in dismay. This is More's argument in his criticism of sixteenth-century Europe, and of course it is also the argument of artists, writers, philosophers, even economists, on both sides of the Iron Curtain today. It is also the argument of Christianity, even at its most institutionalized and compromised, but it is an ever-mounting experiential, existential realization in the very guts of the most articulate Christian leadership.

This is the relevance of More. He is one of the very few thinkers ever to try to construct a model of a community of love while recognizing the fragility and recalcitrance of his material. He did not believe that man was naturally evil. He believed that man was naturally good but prone to mischief. He did not believe that tinkering with the economy and the environment would insure the automatic release of universal benignity. He did believe that it might be possible to construct an environment and an economy based purely upon natural law as distinguished in his mind from revelation (his Utopians are pagan) which would inhibit tendencies to social destructiveness and enable tendencies toward social peace, joy, creativity and familial community.

All down the four centuries since he has been without major influence upon effective political and social thinkers except in his own country. We too often forget that British Socialism, as has been made abundantly clear from the memoirs of every British Socialist leader, is based not upon the materialists, Marx and Engels, nor their bureaucratic and formalist French predecessors, but upon Ruskin and William Morris—Christians, artists and men of sensibility, who were morally outraged by the horrors of an acquisitive society. Moscow, Peking, Washington, Paris, Bonn, these, like Jakarta or Conakry, are simply foci of one world "society of rising expectations" and the very term reveals what drives them and that will all drive the human race to disaster unless the nature of these expectations can be changed.

This is the relevance of More's *Utopia*. Of course, it would not work. It is only a schematic model constructed long ago in a different economic era, but it correctly diagnoses the ill, and the remedies will only be found by seeking to improve and develop its prescriptions. Will this happen? No. In More's day there were 450 years left. In our day it is most unlikely that there are that many months and quite possibly not that many weeks. So we can solace ourselves with the beauty of More's style, its extraordinarily agile and resonant Latin so much richer than that of his friend Erasmus, if we are scholars, or if we are not, the clarity and sparkle of the modern translation edited by Father Surtz. As Engels and Marx used to say, "Freedom is the consciousness of necessity." At least there is considerable pleasure in knowing what hit you and why.

Although Hexter's book, especially as corrected in the final note for the paperback edition, clears up most of the problems of the scholarship of the *Utopia,* what is most impressive about it is his personal, deeply perceptive analysis of More's own tragedy—a saintly man destroyed by the delusion of participation.

1964

20.
The Oxford Conspirators

Books on the Oxford Movement, the development of the Catholic Revival in the Church of England, seem to be eternally popular. They have been written from all sorts of points of view: Low Churchmen who believed the whole thing was, and still is, run by a special committee of the Society of Jesus; Broad Churchmen who looked on it as the triumph of barbarism and superstition; amateur psychoanalysts like Geoffrey Faber who manages to be very penetrating and very silly in the same sentences; and, of course, Anglo-Catholics and Catholic Modernists in the Church of England themselves. Today if we could lift a typical English churchman of the early years of the nineteenth century into the middle of the twentieth by time machine, it would seem to him that the Oxford Movement had won all along the line. Even the most militant Low Churches would seem to him positively papist, in both doctrine and liturgy. Yet the struggle still goes on. Although a middle-of-the-road Anglo-Catholicism with strong Catholic Modernist overtones is the dominant theology of Anglicanism, there are still plenty of Low Churchmen who are horrified by rites like the Benediction of the Blessed Sacrament, practices like genuflection and doctrines like transubstantiation or the Immaculate Conception. On the other hand the most "advanced" wing of the Anglo-Catholic Movement is today the most integralist and maximalist Ultramontane and ultra-Thomist body of opinion left in Catholicism, Orthodox, Roman or Anglican, and it is there that the Latin Mass and the solemn chanting of the Latin Breviary, the strict interpretation of infallibility and the absolute condemnation of birth control still survive. Ultramontanes have always found this all-inclusive ecumenicity outrageous, but before the Council of Trent it was nip and tuck. Had it not been for purely secular political maneuvers, what Anglicans call the Church of Rome might itself well have been such an ecumenical communion.

It is this inability to accept Catholicism as catholicism which results in a peculiar united front between militant Low Church and "Romanist" historians of the Oxford Movement. Both treat it as a "Romanizing" movement, essentially unassimilable to Anglicanism, and, since "Romanizing," inevitably headed for collision with the doctrine of infallibility. Therefore they treat the entire revival as a kind of scenic background for John Henry Newman's long, tortured and tortuous journey to the cardinalate. All but the least informed know enough not to stress its ritualism; while to the more ignorant it's all a matter of bowing and scraping before idols whilst emitting gobs of incense in all directions over a coughing and sneezing congregation.

Father Marvin R. O'Connell tries hard to escape from this web of historical fallacies, but the very title of his recent work, *The Oxford Conspirators,* shows how unsuccessful he is. I know of no book by a Roman Catholic in this century as widely informed, as carefully researched, nor as full of interesting detail and penetrating insights into the various personalities, yet the book is as misleading as the most bigoted in its Romeward perspective. Father O'Connell repeats the old myth so beloved of Anglo-Catholics, of the somnolent, simoniacal and cynical eighteenth-century Church of England. True, these vices flourished, but throughout Christendom it was a period when the Church Universal was most captive to the parochial nation state, the heyday of a debased Gallicanism in France, of the mercantile Lutheranism that was to revolt Kierkegaard in Denmark, and the utter prostration of Russian Orthodoxy to the Czar and Greek to the Turk, while the city of Rome itself was a malarial cow pasture, thinly scattered with palaces, ill-kempt churches and slums, the capital of a semi-barbarous state, ridden with bandits and ruled by indifference and terror. Yet the eighteenth century was a time of some of the noblest saints, of "going to the people," whether in the slums or in the martyrdoms in the forests of America and the cities of Asia. It was also a time that rediscovered, developed and intensified the art of contemplative prayer. In England it was a time of a mass revival of the Christ-centered life led by the Wesleys, the time of William Law, the teacher of both the Wesley brothers and the historian Gibbon, a mystic in the tradition of the great English mystics of the Middle Ages and the teacher of that practical divinity, that family monasticism so English and best known in the life of St. Thomas More. It was also the time of the full flower of that same lay monasticism known as Quakerism. So it is simply not true that Newman and a small band of his disciples woke the English Church like Lazarus from the grave.

Quite the contrary. All the leaders of the Oxford Movement were profoundly influenced by William Law and the Evangelicals, the "Methodists" who had stayed in the Church. That is precisely what the Oxford Movement was, a mutation of Evangelicalism, a return to the evangel, to a life based on that of the Apostles and centered on the living Christ. They did not refer to the movement as Anglo-Catholic but called themselves The Apostolical Movement. From the Apostles they moved step by step through the Apostolic Fathers, through the great theologians of the Patristic period, and the "Councils of the Undivided Church." Their opponents did not call them Newmanites, but Puseyites, because it was Edward Bouverie Pusey, not Newman, who was the leader and the theologian. Newman was the public personality, the preacher, what today we would call the public relations man. His own special group of disciples were characterized by an unstable emotional intensity, excessive scruples and churchiness, and like Newman himself, they were obsessed with the search for external authority. Pusey, Keble, John Mason Neale and all the other great leaders of the Movement who stayed on the far side of the Tiber knew that the basis of Catholic authority was ultimately internal, just as much as did the Quakers. "If thee does not turn to the Inner Light, where will thee turn?" It was not for the pomp and power of the Vatican that St. Thomas More went so wittily to the block. It was, as he insisted again and again, for his conscience.

In his quest for what psychoanalytic biographers call "paternal authority" or a stable super-ego, Newman constructed a raft called "The Theory of the Development of Doctrine" on which he and his personal disciples could cross the Tiber. Once they landed on the other side, the Holy Father, enthusiastically aided and abetted by their more maximalist fellow converts, demolished the raft. Newman spent the rest of his life a frustrated man still seeking authority to submit to, in most cases—for instance, the Irish university—in perfectly needless self-sacrifice.

The Catholic revival in the Church of England was very far indeed from being damaged by the conversion of Newman and his circle. A generation later the Movement had left the universities and gone to the slum churches of the great cities, to jobs that nobody else wanted, merged itself with the life of the poorest of the poor, the people Engels wrote about in *The Condition of the Working Class in England,* and had turned empty, ruinous buildings into houses of prayer filled with humble practitioners of the imitation of Christ, and had far surpassed, not just Newman, but Rome itself in the revival of the interior life, and its outward garb, the simple splendor of liturgy. It was the merging of the radical Catholic theology, quite independent of the Oxford Movement, of F. D. Maurice, the social revolutionary Catholicism of de Lamennais, and the Apostolic theology of Pusey that produced the great Red slum priests like Stewart Headlam who would be considered an advanced ritualist even now and who was the founder of the first socialist organization in England. It was Maurice who realized that England could never be returned to the spiritual life within the confines of the Oxford colleges and who led the way to a Catholicism with the deepest possible roots in the souls of ordinary men. But "conspirator" none of these men, not one, ever was. Newman's, Pusey's or Maurice's apostolates were as public as the loaves and fishes.

1969

21.
The Modernists

This is a book a good many people have been looking forward to, ever since it was announced. John Ratté has made a specialty of the study of the evolution of liberal, radical, progressive and modernist Catholicism in the nineteenth and twenties centuries. Presumably he knows as much about the subjects—plural, each one of these adjectives refers to a different school of thought, a different group of men—as anybody now writing. Yet this is not the book I for one had hoped for. Perhaps it is the generation gap. Ratté makes it all seem very remote. Although he would certainly say he was most sympathetic with Loisy, Tyrrell and Sullivan, here is a case where that infinitely misused term "empathy" can be used correctly. He just doesn't seem to have much *Einfuhling*, much visceral indentification, with the gut agonies of his subjects. The fact that he treats all three men more or less as equals, and as more or less the same kind of "modernists," is sufficient proof of his lack of deep feeling for them. They are actually very unlike, and Sullivan is as remote as can be from the other two.

Alfred Loisy was a late-born member of the French Enlightenment, a rationalist of the orthodox school. When he left the Church, this is what he became, and it is the last lingering descendants of Voltaire, Tom Paine and Robert Ingersoll, who read him today. For all his connexions with German Higher Criticism of the Gospels, he was utterly French. In France the Church is, even today, a social institution, with roots that sink deep through the centuries and millenniums to, not just Roman or Gallic times, but to the mysteries of the caves of the Dordogne, the rites of passage and of the year, that subtly reshape the ceremonies of the Church in remote villages in the Massif Central—but which also still determine the kind and quality of devotion in St. Severin, the parish of the most radical intellectuals, in Paris. It is the almost instinctual urge to preserve the special *tremendum* which haunts French society at its most significant moments that is responsible for the Goddess of Reason enthroned on the altar at Notre Dame by the Revolution, the High Church rituals of the Comteans, and even for the ceremonial sins of Baudelaire, Gourmont and Huysmans. Had Loisy been left to his own devices, and not forced to quit the Church, he would have become the apostle of a ritualistic, agnostic, intensely chauvinistic, social cultus, very like Japanese Shinto in the years just before War Two. Neither the evangelical Jesus, in all ways made like unto us, nor the prayer life of the Catholic mystics, nor the re-creation of a specifically Christian philosophy, like the Fathers of the Church or the modern Russians, meant much to Loisy. It is precisely these aspects of the Church, as well as its Ultramontane political structure, that he wished to do away with.

Sullivan is not relevant, except to show in what a distorting mirror English and French modernism appeared in the United States. Both Loisy and Tyrrell were amongst the least vulgar of modern religious thinkers, and von Hügel was so refined that he was inaccessible to almost all of his contemporaries in the Church. (Which is probably the real reason he was not condemned.) Sullivan was what is wrong with the Church—any contemporary Christian Church in America—pushed to its logical conclusions. He was shockingly vulgar. Ratté quotes some pretty embarrassing things from his published and unpublished writings, but he apparently assumes that no one is likely to go back and read Sullivan. Try it. You can find his novel in most big libraries. Queasy is a mild term for the reaction to a full dose of William L. Sullivan. I suppose he does represent one tendency in modern Catholicism—that tendency which has produced a liturgy in the language of the luncheon clubs and a confessional modelled on Dear Abby. What is modern about it? This we have always with us. Bingo. Many sincere men believe that if you can just talk the language of a spiritually famished society dominated by the cash nexus and with TV tastes, you can convert that society, or at least nibble around its edges. I believe this is a grave error, due to the fact that the clergy simply cannot communicate at all with the socially alienated and corrupted except in the most catastrophic emergencies. Jive liturgies and rock Masses mimic, they do not communicate. Sullivan doesn't mimic—he is a natural-born Babbitt.

Father George Tyrrell is a different kettle of fish altogether. His life was centered on prayer. He was blest with a soul of exceptional natural nobility. His primary vocation was pastoral —as confessor and spiritual counsellor. Everything he wrote was shaped by the passionate concern of a contemplative for the cure of souls, and it cannot be understood properly if divorced from that living context. He was also the only man in the entire movement of reform, from Acton to the American Paulists, who was manifestly what the Church, if it had not expelled him, would have called a saint. Loisy is reasonable, Sullivan is rhetorical, Tyrrell is passionate, and these qualities are applied by each specifically to the love of God and the love of man. Loisy and Sullivan are chauvinists, Sullivan not a little crazy on the subject. Tyrrell never gives up a mystical quest for the City of God. Even after he was expelled, some of the most sensitive and acute religious intelligences in England, both Roman Catholic and Anglican, continued to go to Father Tyrrell for spiritual counsel, if not confession. I can imagine going to confession to either Sullivan or Loisy only on a stormy night when far, far from home, and heavy burdened.

One of the most annoying things about Ratté's book is its constant slight, subtle undertone of depreciation of both Loisy and Tyrrell—especially Tyrrell—but not of Sullivan. Ratté is the master of the gently pejorative, and of the innocent quotation *en deshabille*. Or is this what the book is all about? Is the inclusion of Sullivan with these two large-souled, richly cultivated men delicate exercise in vulgarization by association? Again, both Loisy and Tyrrell are judged by what they became after they were expelled. This is manifestly unjust. Tyrrell lived on only a short while, and always in great mental pain, and he certainly never ceased to think of himself, except in brief moments of despair, as anything but a Roman Catholic. He never even showed any interest in returning to the Anglicanism from which he had come, and where he had hundreds of followers and many more sympathizers. Loisy was no different than countless French priests, from Suger of Brabant to today, who are devout Catholic sceptics.

Most important, it is extremely unjust to portray the modernist movement as an attack on the Church. It was exactly the opposite. It was an attempt to construct a new defense, which would answer the modern challenger, in terms he could understand. The modernists were acutely aware that Darwin, Freud, William James, Einstein, or even James Joyce, defined a universe of discourse which lay outside that defined by the opponents of St. Thomas, and that the old apologetic was simply not relevant. (I don't of course mean that they had heard of all these individuals, some of whom came to public notice after their time.) Tyrrell and von Hügel conceived of this apologetic as founded on a specifically Christian philosophy, something which had not existed in the main tradition of the Western Church since Origen and St. Clement—who did not belong to the Western Church. It is interesting to compare the first tentative steps of the modernists toward a Christian, not a Christianized, philosophy, with the normal development of Russian philosophy from the beginnings to Berdyaev. What seemed an adventure into unexplored territory to them was just the accepted and familiar field of Russian Orthodox thought. This, obviously, is due to the abiding power of the tradition of the Fathers of the Church in Orthodoxy.

So likewise, it was in Anglicanism that the modernists met with their greatest response, and precisely because the Anglo-Catholic movement since the days of Keble, Pusey and Newman had been founded on two rocks—one of which was the Apostolic and Patristic Christian world view. The other was the interpretation of the Christian experience as the experience of Christ —what His experience was, and what others experienced when their lives touched His. Even Loisy, who was hardly a mystic, realized that this meant, beyond Christology and the analysis of texts, the living experience of the Christian community, the fellowship of the Christian experience. As Wittgenstein used to say of philosophy, "What do we do when we *do* Christianity?" On this hangs all the law and the prophets—but the first and great commandment and the second that is like unto it, are forms of prayer, and this Father Tyrrell, counsellor of seekers, never forgot.

Exegesis, philosophy, liturgics, the concerns of *aggiornamento*, bear little resemblance to those of the modernists of the beginning of the century. Roman Catholicism dropped them and passed them by and has come at the basic dilemmas by quite different routes. Not so with Anglicanism. The documents of modern Anglo-Catholic theology and apologetics are not just deeply indebted to Tyrrell and von Hügel, they are all part of an essentially developing tradition. The most reliable historian of Catholic modernism is the Anglican Alec Vidler, quoted often by John Ratté, and in his books Bishop Charles Gore, Father Thorton, Bishop Weston, *Essays Catholic and Critical*, A. E. Taylor, and the rest, march along in order with Tyrrell and von Hügel, nobody breaking ranks in the development of a contemporary Catholic apologetic which has grown up alongside, and quite independent of, the leaders of the world of Post-Vatican Two. This last Advent season, while considering this review, I have read once again Father Tyrrell's meditations on the Spirit of Christ and the Prayer of Christ, *Lex Credendi*. This is Tyrrell at the high point, spiritually, of his career, and it is certainly meaningful still in a way that much of the New Theology is not, and it is certainly intensely, inexpungibly, Catholic.

It seems to me that there are two drives operating today, two contradictory definitions of *aggiornamento*. One is the now long dead Liberal Protestantism which is given lip service in the luncheon clubs and all the forums of the Social Lie, the apotheosis of spiritual vulgarity. If this wins, it means the end of Catholicism, Christianity, religion, all interiority. The other is simply a more developed concept of prayer, and the opening of all life to its pervasiveness. This is not new at all, but Patristic, Apostolic, Evagelical—or if you will, a clarification of the religious experience as such, so that it might be shared by all men, today. Father Tyrrell and Baron von Hügel were amongst the first to be acutely aware of this antithesis in modern religion. It is obvious which side they chose, which is why they are so desperately relevant today.

1968

22.

The New English Bible

Very seldom has any book of any kind been given the advance publicity blow-up that has launched this new translation of the Bible. I understand that the initial print order is one of the largest in the history of publishing. Since the first of the year editorials, pre-reviews, hand-outs, news stories have been appearing everywhere. You'd think it was a paperback, with illustrations from stills of the picture, of *The Life of Christ* by Carl Sandburg, with Elizabeth Taylor and Marlon Brando. However lavish the salesmanship, it is apparent that the interest is genuine, the demand is there. What is this demand? And does this translation meet it?

Superficially, the arguments for a new translation are, as they have always been, quite convincing. The language of the King James Version is archaic. We have an immense amount of material, codices or quoted passages in other early writings, which is much older than the texts available to the Jacobean translators. We know a good deal more about the meaning of the Greek in certain ambiguous passages. We know a vast deal more about the life and times of Christ and His disciples, and even more about the Old Testament days, so that we can interpret the text with greater understanding. We certainly assume that we are far less time-bound and ethnocentric than a group of Anglican divines of the early seventeenth century. We are more self-critical and less likely to phrase the text to fit our own doctrinal or liturgical presuppositions. (The most famous example of this fault is the use of "chalice" instead of "cup" in the Douai accounts of the Passion.)

The clergy, especially the Liberal Protestant or Broad Church clergy, insist that the language of the King James Version is alien to modern congregations, and even more alien for missionary purposes to those, especially "young people," who are outside the churches. The chairman of the committee responsible for the present translation announced it with the words, "I hope we have produced a work which will be read by the younger generation who now regard the Bible, with its archaic phrases, as a stuffy and old-fashioned book." *Time* magazine, expanding this remark, goes on to say, "Despite its many magnificent drums and tramplings, the 350-year-old King James Version might as well be in the original Greek for all the sense most moderns can make of it."

What was that? I would say that this bit of wisdom only indicates that *Time* thinks so little of its "Religion" section that it employs Zen Buddhists who have never read the Bible to write copy. I mean, really.

It is not difficult to suspect a fallacy in the second argument, the one from the change in the audience. The validity of the first argument is simply a matter of information. Have the researchers of paleography and archeology presented us with enough emendations, and emendations of sufficient importance, to warrant an entirely new translation? They have not. There is not a single universally accepted change in the Greek text available to the King James translators which makes the slightest difference in the facts of the Gospel narrative, or in what Catholics call "doctrine, faith and morals." Three hundred and fifty years of research and discovery—in the text, that is—have not advanced the disputed questions of the Virgin Birth, the existence, nature and number of the sacraments, the personality, divinity and humanity of Jesus, the doctrine of the Trinity, the institution of a priesthood, the meaning of the Death and Passion of Jesus, all the other points at issue in the dogmatic disputes of the churches—not one of the questions has been advanced one iota from where they stood in the days of Launcelot Andrewes and Archbishop Laud . . . or George Fox. With few exceptions they are purely verbal emendations which have no influence on the sense of the narrative.

Are we less ethnocentric than the committee of Jacobean divines? This is a dilemma like "Cleon says all Cretans are liars. But Cleon is a Cretan." The King James Version has a definite Baroque splendor. But the new version has a definite British Liberal Protestant tone, sometimes casual, sometimes chummy, sometimes drab. The *koinē* of the originals may have been the common tongue of the Eastern Mediterranean of the first century, but the language of the Evangelists and Paul is more often splendid than chummy, and it is never drab. Robbed of its Baroque splendor, the Book of Revelations sounds rather like the ravings of a crank. Perhaps this is a genuine crux. The fact is that the Apocalypse cannot be translated into the common speech of the suburbs of London and Glasgow, without being totally changed in significance. Only crazy people, who live in the slums, not in the suburbs, talk or think that way anymore.

As for our increase in historical knowledge. The New Testament is one of the largest collections of primary source material for any period of history. It is itself the most comprehensive source which we have on its own time and place in history. It is in a sense self-explanatory, it carries with it its own background material and footnotes. All subsequent archeology and historical research simply broaden and clarify details of the narrative as it has come down to us . . . as far as retranslation of the text goes, that is. Of course, you might write into the original text "the revolutionary discoveries of the Dead Sea Scrolls" and all that sort of thing. But that would not be translation, it would be forgery. The Jacobean divines may have been, like all of us, ethnocentric, but I doubt if they envisaged the Apostles as British courtiers and scholars and members of the House of Lords. It was left for our time to compare Jesus Christ to an advertising agency account executive.

I guess historical provincialism is the key to the matter. The role of the translator is much like that of the actor. The success of a translation is the convincingness with which it projects a foreign or past original onto a modern stage. Are the Jesus and Apostles of the *New English Bible* dramatically believable? Do we feel "This is the way it would have looked to me if I had been there?" Or do we feel that the accidental present is being forcibly projected into the past, like *Hamlet in Evening Clothes*?

In the first place, the *New English Bible* is full of mediocre writing, as well as careless language. One reviewer has pointed to the story of the entry into Jerusalem, where the colt is tethered to a door, "a usage so modern ("tether" hitherto meaning to tie an animal where it can graze) that it hasn't got into the dictionaries." The chairman of the panel of translators, Professor C. H. Dodd, has said that his committee suspected rightly that exact scholarship does not always go with a sensitive feeling for literary style, so the experts' prose was given lightness and grace by another panel of experts, whose names have not been officially divulged. Read that over carefully. Surely one literary grace lacking to Professor Dodd is irony. The Anonymous Lightness and Grace Committee is a notion worthy of Gilbert and Sullivan.

Sometimes provincialism can illuminate the original—but it is not usually our provincialism, but a past or foreign one on which we can gain perspective. Pope is not Homer, but from him we learn to see things in Homer we never would have known were there. T. E. Lawrence's Homer, on the other hand, just seems bad writing. Robert Graves' Homer is as odd as Graves himself. Even after centuries Urquhart is too odd to represent the humanist Rabelais. Do the translators of the *New English Bible* illuminate or distort the text?

Beyond questions of accuracy and lightness and grace, it is a question of tone. The King James translators believed the words of the New Testament in a way that a panel of modern scholars does not. The archetypical, heiratic grandeur of the narrative, as Toynbee has so ingeniously analyzed it, the transfigured schema of tragic drama—this had a significance for Anglican priests of the early seventeenth century that it simply does not have for a liberal scholar or theologian today. Furthermore, that seventeenth-century significance was enough like the original first-century significance that it had for the evangelists themselves so that identification was possible. The darkness of the Passion is not congenial to a committee of modern scholars. Again, the even darker, semi-gnostic speculations of the author of the Epistle to the Romans and the introduction to the Gospel of John are still less congenial. To the early seventeenth century such occult Platonism was more than congenial, it was positively up to date. So a cosmogonic vision like VIII Romans is far clearer, in the plain sense of that word, in the King James Version than it is in the *New English Bible*.

I think the committee did its best work in the Pastoral Epistles, low-keyed passages of narrative in Matthew and Mark and the straightforward historical prose of Acts. (The poetry of Luke, and the gentle, feminine tone of that Gospel seems to have escaped them altogether. Here both Moffat and Knox far surpass them.) It is obvious what is happening. Where the original is secular and "other directed" the modern, secular, other directed translators can identify with it. Where it is not, they miss the essential tone.

Where the actors and speakers of the New Testament are "like us" they seem a little closer, at least for a change, in words that are like ours. Urquhart's Rabelais is a freakish English classic. Jacques Le Clerc's translation is not great prose—but Rabelais really was more like Jacques Barzun than he was like a crabbed Scotch eccentric, so the translation is illuminating. The trouble is, nobody in the New Testament was much like the members of a Broad Committee.

How archaic, in fact, is the King James Version? Of course it is ridiculous to say that it might as well be in the original Greek for all the sense most moderns can make of it. Most moderns seem to make sufficient sense of Shakespeare—he is rather popular on BBC TV—and the Bible is in somewhat less archaic language. An amused *Time* correspondent wrote in to ask if the editors thought "robbers' cave" was less archaic and more easily understood than "den of thieves." Jehovah's Witnesses, the Salvation Army, the Pentecostal sects, Negro store-front churches, these are all groups of common people who seem to get a great deal out of the *Authorized Version*. In fact, it is amongst those sects who emphasize precisely the "archaic" text that evangelism is most successful, and it is amongst Liberal Protestants, who want an up-to-date version, that evangelism is least successful. Perhaps it is the religion that seems stuffy and old-fashioned to the "younger generation," not the language.

I am afraid I took this assignment more seriously than it warrants. I gathered all the recent translations of the Bible I could obtain. I hoped to do an extensive, judicial, even scholarly comparison of them all. It is not worth the space and trouble. What is wrong with them all is that they are not very good. The King James translators were great writers; Goodspeed, Moffat, Rieu, Philips, are not. They are pedestrian, and the New Testament may have many faults, but it is not pedestrian. For my taste the best translations are Father Ronald Knox's, and something that might well have been a monstrosity, the *Basic English Bible*. Father Knox has style, it may be a narrow style, but style it is. The *New English Bible* is close to styleless, it is so obviously the work of a Broad Committee. The *Basic Bible* is an engaging oddity, and it is certainly simple enough for the simplest to understand.

1961

23.

The Bourgeois

Marx says somewhere, and I'd appreciate help in relocating the quotation, that his diagnosis of the ills of capitalism may have overproven the case for collapse. What keeps the system going? Why doesn't it break down immediately? What makes it morally endurable? The survival, says Marx, of more humane social relationships from the older cultures of the Middle Ages and Renaissance. "If you want to see capitalism in all its horror," says Marx, "go to California." Again, Maritain, answering the same objections to his diagnosis of fatal ill, says, "What has kept Western civilization going all these years?" and answers, "The prayers of the contemplatives in the monasteries."

These answers are not jokes. When a culture loses its interiority, when the tiny flame of contemplation in the heart of civilization goes out, chaos and death take over. The time may vary, remissions and relapses may make the chart irregular, but the prognosis is certain. Today we live in a corpse, a Dybbuk, a kind of violent mummy. Western civilization still rides to destruction, but like the dead body of El Cid, tied in his armor to his war horse. In seventeenth and eighteenth-century France there were theologians and spiritual advisors and preachers who could foresee the consequences of the secularization of all life, the reduction of all values to the cash nexus, and who fought a desperate rearguard battle against surrender to The World. They lost, at least as far as the official Church, what Simone Weil called the Great Beast, was concerned. It was not until the end of the nineteenth century that anything resembling a spiritual religion was restored to respectability. By and large that occurred because of the manifest collapse of a secular value system, and its challenge by a new structure of attitudes and sensibility, a movement its opponents have always called "Neo-" Catholicism. Of course there was spiritual life, contemplative confessors and martyrs of prayer, all through the heyday of a sensate culture, but they were underground, whether they were saints now in the calendar or unbelieving poets and painters.

Mostly, when we study the eighteenth century, we concentrate on the founders of Enlightenment and the Age of Reason, and pay little attention to the battle in the Church itself, which led to the victory of a middle-class, secularized, formal religion, Catholic Capitalism, or Capitalist Catholicism. Bernard Groethuysen's book *The Bourgeois* makes it clear how the bourgeois, who once chopped off the heads of aristocrats and priests and nuns, came to bow his own head to the priest at the Elevation of the Host. That accommodation, so convenient to both sides, was prepared by two generations of controversy within the ranks of those who had been given the cure of souls. The spiritual life was left to the poor, the intellectuals, converts and the mentally unbalanced. It is not just that parish life, especially in the towns, became a minor activity of the business ethic. From Stendhal's *The Red and the Black* on, there is a host of novels giving testimony to the overhelming of the seminaries by a kind of systematized lower middle-class greediness. They became simply grubby, ill-shod, ill-clothed, ill-housed, ill-fed, trade schools.

The Church had once been an anthropological religion, like that of primitive people, that penetrated all life and gave the rites of passage and the rites of the year and all the details of commonplace existence a transcendental meaning and justification. This was replaced by a rigid dogmatism of social order. As it says in the Anglican catechism, "My duty towards my neighbor . . . is to do my duty in that state of life unto which it will please God to call me." A new hierarchy of exploitation has substituted for the old hierarchy of reciprocal duties and responsibilities. The language of catechists and preachers is a parody of primitive Franciscanism, but it is the preaching of humility for the humble, and pride for the proud.

The great trouble with the Catholic form of the business ethic was its quest of stability at all costs. It lacked the inherent dynamism of the Protestant forms described so well by Tawney. The Huguenots forged ahead because of a kind of metaphysical instability of world view. The Catholic bourgeois was frozen in a rigid system of computer programming, scholasticism emptied of the moral content that had once given it meaning.

Groethuysen quotes at some length a correspondence between Neckar and Rivarol, the substance of which is, "Only fear of the devil keeps our servants from murdering us." The obvious reverse of this coin is the Marquis de Sade, who simply called all the bluffs. At the top there was left only an Easter bonnet, business contact, church-going, while the foundations in the poor slid away into ever more gross superstition. With the explosion of the revolutions of 1848 it became apparent to men of sensibility that this convenient system was both dangerous and degrading. The Catholic Revival that began with Romanticism fought it for a century, on all fronts, Newman, or Hello, or Maritain, Bloy, or Abbé Brémond, but it was a century before they were talking to anybody but themselves.

I have only one objection to Groethuysen's book. At the end he has a chapter which seems to say, reversing the Emperor Julian, "Thou hast conquered, oh pale *commerçant!*" He hasn't conquered, not yet, though he is still trying. But even if he had, what of it? Groethuysen catches himself in the old nineteenth-century contradiction founded on the assumption that history is value positive. Even Marx, the leading exponent of this heresy, never believed it emotionally, which is the reason for his pro-phetic Hebraic fire. So, finally in our time, the most telling an-swer to the Catholic version of the business ethic has been an eschatological or apocalyptic morality—"He who is near to Me is near to the Fire. He who is far from Me is far from the judg-ment." On the back of the dust jacket the publisher advertises its own answer to *The Bourgeois*—*Priest and Worker, Autobiog-raphy of Henri Perrin,* a miraculous life of prayer, lived in the eye of apocalypse—that "failed."

1966

The Past

24.
Greek Tragedy
in Translation

Nothing gives a case-hardened critic more pleasure than the chance to say, "This is it. No qualifications. Go out and buy it, everybody." I haven't felt like this since I did the first job on Needham's history of Chinese science, and that, after all, was a work of limited appeal. The David Grene and Richmond Lattimore edition of *The Complete Greek Tragedies* (4 volumes; Chicago, 1959) is something for absolutely everybody. As this job has been coming out over the past few years in small volumes I have said that it was a major event in American scholarship, a historical event in translation of the classics, and far from a minor event in American poetry. Since the Renaissance, one of the symptoms of cultural health has been the ability of a given period of national culture to raise translation to the level of high literature, to assimilate the past on the most noble level. Maybe American civilization isn't so bad off as us readers and writers for the liberal weeklies sometimes get to thinking. We have produced something over here to match the great Tudor and Victorian translators. (Yes, the Victorians were great translators. We just aren't Victorians, so they seem Victorian to us.)

Where do you begin with such a feast of good things? David Grene, John Frederick Nims, William Arrowsmith, Rex Warner, Witter Bynner are all very good poets in their own right, Richmond Lattimore and Robert Fitzgerald are, for my taste, especially fine ones, and I have always considered Bynner's translation of Yuan Ch'en's "Lament for His Wife," in *The Jade Mountain*, one of the best American poems of the twentieth century, quite the equal of Pound's more famous translations. Many of the others may have published good poetry under their own names that I am not familiar with; certainly here, working with the Greek text, they come off very well—without any exceptions. Of course it is true that some are better than others, but none is bad. What is more, none is odd—like the exasperating recent translation of the *Odyssey* by Robert Graves—without doubt the most misleading translation in English since the Urqhuart-Motteux *Don Quixote*. None of the plays is anachronistic or a hobby-horse perversion of what the Greeks actually said. They are all clear, accurate reflections of the Greek in well-polished mirrors of contemporary American language and taste.

Not just language and taste, but, although they are far from being playbook "treatments," they are eminently actable—at least they are when the Greek is. I have only the mildest objection. Euripides, on the whole, has been cleaned up. It is not that they have made him better, they have made him just a little more tasty. A lot of nonsense has been uttered, following T. S. Eliot, about Gilbert Murray's Swinburnian translations of Euripides. If Eliot had had more Greek, he would have known that Euripides does sound like Swinburne—given the idiom of his time. He was a hysterical neurotic, and for the turn of the century, Murray did convey very well the special vertigo of his verse. It is a pity he was never translated by Baudelaire, but alas, Baudelaire, financed by an American millionaire, only translated a bit of Hiawatha! Swinburnism is a lesser, more childish thing than "La Cloche Fêlée," but it's the best approximation our grandfathers could find. The translations of the choruses of the "Ion" and the "Hippolytus" that H. D. did long ago, and which can be found in her *Collected Poems*, hit off the Euripidean vertigo exactly, and it is a great pity they couldn't have been incorporated in these versions. But who could dare to raise a quarrel on this score? The translation is more accurate, and lines like David Grene's "Aphrodite has broken her spirit/ With the terrible sickness of impious love" catches exactly the Euripidean accent as he tells the story of that lewd queen.

Not least, as a piece of bookmaking, this is what Hollywood calls a spectacular—but a spectacular in perfect taste. The beautiful typography, the satisfying paper, the chaste decorations, all of which have become familiar as the small volumes came out, have been climaxed by a stroke of genius. The box is an "off black," with a terra cotta band, white letters and two small decorative black animals, and the books—four volumes lined up, Aeschylus, Sophocles, two volumes of Euripedes, in beautifully graded tones of terra cotta, volume for volume from cream to Venetian Red, black vertical lettering and little white people off the vases. What a joy to see.

Why should these books be, as they say, in every home? And why these books especially in every American home? They are so pretty, they are ours and for us, but beyond typography and even translation—we of all people need most the Greek tragedians. Hard as it may be for you and me to believe, irrefutable evidence is piling up inescapably that an appreciable number of Americans really do believe the Great Fraud of the mass culture, what the French call the *hallucination publicitaire*. They only know what they read in the papers. They think it is really like the movies. Try saying to a well-educated American, even a psychoanalyst or a fashionable minister of God, "Life is tragic." Nine times out of ten he will answer, "Oh, well, now, I wouldn't be so pessimistic as all that." He doesn't know that the art of being civilized is the art of learning to read between the lies. He is very far indeed from knowing that the deepest, the most unshakable optimism is based on the tragic sense of life, as one good European once called it. They say our civilization is based on the Bible, Homer and the Greek tragedians. For my taste, the Bible is a dangerous book, because it can be, and with few exceptions has been, interpreted to give guarantees to life that life in fact never offers. Here in these plays, as in Homer, is life as it really is, men as we really are, when we beat our wives or cheat our grocer or plan our perfect societies or run for office or write our poems—but projected against the empty and splendid heavens, and made noble. Take away the costumes and the grand language, it is the same pride, the same doom haunting Orestes that haunts every Certified Public Accountant, every housewife, every Automobile salesman. How much nicer people, and how much happier, they'd all be if they only knew it. Here is their chance to learn.

1959

25.

On Translating Roman Verse

It is a commonplace with amateurs of the philosophy of history, from Upton Sinclair to my corner grocer, that Roman and American imperialism have much in common. We are supposed to have the same mass culture, the same coarseness of fiber, the same stoatish sex habits and we are supposed to be headed at an ever accelerating pace for the same doom. Not only amateurs believe this but Arnold Toynbee has become a world-wide celebrity like Albert Schweitzer, Brigitte Bardot and Sterling Moss by interpreting contemporary capitalist civilization in terms of the decline and fall of the Roman Empire, even though it is the fashion in bona fide scholarly circles to deny that the term "decline and fall" can be properly applied to the history of the Roman Empire. If we are so like them, it is curious indeed that our artistic expression has been, so far, so utterly unlike.

Since Bryant, Motley, Parkman and the *Federalist Papers*, American literary expression has grown ever less Roman. Inspired by the questionable parallel between the two cultures, it would be easy to imagine the list of favorite authors—Richard Nixon's might be Cicero; Eisenhower's, Julius Caesar; Senator

Fulbright's, Livy; Arthur Schlesinger Jr.'s, Virgil; Douglas Fairbanks Jr.'s, Horace. For better or worse some of these people not only have never heard of these Roman authors but seem to make do very well with comic books, the sports page and the stock market quotations. As is well known one of the most famous of the list once boasted that he had never read a book since he left West Point.

It is not just the top dogs of that conspiracy of mediocrity known as the power élite who show no interest in Roman literature; the Latin poets have no more influence on the leading versifiers of our literary establishment than the mordant observations of Tacitus have on the policies or speeches of Lyndon Johnson. There is every evidence in fact that Latin literature in some peculiar way is especially antagonistic to American. One of these matters of fact is that we seem to be utterly unable to translate it. No American translation of any Latin poet has ever been anything but pedestrian and sesquipedalian. They all give the impression of being onerous jobs done in maximum discomfort, bad hours, low pay and terrible conditions. "Pound's *Homage to Sextus Propertius*," you say? In the first place it doesn't even claim to be a translation, and in the second place it is not in American but in Pound's own professionally odd lingo, the last-born utterance of pre-Raphaelitese.

Years ago Horace Gregory translated Catullus and some years later Allen Tate did the *Pervigilium Veneris*. These might pass muster as mediocre examples of the verse of Gregory and Tate but they would be acceptable as translations only to those ignorant of the originals. Even poets deeply saturated with Latin verse like Richmond Lattimore and Robert Fitzgerald have never been able to re-embody it in their native language. As far as I remember, Pound, Tate and Gregory are the only poets of substance who have ever had a go at the Latins. Louis Zukofsky for the last few years has been "translating" Catullus but not into American or even English, but into Zukofsky, a language which notoriously raises more questions than it solves, like the web of Penelope.

I think the reason for this studious avoidance of Latin poetry by American poets lies in the radically different, in fact totally antagonistic, objectives of twentieth-century American verse and

Latin poetry of the Augustan and Silver Ages. We are still in the midst of an anti-rhetorical movement in poetry now two generations old. Commingled with this main current is an effluent which is at least equal in power (like the Missouri and the Mississippi), a movement of intellectual complication and wit which we call, for lack of a better word, metaphysical. Then there is a counter current against the latter tendency, sometimes weaker, sometimes more powerful, the anti-literary objectivist style of presentational immediacy which stretches from the Imagists to Gary Snyder and Denise Levertov. All these characteristics define a universe of discourse unknown to Latin poetry. In addition to this the American language is moving away from its Indo-European origins and is so far from the inflected subtleties of Latin that it is closer much to the syntactical logic of Chinese. Again the acoustic qualities of the two languages are most unlike. Virgil may have been "the molder of the mightiest measure ever wielded by the mind of man" but that measure cannot be reproduced at all in English, much less American, and attempts to do so just sound like comic parodies of Longfellow. I for one wish this was not so. Horace is one of my favorite poets; a loyal companion and a sovran antidote to the irascible subjectivity that is called the modern temper. I would love to translate him but, as I sit here writing this, and turning over in my mind the snows of Soracte, the chirring bracelets, the lissome slave girls, the crystal spring water, I realize only too well that I haven't the vaguest idea of how even to begin.

Such qualms, if he's had them, have never deterred Rolfe Humphries. If he keeps on and lives long enough he should eventually get through to Claudian. He's done Virgil, Ovid, Martial, Juvenal. The kindest word to apply to these translations is dogged. He's kep' at it. And once in a while he achieves a certain felicity, but it is so brief that you wonder if it hasn't been an accident. As the Fuller Brush men say, "Just keep at it and the Law of Averages will take care of you."

Constance Carrier's *Propertius* is no better. In addition she quite misses the neurotic melancholy, the masochistic anguish of Propertius. He is one of the few classic writers, possibly the only one, afflicted with the modern temper, but fouled up as he is, he still is eminently masculine and I doubt much if he could ever be translated by a woman. A talented enough woman could conceivably project herself into a man's role but not likely into the role of a perverted man. We have seen fairly recently this doubled and re-doubled mirror image projection fail in an attempt to translate the modern Greek pederast, Cavafy. Constance Carrier does no better with the masochist Propertius.

James Michie's *The Odes of Horace* includes the Latin text to which it provides a moderately amusing pony in meters that sometimes resemble remotely the original. Of course you wouldn't know all this unless you read the Latin in the first place. As English verse his translation is not always doggerel but it isn't often a great deal better. Michie, by the way, is English, not American, and it is unquestionably easier to bring over at least a little of Horace into English than it is into American. Horace has always been a sort of shadow Poet Laureate of Great Britain. One of his best Victorian translators called him "an eminently clubable man." I just can't imagine Horace in American, least of all that aspect of him. What kind of poet would a "clubable" American be?

One trouble with most of these translations is that they are in rhyme and since rhyme necessitates an unreal distortion of word order and padding or omission from even the most glib versifying translators and since much of the beauty of the Latin verse depends on the ring and clash of its peculiar acoustic properties and syntax, a rhymed translation is almost certainly foredoomed to failure. The best American translators in the twentieth century, whatever language they translated from, used unrhymed free verse. I am no passionate propagandist for free verse. This is simply an evident fact and it is extraordinary that people persist in ignoring it.

The Roman Comedies is a reprint of selections from the Roman drama in the Random House Lifetime Library now twenty years old. They weren't very satisfactory renditions then and time has staled them. It's too bad. Lacking the Attic new comedy, these plays are the archetypes of formal comedy from Japan, China and India to Hollywood or the Berliner Ensemble. You'd never know it. I doubt if the peculiar rhythms of Plautus, a little like a clodhopper Paul Fort, could be rendered in any other language but his own, not even the Latin of two generations later. However, somebody, some day, should be able to transmit something of his muscular tension and his vibrant guts. There's nothing of it here. There's nothing of Terence, either. He had the disposition of an exquisitely cultivated and subtly sarcastic hairdresser. God knows, there's still enough people like that running around, but I guess they don't read Latin, though quite a few write English.

Hubert Creekmore is a most conscientious translator, but he never catches the iron ring of Juvenal. He does get across the bitter flavor of his ironic bawdry and he picks up most of the jokes and manages to be quite funny. Like the rest of these translators some of his wittiest passages owe their effect to their wry commentary on the Latin, and so go past those who don't have the original tongue. I'm afraid we'll just have to face it for a while yet—the best translator of Juvenal is still Sam Johnson.

This is what's missing in all this stuff, the clang of Roman iron on Roman bronze. From Dryden to Johnson the English Augustans may not have had the genuine Roman temper but they could manage a reasonable facsimile thereof. I am inclined to think that if we had diagnostic instruments of sufficient sensitivity we would discover that Roman and American civilizations are as unlike as any two great imperialisms in history.

French civilization is like, but in a minuscule way and ineffectively. France is always striving to become a petty Rome, to the distraction of the rest of Europe. For this reason a showy job of well-bred *vulgarisation* like Pierre Grimal's *The Civilization of Rome* catches something that the most learned Latinate American might miss—the spirit of Roman formalism, legalism and *gloire*. These of course are French vices and they are only minor Roman virtues, but at least they're Roman. So Grimal's book gives the feeling of Roman culture or at least a portion of it. The reader comprehends even if he does not understand. Roman civilization was based upon law on a clearly defined hierarchy of values and as clearly defined a hierarchy of power. It was pessimistic because it was rigidly traditional. At the end the original endowments of Roman civilization were still there; they had only withered. In the entire structure of the culture there had been no significant growth. Whatever novelties had occurred had been purely formal. The first large-scale genuine novelty, Christianity, that intruded into the structure exploded it. The interrelationships of the basic values of the culture were likewise formal as were the spiritual relationships of actual men. What this means in literature is that the literature was rhetorical—that is what rhetoric is.

It is hardly necessary to point out to my fellow citizens at this late date that American civilization is polyvalent, experimental, optimistic, fluent, and sensuous like the Greek and the basic relationships of its society are at least dynamic and strive to become organic. It's easy enough to translate this into a literary esthetic. So translated, it is obvious on inspection that we are dealing with something which can never be put in a one-to-one relationship with the items of the Roman world-view. The relevance of this conclusion to the difficulties of translating Roman verse into American is patent.

1969

26.
Of Myths and Mythmaking

Jung, Jane Harrison, Frazer, Francis Cornford, Robert Graves, —"The Greeks and the Irrational," —a large percentage of the Bollingen Library—but above all Jung, —this is all popular reading today. The breakdown of the French Revolution produced an anti-rational reaction in the arts and in speculative thought. The Romantic movement covered this ground once before. Today we can draw the easy parallel—the breakdown of the socialist revolutions of the twentieth century has produced a new Romanticism and a new emphasis on the irrational elements in society and human behavior generally. However, those who think this parallel comforting may be made uncomfortable if they pursue it far enough, because of course the French Revolution and the rationalistic synthesis which accompanied it did not break down, they were violently suppressed. It is obvious that even if there were no hydrogen bombs, social and political relations today are so irrational that they will become totally lethal suddenly and soon. This is no reason to assume that men are inherently irrational in their behavior, and those who in the past made that assumption were simply pamphleteers for counter-revolution. The apologists for The Myth in our time or in the first quarter of the nineteenth century do not claim that men need the irrational as a tool to master the environment and live together peaceably and equably, but that they need it as a weapon to master each other and to avoid the problems presented by the environment.

A myth is a symbolic embodiment of an emotional and collective solution to environmental or interpersonal problems. Is there such a thing as a "true myth"? No, because a myth owes its symbolic character to its falsity and it owes its emotional tone to the drive of the personality to overcome the inadequate satisfaction which is the result of its falsity. It is "symbolic" to the degree it does not reflect reality, not to the degree that it does. A definition like this cuts through a lot of the muggy fog of irrationalism and sentimentality which surrounds the discussion of myth, especially amongst literary men. "Science is the critique of myths," wrote W. B. Yeats. "There would be no Darwin had there been no Book of Genesis." In a special issue of *Daedalus* devoted entirely to the subject of myths and mythmaking (Spring, 1959), Harry Levin closes the first essay with that quotation. This sort of talk is very chic today. It thrills neurotic nuclear physicists just like it used to thrill what Moore called "Willie Yeats' train of duchesses." Like lots of myths, it's startling, but it isn't true. In fact, like lots of myths, it is presented in that startling fashion precisely to cover up its falsity. Exactly the opposite is of course the fact. The important thing about it, like lots of other myths, is its context. Just because we like his poetry is no reason why we should persist in deluding ourselves. It's about time that somebody stood up and said that William Butler

Yeats was an avowed Fascist, an extreme example of the counter-revolutionary Romantic. He was not just against Marx or Dide-rot, he was against Montaigne and Erasmus. Of course he believed in myths—he believed in duchesses. And he believed in these irrational things because he was unable to cope rationally with himself, other people, or his physical environment. This was not his fault. Society did not make available rational instruments of sufficient power to accomplish the ends he sought. His predicament was not unlike that of the typical juvenile delinquent.

Yeats may have fancied that he "constructed Great Myths by which men could live." He did nothing of the sort. He constructed poems. We are compelled to believe myths, by their own rhetoric, by our need, and usually by outside forces as well. We do not believe works of art—we enjoy them. A work of art is a fact, like a potato, a pet dog, a vulva, a bottle of wine, and is finally enjoyed in the same way. Those who, in our day or Coleridge's, persist in confusing art and myth are always up to something. They are not interested in providing enjoyment, but in exercising power. T. E. Hulme, D'Annunzio, T. S. Eliot, Georges Sorel, the mythographers and their apologists, these are the boys who really believe that "art is a weapon," they are all more or less politicians *manqué*. The real reason Mr. Eliot disdains Signor D'Annunzio is simply that he was so successful. Both are vendors of coercive and rhetorical myths.

It is necessary to say all this because the literary contributors to the *Daedalus* symposium are all adherents of the Eliot-D'Annunzio thesis. (Does this coupling shock you? Take away the garlic, the energy, and above all the success, and they are really very like.) Professor Schorr, a well-known academic disciple of Mr. Eliot, says, in writing about Blake, echoing directly Mr. Eliot on Blake, "Great literature is impossible without a previous imaginative consent to a ruling [dig that "ruling"] mythology that makes intelligible and unitive the whole of that experience from which particular fables spring and from which they in turn take their meaning." This just isn't true, although, like so many untrue things, it is good Eliot. What makes Dante dull is precisely his mythology, his spiteful God, the embodiment of his spiteful and unforgiving self. What makes Blake's later works dull is precisely his slightly lunatic desire that people should *believe* them. What makes Homer great is that he believed nothing except the evidence of his senses and the testimony of his reason. Least of all did he believe the "myths" which he used with such consummate irony.

How many of the greatest artists of the world have been precisely destroyers of myth. Not just Homer. Professor Schorr, with truly Eliotic comprehension of a text, introduces the remarks I just quoted with another quotation from Wallace Stevens. Wallace Stevens writes: ". . . we live in an intricacy of new and local mythologies, political, economic, poetic, which are asserted with ever enlarging incoherence." Read that over again, Professor Schorr. It has perfectly Stevens' tone, that old apostle of animalism and sceptic faith, and it might have been uttered by Sancho Panza.

The contributions of the anthropologists and sociologists to the *Daedalus* symposium are on the whole much sounder than those of the literary men. I do wish, however, that disciples of the Swiss Mahatma would drop this unpleasant tic they've picked up from their master of talking about "science" when we all know that there is nothing whatever scientific about them, least of all when they quote that irresponsible windbag, Frobenius, as Joseph Campbell does in the leading paper on "The Historical Development of Mythology."

There is not much question but that the anthropologists and sociologists in the symposium are the only sensible contributors. The literary people are talking arrant nonsense. Mr. Levin seems to think that he and his friends have converted the scientists to something. "When a society comprising as many scientists as the American Academy of Arts and Sciences entertains such a topic sympathetically as well as critically, it is a perspicuous sign of the times." What on earth does this mean? Congresses of folklorists, anthropologists, sociologists, comparative religionists have been entertaining this topic sympathetically, critically and *ad nauseam* since it first became fashionable a hundred years ago. That literery men and psychogogues should now be getting in on the act is not a perspicuous sign of the times, it is an ominous one.

By far the best contribution is an all too brief paper on "World Interpretation and Self Interpretation" by Ernst Topitsch. I don't doubt but what the belle lettrists and Jungians feel uncomfortable in his company. He believes in what they call the Myth of Materialism, or Rationalism, or Scientism, or maybe even Economic Determinism. For comic relief there is a bit by Marshall McLuhan on "Myth and Mass Media." Marshall McLuhan is a Canadian Professor of English and Chairman of a seminar on Culture and Communications. May be, but he sounds like a very young Madison Avenue type who had been reading too many books.

Since Blake and Sorel figure so prominently, it might be well to close with the observation that the myths with which they proposed to wage war on an industrial and commercial civilization have been proven failures, precisely because of their mythic nature. What survives is their passionate realization of the necessity for the declaration of war. Blake, William Blake himself, is the viable myth, not Los or Enitharmion.

1959

27.

Sir Thomas Browne

Jeremy Taylor, Thomas Browne, Richard Burton, Thomas De Quincy, Walter Pater—the last generation, devoted to a plain, hard style, lumped together all writers of prose with a capital P. Purple patches and set pieces were not just at a discount; they were not read at all. Even the ceremonial wit of Gibbon was too much for those who thought Hemingway sounded like real talk and Raymond Chandler sounded realer still. Today when we pick up a copy of *Men Without Women* or *The Big Sleep* it sounds as literary as the blank verse of Webster. For almost all purposes, however impractical, the plain style is unchallenged today. What little fancy writing there is is archaistic and deliberately returns to writers like Browne or Jeremy Taylor and bypasses completely the fancy writers of the Edwardian period and the Revolution of the Word of the years between the wars. If there are any disciples of James Joyce abroad, I am not aware of them, but Edward Dahlberg continues to astonish the latter years of the century with deliberate imitations of *Holy Dying, Vulgar Errors, The Anatomy of Melancholy* and Philemon Holland's translation of Pliny's *Natural History*.

There is no limit to the curious things that our affluent society manages to find to do with its leisure. Jazz trumpeters transcribe Guillaume Machaut. Gibbon, illustrated by Piranesi, decorates the bedside tables of the Jet Set. Technocrats in their garden suburbs lay aside their slide rules and marvel over the elegant theorems of Diaphantos of Alexandria in the long winter evenings. Years ago, I bought in Foyles', on remainder, the first edition of Geoffrey Keynes' *Works of Sir Thomas Browne*—the special issue on handmade paper—for three guineas. Today it is unobtainable at any price. It was one of the finest jobs of bookmaking of the Twenties and I treasured it for years along with the MacKenna *Plotinus, The Complete Works of Sturge Moore* and other items of that kidney. Alas, I no longer have it though I have clung to the Simon Wilkins edition of 1836 in three-quarter olive-green levant, one of the finest editorial jobs of its day. It is very good now to have Keynes' editing, augmented and corrected, and reduced to four compact volumes.* The beautiful typography, I imagine, is Sean Jennett's, the man who gave Faber and Faber books their characteristic style. The binding is gray buckram, stamped with gold on maroon, the top edges colored, the paper, as so rarely now, certainly looks like it would last my time. I say all this, not altogether tongue in cheek, because Sir Thomas Browne is still a bookman's author, however much his popularity may be growing.

* *The Works of Sir Thomas Browne,* edited by Geoffrey Keynes. 4 volumes; Chicago, 1964.

Why read Sir Thomas Browne? For amusement. There is no better bedside reading. It is no accident that so many of his chapters close with melodiously fingered, long-drawn-out linked cadences invoking sleep. "To keep our eyes open longer were but to act our *Antipodes*. The Huntsmen are up in *America,* and they are already past their first sleep in *Persia*." But there is amusement and amusement. Like all the finest amusers, Sir Thomas Browne communicates a unique and precious quality of soul. At thirty-two he had made the Grand Tour and seen all that was necessary of the great world and graduated M.D. from the University of Leyden. A Londoner born, he settled in provincial Norwich, married and raised a happy family who became, each of them, a distinguished person. While the world fell apart in civil war, Commonwealth and Restoration, he exercised his massive intellect in the calm pursuit of the infinitude of five-fold patterning in Nature, in the origin of the gypsies, in why black bears sometimes have white spots, in the superstitions of the countryside and in the curious customs of the antique inhabitants of the neighborhood. *Religio Medici,* though written early, proved a summation of his life. He was a kind of ornate Montaigne and it is not for nothing that the Continent thought him a Catholic sceptic and so translated him, while the Vatican decided he was an agnostic and epicurean and so condemned him. In his letters, especially to his family, the ornateness is modulated but the taste for curious examples never tires, although in personal intercourse, he tends to take his engaging instances from actual fact and personal history rather than books, and so his letters have a simple humanity still more Montaignian. In Wilkins' day, most of these letters were unknown. Geoffrey Keynes gives us four hundred pages at least as delectable in their way as *The Garden of Cyrus* or the *Vulgar Errors,* at least as wise and less quaint. Far be it from me to scorn Sir Thomas's quaintness. It is as precious as anything among the oddities of art, but more precious still is the slow reverberation of a personality which grows through a lifetime of possession. That, of course, is what he is—one of the very few authors you discover in youth, buy for your own as soon as you can afford it, and read off and on all through your life.

"Blesse mee in this life but with the peace of my conscience, command of my affections, the love of thy selfe and my dearest friends, and I shall be happy enough to pity *Cæsar.*"

1964

28.
Coleridge and the Lability of Affect

CHICAGO REVIEW
THE UNIVERSITY OF CHICAGO
CHICAGO, ILLINOIS

Dear Mr. Rexroth,

If you haven't yet written the Coleridge review*—could you possibly use it as a vehicle for an article on Zen Buddhism? A good part of the summer issue will be devoted to Zen ("Zen in the arts"—Hesamatsu, "Buddhistic Meditation in the woods"—Kerouac, Zen poems from Whalen and Gary Snyder, "Zen Boom in America"—Alan Watts; so how about "Zen and the notebooks of Samuel Taylor Coleridge"?).

Cordially yours,
Edward Leibstone

Hum. Or, to speak in the *langue verte* of the *métier*—OM. It seems to me that several assumptions lay behind this postcard. That I like Coleridge. That I am part of the fad for Zen Bud-

---

* *The Notebooks of Samuel Taylor Coleridge,* edited by Kathleen Coburn. Volume 1, in two parts, text and notes. Bollingen Series L, New York, 1958.

The Sacred River. Coleridge's Theory of the Imagination, by James V. Baker. Baton Rouge, 1958.

dhism. That I think there is some connection between Coleridge and Zen Buddhism, whether of the Japanese, San Francisco or Greenwich Village variety. None of these assumptions is sound. There is something that Coleridge does share with many, but not all, of our native Zenists, and that is a certain kind of personality, or personality disorder. Nothing could be further from the ideal Buddhist personality, Zen or other.

Coleridge had a badly disorganized mind. He was incapable of sustained attention, consistent thinking, persistent work, and he suffered from what the psychiatrists call great lability of affect. He was very untidy in his life and inside his head. In some ways he might be called the first hipster. He took dope. He was an inveterate religious window-shopper. His approach to literature was subjective to the point of being barrenly emotive —he "dug" the plays of Shakespeare, for instance. Reading him it would be quite impossible to tell what Shakespeare altogether or any play separately was simply *about*. In fact, in complex cases, the major tragedies or the great romances, it is obvious that he didn't have the foggiest. His mind was as muddy as yen-shi soup. He could take the clearest ideas and make them hopelessly obscure. He liked them that way. Vagueness, indefiniteness, obscurity, excited him. All the moral and intellectual qualities which the eighteenth century abhorred, he liked best —in fact, he dug them. As a thinker and esthetician he is renowned for his theory of the imagination. Numerous books have been written on this subject. None of them agrees as to what Coleridge's theory was. The most fun to read is I. A. Richards' which undertakes to prove that Coleridge meant exactly the opposite from what he said. This is a fruitful—sort of Zenny?— approach. Mr. Richards' mind is a more amusing place than Coleridge's. There are many confusing books in Muirhead's Library of Philosophy, the most confusing is his own *Coleridge as Philosopher*. Husserl and Heidegger can't hold a candle to it. I read it as a boy and it was one of the major influences that turned me away from Germanic Romantic metaphysics for good and all, and for that I am grateful.

What then is the reason for this century and a half of imposing reputation? Who likes Coleridge and why? Reactionaries. Coleridge and Wordsworth started out on the frivolous edge of the

Left of the French Revolution. Wordsworth, who had the moral fiber of a rabbit or sheep or some other herbivorous animal, folded up when the heat was turned on in the Napoleonic Wars—when it became obvious that the Revolution meant business—business that would hurt British business. Coleridge went on, as did the Germans, to lay a swampy philosophical foundation for the Europe of Metternich. We forget that the essence of Romanticism is precisely Restorationism—the vague mystery and terror of pseudo-medievalism. Out of Coleridge does not come Baudelaire, but Walter Scott. Against him stand the intransigents —classicists and Jacobins—Burns, Blake, Landor—the apostles of that French Revolutionary *virtu—clarté*. Out of Walter Scott comes the Myth of The South and the pillow-case head-dress school of American poets and critics, just to bring things down to contemporary cases.

How curiously like is Coleridge's career to that of the editors and contributors of one of America's best-known quarterlies. The first volume of notebooks covers the years 1794 to 1804, the years that made all the difference. Walks amid the hills and waters of the Lake Country, chemistry experiments, readings in the Byzantine Neo-Platonics, notions for poems and books that never got written, growing fright at what was going on in France, religious speculations that seem extraordinarily super-stitious in 1957, brief paragraphs of painstaking analysis of specific sensations, and with this, a constant running commentary on his sensibility as such, a seeking of maximum irritability—a kind of beginning of the reasoned derangement or at least exacerbation of the senses. It is in these latter passages that Coleridge shows at his best—just as his best lines as a poet are concerned with careful scene painting in an occasional and often unfinished poem. At least he had a vast and hungry mind, and poking about in it, as you can in his notebooks, is certainly interesting. There is no question but what Coleridge is interesting as a person—a character—and if you want to take him as, unless you are very naïve, you have to take Leonardo or Goethe or Marcel Duchamp, well and good. Everything he wrote is really "Notebooks," "Aids to Reflection," "Biographia Literaria." There is only one trouble with it all, taken that way—it's all so endless and amorphous, and, like certain other, similar people,

De Quincey, another hipster, there is something a little sickly sweet about it all—like the taste of opium. There are a number of sickly autobiographers, Amiel, Bashkirtsieff, Richard Jeffreys, Barbellion, James Hinton—this is Coleridge's set, he is the greatest of them, but it is here that he belongs. And like them all—he palls on one—he's so *morbid*. He's at his best at his healthiest, describing the shape of a cliff or the flora along a waterfall on Scawfell. He is at his best when he is most like Wordsworth, when he comes nearest to fulfilling the program they set themselves in youth. And this he does only by the way, by accident. His philosophy is vague and pretentious and gets nowhere. His major poems are dreadful things, as cooked as Poe and no more wholesome. If he believed that the imagination is that activity of man by which he apprehends aspects of the universe considered ultimately as an organic whole, he never said so clearly, in so many words.

With Miss Coburn's work I have no quarrel. I found it entertaining reading, with a certain melancholy wistfulness about it, and her own work, her scholarship, her volume of notes on Coleridge's notes, is stupendous. With Mr. Baker, well, "His treatment of meter, however, is more satisfactory than Wordsworth's, and this is not remarkable in one whose mastery of it in *The Ancient Mariner* and *Christabel* is little less than miraculous." I guess stuff like this goes over down in the land of Sidney Lanier and Edgar Allen Poe.

What has all this got to do with Zen Buddhism? Practically nothing. Coleridge, like Cardinal Newman, inhabited a region at the other end of the universe from the world of the Zen masters, the greatest haiku poets, ink painters like Sesshu, the inventors of modern Japanese sword play or ju-jitsu, or for that matter the admirals who planned Pearl Harbor. Zen training is designed precisely to get rid of every trace of just those things that occupied Coleridge the most. His poetry is rhetorical. Latent of course is the bright imagism, the gracile phrase of Bashō or Issa or Wordsworth—but he threw it all away for the jimcrackery of *Xanadu* and the prurience of *Christabel* and the plain silliness of *The Ancient Mariner*. All of his thinking, like his poetry, is permeated with the urge to exert power—to get other people to do things. What gives him his pathos is his own knowledge that he could not really affect others. His dreams of power do not end tragically in impotence, they begin pathetically with impotence as the secret presupposition. A Marxist might say that he reflects very clearly the position of the former guiding, clerical class in Great Britain as it saw itself overwhelmed by the Industrial Revolution. Compare him with Baudelaire! They both took dope. They both invented a number of literary fashions that have endured to this day. But Baudelaire is the Romantic who destroyed Romanticism. In fact he destroyed the Social Lie of the whole epoch from the French Revolution to the present. And he did so because he saw "Life," the life of modern man, steadily and whole in a way no British poet ever did or would. It is that steady gaze which is one of the stigmata of Zen. Bodhidharma looked at the wall until his eyelids dropped off and the wall was no longer there. But this is Zen of a sort:

Entry for December 1803, around Christmas

What a beautiful Thing Urine is, in a Pot, brown yellow, transpicuous, the Image, diamond shaped of the Candle in it, especially, as it now appeared, I having emptied the Snuffers into it, & the snuff floating about, & painting all-shaped shadows on the Bottom.

1958

29.
Tolstoy's Interior Kingdom

Every day, all states do things which, if they were the acts of individuals, would lead to summary arrest and often execution. By and large, organized society functions on the basis of an elaborate system of checks and balances. What is checked and balanced is not just the various "powers" of government, as we are taught in civics classes, but all the frauds and violence of institutionalized mankind. In the thousands of years since the Neolithic Revolution mankind has worked out an elaborate system of focusing and using its own destructive impulses, or, where they cannot be used, of neutralizing or aborting them. Machiavelli, Hobbes, the Social Darwinians, the Realpolitikers, and the vast majority of just the conventionally minded, the practically minded people who want to get something done, the majority has always accepted this situation, justified and even glorified it. When we speak of "civilization" this is always a big part of what we are talking about. These are the Emperor's new clothes—"The Social Lie."

From the beginning of organized society, or at least from the beginning of written documents, there have always been people who challenged and rejected this state of affairs. Usually they have been members of the Establishment themselves, Buddha, Kropotkin, Tolstoy were princes. Obviously, the mute inglorious sufferers who have always borne the burden of "The System" are unknown to history, except in moments of social turmoil when some renegade from the ranks of the literate and privileged has spoken for them. It is hard to say of any given period of history or of any people, even our contemporaries, how acceptable the actual bulk of society finds the principles upon which it is organized. As a matter of fact, most people except politicians and authors work out for themselves, in secret, ways of living which ignore organized society as much as possible. After five or six thousand years much of life is still private, extraordinarily resistant to the mechanisms of civilizations, even, or perhaps especially, in the most powerful and authoritarian states. What is called "growing up," "getting a little common sense," is largely the learning of techniques for outwitting the more destructive forces at large in the social order. The mature man lives quietly, does good privately, assumes personal responsibility for his actions, treats others with friendliness and courtesy, finds mischief boring and keeps out of it. Without this hidden conspiracy of good will society would not endure an hour. We all "live Jim Crow."

Tolstoy was the perfect type of discontented aristocrat. He had a great deal in common with Buddha, but he also shared many characteristics with Byron, with Bakunin, with Kropotkin. The thing that distinguishes men of this type is that they take their aristocratic profession seriously. They believe the Myth of the Aristocrat, the Platonic Guardian, responsible for the good and welfare of his fellows. Most members of the upper orders are mature enough to learn, early in life, that aristocracy is just another one of the many social hoaxes. The literature of the world from the Egyptians and Greeks to the present is full of guides and manuals, "The Mirrour of Princes," "The Regimen of Rulers," "The Courtier," "The Governour." There is little evidence that the class to which they were addressed ever took them very seriously. But a few always have. The vast majority are of course unknown, tragic noblemen who gave themselves to their people—who consumed them, or who consumed themselves with frustration and blew out their brains in tumbledown mansions. They are great favorites with Romantic novelists. Literature is full of them. A very few have been writers, able to articulate the utter contempt of the believing aristocrat for the cobwebs of vulgar lies and compromise which envelop society—the society which they feel they should have been permitted to govern or lead, strictly in the paths of their own noble idealism. Except for the tiny number who have managed to found religions, mankind has judged most of these people to be self-deluded fools.

In the eyes of the world, Tolstoy was such a fool. A hero of the seige of Sebastopol who became a pacifist, a passionate gambler who freed his serfs before the Emancipation, a young rake who in later life denounced the music of Beethoven, women's sweaters and unchaperoned canoe trips as immoral in themselves and snares of still worse immorality—Tolstoy is not easy for the mature to take seriously. His religion is an expensive one—if it were literally put into practice organized society would collapse and it is open to question if it could ever be rebuilt afterwards.

The Kingdom of God is Within You, like other specifically religious writings of Tolstoy's, attempts to "prove" that his religion was identical with that preached by Jesus Christ. These arguments have relatively little cogency with us today. We are not worried about the integrity of the original Gospel. We value

Albert Schweitzer's Christology, not because of its historical soundness, its reconstruction of the "True Christ," but because it has served as the symbolic vesture of Schweitzer's own world-transforming religion. So with Tolstoy, what is important about his religious writing is not his scholarship, which is make-believe, or his criticism of others, which is makeshift and utterly intolerant, but his vision.

Whatever the Gospel of the authentic historic Jesus was, it was apocalyptic. The world as it is was weighed in the balance and found wanting. To this degree both Schweitzer and Tolstoy are "True Christians." There is, however, an essential difference between the two men. Committed to an ethics of apocalypse, a moral code of life lived always in the immanent eye of Judgment, Schweitzer has assumed the role of, to use the title of the Pope, a servant of the servants of God. Rather than attack society head on, he has preferred to subvert it with mercy. Tolstoy was closer to the pattern of his Master. He was intolerant of dogma, a compulsive anti-ritualist, militantly meek and aggressively mild, and, in spite of his professions of other-cheekism, unforgiving of the weaknesses and follies of his fellows . . . especially of his fellows in the ruling classes.

It is not the custom nowadays to take Tolstoy seriously as a thinker. Fiery apostles of nonviolence, loud denouncers of public and private hypocrisy do not make good colleagues or neighbors. Since all men are by nature fallible and foolish, society gets great delight in pointing out the hypocrisy and violence of such as Tolstoy. True, he was a crank, with all the weaknesses of a crank, but, as cranks sometimes are, he was far more right than the majority of men who profess to speak for the majority of all the other inarticulate human beings. Furthermore, he was not a thinker in any substantial sense, he was a prophet. Prophets are supposed to be cranks. Nobody expects Jeremiah to show the wisdom of Solomon. Unchallenged by the prophetic wrath of Jeremiah, the wisdom of all the Solomons of history leads only to perdition.

Tolstoy was also a great artist. Although he thought otherwise, he was singular amongst all the artist prophets of modern times in being able to keep his prophecy from corrupting his art. His great novels are humane, lucid, all-knowing and all-forgiving.

Yet they make no sacrifice of his principles. In contrast, Blake is turgid, Byron, whom few people remember was once a prophet, is plain silly, D. H. Lawrence all too often bogs down in a mishmash of sentimentality that is neither art nor prophecy.

Possibly this is so because Tolstoy is more nearly right than they are. He may have been a crank, but he concentrated on essentials. Whatever the disputed teachings of Christ were, it is apparent that they have not been embodied in the practices of the organized Christian churches. "Do not resist evil with evil." "Respect the personal integrity of each man." "Assume direct personal responsibility for the moral world which surrounds yourself." "Never delegate your moral responsibility." "Seek out all opportunities for direct, creative ethical action." "Avoid violence, anger, the invasion of others, refuse bloodshed, and all kinds of theft and lies, covert or open—especially in their approved and institutionalized forms." These are fairly simple commandments. Authority for them can certainly be found in the Sermon on the Mount and the great parables. What is more important, they are not at all difficult to carry out. The great churches have indisputably compromised the simple ethics of the Gospels, and yet, Protestant and Catholic, they have always represented the Christian ethic as extraordinarily difficult and even unpleasant. It is nothing of the sort. Many Buddhists and most Quakers, many simple monks and nuns, millions of humble housewives who attend daily Mass or Wednesday Prayer Meeting, live this way with ease and joy.

Untold numbers of people have lived like them, grinding corn in the adobe huts of Babylon, punching time-clocks in Detroit. It is due to them that we have got as far as we have—that we are here at all. Over their heads their betters have fought the battles of the Social Lie and made history. This is the secret of Tolstoy's religion—in the final analysis, it is not cranky or odd at all. It is common. The significant thing is that, by and large, give and take a few pathetic sins, men do not behave in their daily relations with one another as states and churches and even abstractions like classes behave on the stage of history. If they had, we wouldn't be here.

1961

American Writing

30.
Jack London's Native Sons

As a member of the penultimate generation of San Francisco writers, I am far from an ideal person to talk about Jack London. His memory and his literary set, most of whom survived well into my time, were a blight over literary Northern California up until the population turnover during and after the Second World War. Gertrude Atherton, Kathleen Norris, Sara Bard Field, Marie DeL. Welch, George Sterling, James Hopper, Charles Erskine Scott Wood, the Native Sons and Daughters of the Golden West and their adopted brothers and sisters are people I prefer not to recall. For us middle-aged locals they represent a bygone despotism of mediocrity, which may not have inhibited our youth, but which certainly made it uncomfortable the rare times we encountered them. Outlandish as it may seem to the rest of literary America, their few survivals and their many descendants still control cultural backwaters and undrained sloughs in literary San Francisco and at the University of California, Berkeley. At the name of Jack London I bristle like a hedgehog at the sight of a hairbrush.

Like Sinclair Lewis's, Jack London's biography was his own best work of art. But this is no compliment. He was no Goethe. His life was eventful enough. He grew up in a world of lower-class charlatanry and scuffling that has been one of California's special characteristics ever since 1849. He was a hobo, oyster pirate, boy soap-boxer, sailor, harvest hand, a member of Coxey's Army of the unemployed. His experiences in the Alaska Gold Rush provided him with the best copy for fiction for the rest of his life. He was a flamboyant war correspondent. His adventures in the Russo-Japanese War, as arrogant and foolish as those of any old-time Chicago police reporter, are scarcely believable today. His first marriage was conventional enough; his second was a boyish orgy of misplaced romanticism. While he was still young (he never became anything remotely resembling mature) he became one of the ten most popular writers of the world in any language. Success set him off on the pathetic career, not of a gentleman of letters but of a kind of Great Laird, a provincial Walter Scott. Like Scott, this brought him nothing but financial disasters and heartbreak. As his friend Upton Sinclair has pointed out, the real tragedy of London's latter years was caused by nothing very profound but, like so many other American writers, by alcohol. He quite simply drank himself to death. Today his fictions, once so enormously popular, are scarcely read, even by adolescents, except in Russia. They are about on the level of taste of current Russian pulp fiction and they give about as accurate a picture of the American society of their time which is why the Russians read them. There are few people indeed left in the West of any age boyish enough to enjoy London. Biographies of the man, however, have enjoyed great popularity. Plenty of people still refuse to grow up and drink too much. Unlike London most of them do it very uneventfully with a paucity of local color. So they find considerable glamor in his tale of troubles. I am not sure that growing up consists in learning from experience but London did neither. I doubt if there is anyone writing today whose attitudes on every subject and in every situation are as childish. London has been psychoanalyzed by later biographers and critics *ad nauseam*. There's no question but what his relations with George Sterling were as homosexual as could be. Whether they found overt expression is of no moment. They were sufficiently comprehensive in their only moderately covert form. Similarly, his relations with women, both in life and in fiction, have been described enough times as persistent refusal to accept woman as anything but a deformed boy. London practically invented the heroine as Good Chum. The homosexuality is not the point but the immaturity is. There are simply no adults anywhere in London's fiction. It is impossible to take seriously sea captains, goldminers, entrepreneurs, revolutionary leaders who behave like newsboys, playground bullies and Eagle Scouts. True, such people do, in fact, often behave like such children, but the author has to know it. London never did and so his own life was the tumbling misadventures of a great, big, lovable child. When he is a child, it is exciting reading. When he comes to man's estate and it is time to put aside the things of a child, the long-drawn-out kyriale of his pranks becomes monotonous. So much so that finally it passes from plain monotony to artistic monotony like the exhausting dilemmas of Kafka's Gregor. There was no solution for Gregor except insecticide. So, as London's life becomes more and more enmeshed in the follies of ungovernable immaturity, you feel that if alcohol had been unknown it would have had to have been invented especially for him.

I do not buy his Socialist idealism. He was intransigent amongst municipal Socialists and the potters, weavers and barefoot dancers of the Berkeley Hills. His connections with the labor movement were minimal, always on a Great Man basis, and he always came down on the side of moderation and seeing all sides of the question. At the final showdown, the question of supporting the First War, he weaseled out, and became a professional patriot and, in a maneuver that would be shocking if it were not so infantile, did so by writing his former comrades a scolding letter accusing them of being not revolutionary enough.

Nobody today would claim Jack London as a stylist. His most tender love scenes and most tragic deaths are described in a nauseating, dated journalese. He is still advanced as a great storyteller. Maybe he was for his day. He is one of the first journeyman commercial spinners of tales. Today there's more of this stuff on the market than all the presses can absorb and since it is an easily teachable skill, the quality, slick, or pulp, or comic book, is incomparably better. It is interesting to note that this is the one thing that London always insisted he could not do—plot. He bought his plots and I'm sure would have welcomed those dial-your-own-plot machines that are advertised in the shoddier writers' magazines. I am far from putting down commercial fiction. In fact, I sometimes think it's all that will survive this over-refined time. But compare Ernst Haycox, Gordon Young, Georges Simenon, Raymond Chandler. Two narrative sentences from any one of them is sufficient criticism of London. The style not only is the man, it is also the plot. Otherwise those plotting machines would really work. The great storytellers are the great stylists, whether Defoe or Homer, and great stories are about adults and their conflicts and problems. Even in the field where the human relations which prevail in newsboys' dreams are making their last stand—science fiction —we demand greater maturity than can even be found in *Martin Eden*. Even the childish amongst us have come to prefer the *habiliments* of adulthood. Even sexual intercourse now takes place in space-warp. So London's best stories are about dogs. I, as a man, think they're better, but maybe if dogs could read, they'd think they were kind of silly.

1964

31.

The Letters of Carl Sandburg

Carl Sandburg and Robert Frost were perhaps the last American poets of great importance to enjoy a normal relationship to American society and to be accepted by the dominant culture. Today most people under fifty, and certainly practically all members of the sub-culture of secession which is now turning into a counter-culture moving toward dominance, as well as the old-line intellectuals of the literary quarterlies, all these alienated people dismiss Sandburg as a kind of foxy grandpa of the Establishment—Eric Hoffer with a hoe. Sandburg may still be popular with the people of whom and for whom he wrote—just folks. Today the prairie towns are being deserted for Southern California and you can buy a beautiful home built by a wealthy retired farmer at the end of the century on a quiet street heavily shaded with maples for $3500, one-twentieth of what it would cost in Babylon-Under-Smog. Carl Sandburg's young days as they are revealed in these letters will never come again. Only a little while ago everybody would have read them because Sandburg was like everybody else. Today if they were to be read by an aging young poet in a Nehru jacket jetting over the Atlantic to Spoleto for more money than Sandburg earned in a year at the same age, they must seem as strange and old and far away as the verse letters of Sir Thomas Wyatt, the lover of Anne Boleyn, or the Epistles of Horace.

The problem is to make Sandburg acceptable at all to a generation to whom his life is outlandish, or, where it has survived in the family background of some people, is bitterly resented. A large percentage of the suicidally disconnected youth of the East Village and the Haight-Ashbury come precisely from those little backwaters of cultural lag—the bosky towns and suburbs of mid-America where in Sandburg's day the future seemed already to have arrived and to work.

The most impressive thing about *The Letters of Carl Sandburg* is the endurance of a man and the vanishing of a society which they portray. The first letter is from twenty-year-old Private Charles Sandburg at war in Puerto Rico. He enlisted in April 1898 and was home in September. We can watch him grow up in letters to his family and friends, maturing all through his twenties, becoming a Socialist organizer, a Lyceum lecturer, and in his thirtieth year marrying Lillian Steichen, the daughter of the famous photographer and herself a Socialist activist. Sandburg's life is no different from that of many thousands of young Middle Westerners. His values are the same; his politics are more Populist than Socialist and his culture is guided by Elbert Hubbard, a sort of commercialized William Morris for provincial America, and by the Chautauqua circuit, small-town America's summer adult education under canvas.

There isn't anything wrong with this way of life at all. Today its values have been caricatured and are the false rallying cries of reaction. They were not then. In the years before the other

war it was easy to believe that Whitman's vision of America was
about to come true, that the latter part of the century would see
a community of love and a comradeship of creative work "from
sea to shining sea." The war made the difference to Sandburg
as it did to America. The crucial letter, the pivot on which the
book turns, is to his wife, dateline New York, December 27th,
1918. His baggage was held up in New York after five months
abroad as an N.E.A. correspondent. In Stockholm Michael
Borodin, whom he had known in Chicago under the name of
Axelrod, gave him a draft for $10,000 to deliver to Santeri
Nuortava, a Finnish Socialist who was to become one of the
founders of the American Communist Party. American and
British intelligence officers and an assistant district attorney
spent three hours sweating Sandburg and insisting on a direct
answer to the question, "Which group do you personally favor,
the Liebknecht-Luxemburg Spartacans or the Ebert-Scheidemann
government?" He insisted that he didn't prefer either of them
but was inclined to favor the German Independent Socialist
Party, whose position was in fact at that time much like his own
or his fellow Midwesterner's, Eugene V. Debs. The authorities
confiscated the $10,000 and considerable of the documentation
of the first year of the Russian Revolution that he had brought
back in his luggage. They did, however, permit him to keep a
document which purported to be the Czarina's last love letter to
the Czar which later Sandburg was to report to his wife "is going
big." From this point on Sandburg changes and year by year
becomes more assimilated to the new society which was emerging
in post-war America. His attitudes, which were authentic in the
older America, persist, but since they have less and less relationship to reality they become more and more sentimental. The
tears of the Czarina win out over the $10,000 trust of the
Socialist movement. Sandburg never seems to be aware of this
in the slightest. He goes right on living in the intellectual and
moral world of the first Debs presidential campaign. Least of all
is he ever aware that in the book that occupies much of the
middle of his life, his *Abraham Lincoln,* he was busy creating a
sentimental myth designed primarily to shelter himself. His
greatest contribution to American culture in those years, his
Song Bag and his concert performances of folk song, he writes

little about and dismisses as work. Today one of the principal foundation-stones, perhaps the cornerstone, of the counter-culture, is the American folk song. It is through songs that Sandburg first made popular that the old free America in which he grew up was to transmit, as through the narrow channels of hundreds of capillaries, its value system, its life blood, to a generation that ignores him or looks on him as a joke.

In the letters we watch too the toning down, sentimentalization and emasculation of the old spirit that speaks so fearlessly in the first three books—long embarrassing arguments with his publisher, Alfred Harcourt, over strong language and even the inclusion of two of his finest poems, one to Billy Sunday and the other to a trade-union dynamiter. He still thinks the later books, *The People Yes* and *Good Morning America,* challenge the fraud and evil of the new society in the same way that the *Chicago Poems* did that of the old.

What stands up through all the book to the very end is the correspondence with his wife. Sandburg was an American intellectual who grew up long before musical beds became the principal work and play of American intellectuals. In youth he became the good husband of a good wife and so he stayed. "Silver Threads among the Gold" was not a sentimental song to him, it was a fact. What he saw in Lincoln above all else was steadfastness. This may be disputable, but the letters reveal that steadfastness was Sandburg's own first virtue. Toward the end of his life he is still writing to the few surviving friends of his youth. He was loyal to people. It is not his fault that the ideas that engaged his loyalty changed imperceptibly into something else.

The correspondence of most of the world's leading poets is not very nice reading and some of it is shameful. There is no necessary connection between being a good man and a good poet. These letters reveal Sandburg as a very good man indeed and what is more they reveal the American Middle West that produced him as a society which could produce good men who were good poets and vice versa and take it for granted that that's the way things had ought to have been.

1968

32.

Sinclair Lewis

Mark Schorer's *Sinclair Lewis* is the best literary biography by an American since Matthew Josephson's *Zola*. I only hope they put it in the moving pictures and Mark Schorer and the Lewis estate make as much money as was made on Paul Muni's *Zola*. But who would play Sinclair Lewis? Lee Tracy played him once, in a picture about Dorothy Thompson and Lewis in Russia which was almost as funny as *Ninotchka*. It is a pity George Arliss is dead—there is just enough resemblance to assimilate Red Lewis to Disraeli and Richelieu and the rest of that handful of historical great figures my generation grew up believing all looked practically alike, give and take a little putty and grease paint. It would be an unsavory role, and the makeup job would be formidable. He was an ugly man, Lewis, physically, mentally, morally. This is the great over-riding subject of Schorer's biography—ugliness. Other tragic flaws have made other tragedies down the long history of literature—pride in the Greeks, anger in Lear, lust, accidie, even gluttony. I wonder if Mark Schorer is completely aware that he has written a great tragedy which springs almost wholly from the fact that its hero had the esthetic appeal of a scorbutic rhinoceros . . . and knew it only too well.

Reviewers have seen fit to laugh at Schorer's incredible mass of detail—"the four cords of wood that Dr. Lewis asked his son to chop on Feb. 23, 1903, were really 4 ¾ cords." But this sort of thing is precisely what makes the cheese so binding. With all the Lewis papers and nine years to work, Mark Schorer, an anti-naturalist as far as his own taste is concerned, has chosen

to erect an enormous Great Pyramid of naturalism as a monu-
ment to a flimsy, provincial and tragic successor to Zola. Here
is one place where hypertrophy itself becomes a discipline. The
effect is stunning, practically stupefying. It is also convincing,
and more than that, interesting. These are qualities I for one do
not find in Lewis himself. Except for the purposes of my own
education as a critic, I find Lewis's novels utterly unreadable.
Forgive me for laboring the point, but I am actively unsym-
pathetic to Lewis's literary theories, and I find his stylelessness
revolting, his plots put together with pins and his characters cut
out of paper. (I am not, however, an anti-naturalist, I think
Dreiser one of the few genuine stylists of the first quarter of the
century in this country.) Furthermore—I don't agree with Mark
Schorer's critical ideas as they have been revealed in his previous
books either. In other words, I was a bad choice for this review.
But I think the book is extremely important and even more
absorbing reading than it is important.

Lewis's career raises the whole problem of alienation in
America. Who is alienated from what? France is a country with
twenty aborted revolutions in two centuries. De Sade, Rousseau,
Laclos, Restif, they started out alienated and by the time two
generations of barricades had risen and fallen, Baudelaire was a
man at cross-purposes with his society at every point. Salinger,
Mailer or Ginsberg, these people have disaffiliated themselves
from a world hell bent on destroying itself. The Dadaists exhibited loaded revolvers pointed out of picture frames, a string
tied to the trigger and a card "TIREZ S.V.P." It is a commonplace
of American criticism that Lewis was part and parcel of the
world of Babbitt and Gopher Prairie, but that is not what I am
getting at. Rabelais, Aretino, Machiavelli, Swift, even G. K.
Chesterton, all satirists must necessarily be part of the world
they satirize. It's something more fundamental.

Elmer Gantry is really the only work of satire Lewis wrote.
It is, incidentally, the only one which seems to have shocked just
about everybody. It is a farce, a charade, an angry explosion of
stereotypes. Yet it has a kind of justice, and it has humor, more
humor than Lewis ever showed before or after. The other books
mostly are mediocre representatives of a century-long movement
that has been dignified with all sorts of critical metaphysics, but

which is really the movement of provincials struggling to de-provincialize themselves. Perhaps that is why the leaders have been Sicilians, Norwegians, Middle Western Americans. Trollope didn't give a damn whether he was provincial or not. Neither did Wells, he had bigger fish to fry. But the really shocking thing about Shaw is that he did—his wing collar never ceased to abrade his neck.

I don't remember what happened to Carol Kennicott—but I know what happened to Norah when she left the Doll's House, she went to the city and got a job. Lewis fought his lower-middle-class background with nothing but his nerves, and when he broke loose he had nowhere to go but to Harry's Bar.

I know I sound like an old-time *New Masses* critic. They were always taking the social critics of their day to task and urging them to join up—"take a positive stand." Pasting stamps in a party book or getting socked on the picket line was not the solution, but in a sense they were right. You can't just go nowhere. It is horrifying to read about Lewis in his old age hanging around the Doni, Leland's Bar, Harry's Bar, the Via Vittoria Veneto, with all the other witless victims of Momism. Satire may be a method of constructing a system of values, that is, the satirist may not start out in a very well-organized fashion. But eventually all great comedy comes from the solidest wisdom and the firmest personal base. Lewis's rejection of the America of his day seems almost unmotivated—the only clear motivation was his bad complexion. He was uncomfortable when asked out.

The saddest part of the book is the story of his marriage to Dorothy Thompson. Doubtless she was the very archetype of the American Mom on the rampage—but he knew that when he married her. That's what he wanted and that is what he always pretended he got. But he didn't. For years the poor woman tried her best to be a wife and mother. It is heart-rending to watch this middle-aged career girl struggling to love, honor and obey a man who is only interested in hitting Mom over the head with his bottle of formula.

The tragedy of Lewis is not the tragedy of a writer at odds with his society, it is not the tragedy of an *aliené*, it is not even the tragedy of a self-educated provincial on the make. It is part of the vast tragedy of male and female in America, the

dislocation of function and responsibility which has baffled and
frightened all outside observers, and some natives, from Tocque-
ville to the present day.

1961

33.

The Stories and Plays
of William Carlos Williams

Obviously, some playwrights have been very great poets, but
few poets who who were not primarily dramatists have ever
been good playwrights. Even fewer poets have ever written
readable prose fiction. Longfellow wrote a novel. So did Swinburne. Ghastly productions, both of them, though for opposite
reasons. Almost all the great nineteenth-century poets whose
portraits decorate the corridors of grammar schools tried their
hands at playwrighting. Their work is not only dull and un-
dramatic, it was a failure with audiences in their own day.
Curiously, only Swinburne and Shelley, neither of whom we
ever think of as thinking dramatically at all, wrote plays that
are still performable. We may think of the verse of *Atalanta in
Calydon* as on the level of the taste of the hero of *This Side of
Paradise* but the fact is that staged it is a remarkably effective
play and more convincingly Greek than Gilbert Murray's translations of Euripides into pseudo-Swinburnian verse. Shelley's
The Cenci is always being revived somewhere and is a *tour de
force* of deliberate archaism, a genuine Elizabethan tragedy of

blood. Lots of people think it is the best thing Shelley ever wrote.
I imagine this would be T. S. Eliot's opinion. Swinburne's cycle
of plays on the career of Mary Stuart contain some of the finest
dramatic writing of the nineteenth century and certainly could
be put on now, if drastically cut.

The point is, these are archaistic, literary plays, although not
really closet dramas. So are the Noh plays of William Butler
Yeats, the only truly radical innovations in the English theatre
in my time. Properly performed they are gripping, practically
hallucinatory in their effect, but they are hardly about ordinary
folks encountered in the streets of twentieth-century Dublin.
W. H. Auden? Except for his first playlet—the symbolic mythic
Paid on Both Sides, his work seems to have failed as drama. Who
else? Is Hardy's *The Dynasts* a play at all? Of course not.

William Carlos Williams is the only major poet I can think
of who has written effective, more or less realistic, plays about
contemporary people. This is a strange state of affairs. Look at
the French theatre. Not just Cocteau and Claudel—even people
as unlikely as Francis Jammes or Guillaume Apollinaire wrote
plays and saw them performed. Ibsen, don't forget, always
thought of himself as a poet.

I think this lack in the English-speaking stage can be laid
simply at the door of its arrant commercialism. It is absurd that
the doggerel of Christopher Fry or Maxwell Anderson should
see thousands of hours of successful production. T. S. Eliot
managed to force his way into the theatre by virtue of his
tremendous prestige, in Broadway terms a hot commodity. His
plays of course are not more or less realistic ones about contemporary people, and furthermore, they are not very good.

Williams has been fascinated with show business, the real
Broadway thing. He has tried to write in those terms. To a
Turkish student of contemporary American literature, his plays
might look like some of the deeper excursions of the commercial
theatre. They undoubtedly look that way to Williams, and he
has never been able to understand why nobody else agrees with
him.

They have an absolutely veridical diction, a sweet ingenuousness, a simple, country-doctor kind of morality, and considerable
constructive skill. Properly performed they should knock an
uncorrupted audience into the aisles. Alas, point by point, these

are precisely the virtues Broadway does not want, and generations of absorbing the opposite vices has certainly corrupted any possible commercial audience. Even so, when some off-Broadway or university theatre does perform one, it turns out to be successful enough. *Many Loves* ran in repertory for a year at the Living Theatre.

Anyway, now in one volume, *Many Loves and Other Plays*, are all of Williams' plays except the whimsical poetic one-acters of his youth. They're in print. Somewhere a few copies may survive the holocaust, and comes the Revolution they may be a great success at the Kropotkin Theatre on Luxemburg Avenue. Anyway, somewhere, in some less naughty world than this. Meanwhile, let's hope the college drama groups take them up.

With few exceptions, poets would be well advised to write prose only for money. I know, I am a poet and I write prose only for money. They are two radically different arts. The only thing they have in common is words. William Carlos Williams is not only the finest poet writing in America, the master of those (of us, all of us) who know. He is also a consummate master of prose. Yvor Winters, a master too—of the rash statement, once said that a chapter of *In the American Grain* was the finest prose written by an American. Granted he was rash, but he had something. *In the American Grain* is a collection of evocative essays on American history. Williams' fiction is about real people in real situations, some of them unbearably real—both situations and people. His stories are even more evocative than those essays, but in a most subtle fashion.

This is not realism, let alone naturalism, although to our Turkish student it might seem so. What is it? It is in the tradition of Stendhal and Flaubert as it branches off into Chekhov. But it is this tradition pushed to its ultimate of clarity and modesty. I think it could be called an excruciatingly poignant Imagism, in which the completely realized real has come to symbolize the still more real that hides behind the colored face of phenomena. Remember when Emma notices that Charles Bovary takes from his pocket a jack-knife—"like a peasant," says poor Emma, and all the foolish tragedy of that silly woman hits you like a blow? Remember Chekhov's mocking description of his own methods to a bookish girl—the flash of light on a pond on a lonely, seedy Russian estate?

Theoretically, piercing little fillips to the sensibility of this kind should "enliven" naturalistic narrative like olives in cocktails or cherries on sundaes. In Williams they are the continuous stuff of his art. This sounds barbarous. Katharine Mansfield tried something like it and was awfully barbarous. In Williams it comes off. It always comes off, as it does not in his special colleagues, whether Pierre Reverdy or Katherine Anne Porter.

This, incidentally, is what Huysmans, a reformed naturalist, meant when he coined the word "*surrealisme*," not the pseudo-Freudian mish-mash that appropriated the name. Huysmans, *helas,* was barbarous past belief, and never came off at all.

Not for nothing were both Chekhov and Williams doctors. Williams' narrative is a continuous surgical interference with the nervous system, and it is an interference which adds up to meaning on the deepest levels. So the fifty odd stories in *The Farmer's Daughters,* the collected stories of William Carlos Williams, are amongst the most precious possessions of the twentieth century in any language. And when they come to ask, "What were they like?" we can say, "This is us."

1961

34.

McAlmon and the
Lost Generation

For those of us who knew him, Bob McAlmon was always something of a problem. He certainly never made himself easy to like, and as he grew older, more embittered, more alcoholic, he became about as difficult as could be imagined. Robert Knoll in this book speaks several times of his engaging charm. True, in his heyday he could turn on very winning ways, at will, even in the midst of a savage hangover. Most important, in his heyday he had power and the imagined disposal of fabulous sums of money. The combined wealth of Harry Crosby, Peggy Guggenheim, James Laughlin, John Quinn and Nancy Cunard would have been small potatoes beside the Ellerman fortune. So he had lots of friends. Prematurely old, sick, wandering around the West in a mild state of alcoholic hallucinosis, living on his relatives, he had few indeed.

James Laughlin is a very good poet. Peggy Guggenheim is a master—or mistress?—memoirist. So is Caresse Crosby. Harry Crosby was the very archetype of the demented and alienated poet. Nancy Cunard was one of the better imitators of Eliot's *The Waste Land*. So it went. But nobody took them seriously. Why? They were rich bitches and rich bastards whose only function was to be conned. Writers and artists are really exceptional swine. They seldom pay any attention to their colleagues' work except to ferret out crevices into which to stick the daggers of one-upmanship. After a lifetime of experience in the faubourgs of bohemia I have come reluctantly to the conclusion that with few exceptions they are parasites first and creators afterwards— the "creation" was thought up along in high-school days to justify the already ingrained sociopathology. Wave a little lettuce at them and they can see nothing else, least of all the human being doing the waving—no matter how talented or handsome or beautiful.

McAlmon started out as possibly the most promising of the ultimate generation of Populist writers—a contemporary of Evelyn Scott and Lola Ridge in Greenwich Village. He made a sensational marriage to a woman of immense wealth. He believed, after a short while, that he had been tricked into a marriage of convenience. Looking back on it from my own intervening years of sad experience, I am inclined to think that he was in fact deeply loved. He didn't think so, and the inability ever to believe, after that, that he was genuinely loved corroded his soul. Most writers are mildly schizzy and lovelost. Like Trotsky, who believed GPU men were hiding in the bushes, McAlmon had objective grounds for his pathology—but pathology it was nevertheless.

With an infinitesimal portion of his wife's wealth he ran one of the historic publishing ventures of Paris-America in *cette belle époque*. He published everybody of consequence. Everybody was indebted to him, or if they weren't they were busy trampling others senseless in their efforts to become so. McAlmon was not a fool, he knew where he stood. For, you see, he was not naturally a rich man. He was not buying off the guilty burden of steel mills, copper mines, banks or shipping empires. He was handsome and engaging and fresh. He could get layed any time he wanted, by almost anybody, for free—at least if he went about it incognito.

What he was naturally was a writer, and a rather simple but most canny one. His mind had been shaped in windy nights by oil lamps in farm houses in the cornfields of the prairie states. He had watched the well-known collapse of the Protestant ethic at the seismological epi-center. He had seen the very Norahs and Heddas themselves go off to Self-Determination, in their starched shirtwaists, smoking pistols in their hands, castrated males writing on provincial floors behind them, like rattlesnakes made harmless with one slug of a forty-five. He knew, as it were, the score.

This bitter knowledge gave him a style that at moments rose to the level of the best epitaphs in *Spoon River*. At its worst it never lost that bumbling clumsiness that is a precious ingredient of the charm of one of our greatest prose stylists—Theodore Dreiser. What I am trying to convey is that Bob McAlmon was a bona-fide Autochthone. It would be hard to find anybody less like the French poets and novelists of the Late Dada and Early Surrealist Periods. Yet it was people like Philippe Soupault, Louis Aragon and the rest who understood him best in those days and who to this day remember him with fondness. "What ever happened to McAlmon?" Everybody asked that question for twenty years. The French asked it with affectionate nostalgia, the Americans patronizingly, with contempt. After all, *they* had arrived, and where was he? And who remembered that they had been given their first ride on the greasy golden toboggan of success by Robert McAlmon? Nobody, at least nobody who was anybody. Everybody had forgotten.

For years a few people, Bill Williams, myself, three or four others, tried to get him published in America. Nobody would touch him, or if they did, Bob, sick, drunk and hostile, made himself so extraordinarily disagreeable that they dropped him. One of Scribner's leading authors—Hemingway—stormed into Perkins' office and said, "If you publish McAlmon I will break my contract." He was, in the estimation of his then colleagues and associates, one of the leading writers of the Twenties and Thirties, one of a group who have all become twentieth-century classics. He never even so much as achieved publication by a "bourgeois publisher," unless you call New Directions "bourgeois" which it sure wasn't in those days. Laughlin published in America his one "published," in the strictest sense of the word, book, a volume of verse called *Not Alone Lost*. Nobody bought it but me, Bill Williams and three or four other people. It is the poorest-selling title in New Directions history. Caresse Crosby published in Paris in her premature paperback series his collection of stories, *The Indefinite Huntress*. Nobody bought that either. The title story of an Ibsen girl he knew with the Greater Intimacy is *Spoon River* with a vengeance. Sad, wise, deeply resonant, few better insights into human motivation have come out of the prairies. Why didn't anybody buy it? Gee, you'd think the movies would have bought it for the title alone. It is the perfect marquee identification of all the lovelost heroines, seeking, seeking, through the twentieth century, the century, as they say, of the common man. I'm not being flippant in what to me is a pathetic and tragic case—but it is the ideal title for the sure to be issued *The Marilyn Monroe Story*.

And so for Bob, too. He was an indefinite enough hunter. What was he hunting for? To write well, utterly without bullshit, and to understand human beings. He wanted nothing but compassion and the other side of the coin of compassion, which is style. To find this pot at the foot of this rainbow you have to be loved, I guess, and if Bob was ever loved by anybody except the wife in whom he did not believe, I never heard of it. Yet we all loved him, even after he was gone, with his flopping gait, his stinking breath, his rumbling guts and his raling lungs . . . Korsakoff's Syndrome . . . in the last years he was disoriented in time and kept slipping off, back to that damn yacht in the Mediterranean and confabulating myths and *Märchen* of bygone days in the first one-piece bathing suits. We all loved him. And who were "we"? Bill Williams, Ezra, me, his brothers and sister, and three or four other people, anybody who was anybody, and a woman in England, growing old with her inaccessible memories.

Robert Knoll, author of *McAlmon and the Lost Generation*, is apparently a professor at Nebraska, which university has inherited the McAlmon papers. It is easy for the remnants of the avant-garde to say he is making a career of poor old Bob and doesn't really dig him. OK. Why didn't they? This book is a collection of stories, strung together on excerpts from his auto-biography, and eked out with explanatory comment by Professor Knoll. I can think of more satisfactory ways to handle McAlmon —or can I? After all, though he was, in his own eyes, above all else a dedicated writer, he was, as dedicated writers go, an exceptionally human one. The human man is here, and the stories into which he spoke as he lived.

1962

35.

Pagany

Recently I got hold of a complete, bound file of Richard Johns' memorable literary magazine *Pagany* from the University of California library. As I looked through it it was just like Proust's *madeleine*. My own youth came back like a total hallucination of the senses, the very sight and sound and smell, taste and touch of forty years ago. What affected me most poignantly before I had read any of it at all was the sight of my own typography for the ads of various and sundry other literary magazines of the time. They must have been the first examples of Bauhaus or Comfuturist typography in America done in the days when Rodchenko, El Lissitsky and Moholy-Nagy themselves were young. It's not that my own youthful efforts were important in themselves; it's that *Pagany's* lifetime spanned the breakdown of the international avant-garde as the world economic crisis shut down and a quite different kind of literature emerged.

The earliest issues of the magazine are full of contributions by Americans who bear an apparent relationship to writers like Blaise Cendrars, Pierre Reverdy or the young Louis Aragon. Many of them are now unjustly forgotten. They believed and hoped that the arts would be the instrument of a fundamental revolution of the human sensibility as such. They believed that the word or the pictorial image could be used to subvert the dead syntax by which human self-alienation had been grafted into the very structure of the brain and nervous system. They believed that the Revolution of the Word would liberate a new life-meaning for man and sweep away dead shells from which meaning had been exhausted or had turned malignant.

This does not mean Art for Art's Sake. Quite the contrary. The term itself had become a slander turned against its inventors by the squares—in those days the labor movement called them scissorbills—the guardians of conventional culture. Let's not forget that Oscar Wilde himself was a far saner and more trenchant critic of society than his disciple Shaw, an Oscar Wilde diluted with whey and hyped up with red pepper. The advance guard of international culture from 1870 to 1929 had already laid the foundations of what now we call the counter-culture, and those foundations were certainly grounded in a maximum sense of responsibility to the people—"*paganus*—a person, or relating, or belonging to a person in civil life, a native, the opposite of *miles*, a soldier."

I would like to avoid singling out names because all of *Pagany* is important, but I would like to point out that its American writers were at least the equals of their European contemporaries. John Dos Passos' pieces that eventually went to form *U.S.A.* were sections from what is unquestionably the greatest achievement of *unanisme*, certainly an incomparably greater work than the tedious, many-volumed production of

Jules Romains, the inventor of the term. This is true of the poetry too. Many a long forgotten or suppressed American poet was a far better writer than, say, Philippe Soupault, who already enjoyed a very substantial world reputation and who now seems pretty thin stuff. Long forgotten or suppressed but now being resurrected, ferreted out in libraries, by inquisitive poets of the present generation, ever becoming more conscious of their own ancestors, they were the first architects and bricklayers of a New Jerusalem that yet may never be built.

Then midway in the course of the short life of *Pagany*, the economic and social collapse of the dominant society began to make itself felt. As Louis Aragon was to say a few years later, "We do not need to manufacture our own synthetic apocalypses; we can find them every morning in the newspapers." Under the pressure of catastrophe, writers and artists all over the world began to turn to attack the specific social evils from which they had thought they had escaped by concentrating on the underlying, fundamental Lie. Richard Johns was especially sensitive to this great turn, and published some of the earliest and finest writing of the kind that was eventually to be debauched and destroyed by the slogans of falsification—Prolecult and Socialist Realism.

Only recently Stefan Heym said, "We will never have a true Socialist Realism until we are able, unafraid, to describe the boredom of Minsk." For this self-evident truism he was broken by the East German government and became a not-person, like the folk-singer Wolf Biermann, who sings precisely of the soul of man under Socialism, the human self-alienation that still endures behind the interpersonal iron curtains of slogans and shibboleths.

Time was when the little toy dog was new and the soldier was passing fair. As the literature of social criticism and protest arose in America, it was still fresh, still undisillusioned. This freshness was not naïveté, but the voice of the unbroken heart of young men and women who were certain that the future belonged to them and the people for whom they spoke. Richard Johns was especially discriminating of the values of this kind of writing. There are no slogans, no stereotypes. He would not have printed them, and anyway it was before enforced stereotyping. It's sad to read over the work of some of these people. Where are they now? Only a handful of them are still left working away past the age of retirement in the skilled building trades, working on the walls of the New Jerusalem, their hair white or very gray, but still calling down to their tempters, "I'm working on the wall and I can't come down."

Pagany was a mirror, admittedly not the largest, of the conflicts and the communions, the victories and defeats, of a pivotal moment in the history of Western culture. Today when a whole generation has seceded from the Social Lie and has demanded the freedom to discover meaningful, significant lives in the Community of Love, it is good to have a collection of things where they can see, like notes in a sealed tin at the summit of a Himalayan peak, that climbers had believed hitherto inaccessible, that there had been others here before them.

1969

36.

Henry Miller: The Iconoclast as Everyman's Friend

I.

Henry Miller is a baffling man. He is the perfect salesman. He believes every word he tells the customers. Few drummers who peddle the ordinary run of commodities have blind faith in their lines. They take it all with a grain of salt, it's just another pitch. House-to-house peddling on a strictly commission basis is another matter. There the motto is, "Sell the salesman. He'll sell his aunts and uncles and friends and neighbors. When he's used them up, he'll quit and we'll get another salesman." It's all done by combining the Law of Averages and 100 per cent turnover.

Henry Miller is an elderly gentlemen who bears a distinct physical resemblance to a very successful salesman of brushes or photo coupons. The resemblance is more than physical. He enjoys the same blind faith in his product. In his case the product is alienation. He is convinced that he is a scorned and rejected prophet. He believes that the artist in America is a pariah. He believes that he has been persecuted because he was a great artist and an even greater thinker.

Writers talk like this to the customers. It is handy when you want to make a girl or when you've been arrested for stabbing your wife. Does anybody really believe it? Yes, Henry Miller. In actual fact, for years he has lived an extremely comfortable life. He has a nice home below Big Sur, where his neighbors are mostly millionaires. Few writers in our time have received more lavish adulation. He travels about, judging movies at Cannes and novels in Majorca. He has been suggested for the Nobel Prize. When his bestseller *Tropic of Cancer* got in trouble in suburbia, the leading literary academicians—whom he despises —came to his defense and talked learnedly about the profound social and moral significance of a book which is simply a traditional picaresque comedy. He is a respected and even revered member of the American Establishment, considerably more so than Engine Charley Wilson or Wayne Morse. But he refuses to believe it. He believes in the comforting myth of his own iconoclasm.

Stand Still Like the Hummingbird is a collection of such myths, Henry Miller the boss iconoclast, bestowing his accolade on his fellow iconoclasts. It is all very excited and exciting. It sounds precisely like the funny conversations in the *Tropics* and *Black Spring*. The only trouble is, thirty years have gone by and Henry Miller is no longer a poor boy with holes in his socks, arguing about Dostoievsky by gas light and picking up file clerks on the Brooklyn subway.

The results are hilarious. One of the most hilarious essays in the book is a puff for Ionesco, another boss iconoclast. As a matter of fact, the essay is mostly taken up with the expensive adventures of a successful author touring France with his children (namely, H. Miller) and a totally uncritical repetition of Ionesco's own sales pitches. Ionesco, of course, is the exact reverse of an iconoclast. He is a practically perfect example of a man who has turned the postures and argot of alienation into an immensely fashionable and profitable and very, very gimmicky—commodity. Ionesco an outsider? I'm laughing . . . almost as much as I laughed over the picaresque bawdry of *Black Spring*.

II.

I have been collecting clips of the response of the newspaper book-reviewers around the country to Henry Miller's *Tropic of Cancer*. It has not been good. Few have minded the bad words, some have even reviewed the book without mentioning their existence. Most of them have had deeper moral objections. They object to Miller's windy generalizations and empty profundities. A couple quote Nelson Algren's remark that the big trouble with Miller is he thinks he thinks. Several point out that the sexual encounters bear unmistakable signs of fantasy rather than empiric knowledge. Almost everybody says that continuous ranting accusation of collapse and bankruptcy levelled against Western civilization is totally misconceived; the West may be collapsing but Miller's accusations are not correct diagnosis, and the rant is stereotyped. The most fundamental objection occurs again and again—there are no people in the book. It is written without sympathy or insight, Miller doesn't like people, in fact he doesn't know they are out there. He is anti-human and anti-humane. What all this adds up to is the judgment that Miller is a barbarian within the gates, an uncultured and unculturable man, one of Toynbee's Internal Proletariat.

I agree. The newspapers are perfectly right. Back in the days when he was being discovered Cyril Connolly did not compare him to John Locke or Walter Bagehot. T. S. Eliot did not liken him to Matthew Arnold or Henry Adams. This is the voice of the outcast who can never get in. He doesn't know where in is or what it is. His descriptions of the motives and mores of the Paris or New York around him are irrelevant fantasies, as unreal as the notions of a millionairess or a neo-beat intellectual on the prowl in Harlem. The indictment of a criminal is based on law, the codification of social relations. Miller's indictment of society is not based on social relations at all but on his inability to have them. This is the moral Bowery speaking. Over the years since the *Tropics* Miller has accumulated a vast mound of "speculative" writing under his byline. It is, all of it, not just wrongheaded and wrong in facts and taste—it is excluded from the universe of discourse, the travel diary of a philosopher who always put up in the Mills Hotels.

Yet Miller is not Little Joe Gould or even Restif de la Bretonne. He is not a naïf. True, he thinks he is, and he is always writing letters to critics telling them that the *Tropics* are not works of art but "just the way it happened." Rereading *Cancer* at this late date it is apparent that it is not a *"récit,"* it is unquestionably a construct. The comparison is with *The Satyricon*, not with *Monsieur Nicholas*.

The Satyricon, even in the fragments we have, is a great comic novel. Restif's book is not comic at all. It is funny often enough, but when it is it is pitiful, because we laugh at Restif himself. We never laugh at Miller. We share with him his vulgar, delinquent Brooklyn Boy horse laugh and razzberry. True, the greatest comedy is the most humane form of letters. Miller is not Rabelais or even Swift. The characters in the *Tropics* rattle against each other like pebbles in a couple of maracas. But this is true of *The Satyricon* too. At least Miller knows he is being funny.

Twenty-eight years have gone by since *Cancer* was first published. Since then its form has become the most fashionable in modern literature. We are being overwhelmed in a pandemic of *récits*—especially French ones. The Underground Man has become literary Top Dog. An admitted ex-male prostitute and studbuster has reached the windiest pinnacle of international *réclamé*. The corridors of American publishers are crowded with Columbia Creative Writing Majors disguised as switch-blade artists, dope fiends and violators of the Doyle Act.

There is only one trouble with all this stuff. It is soaked in unfathomable solemnity and pompous rhetoric. In all Genet or Kerouac there is nothing to compare with Miller's Hindu and the bidet, or the Imaginary Rich Girl. I'm sorry. I just don't believe Henry when he expands and augments Count Keyserling, or recommends a Dream Book, or worries at breakfast over the astrology column in the morning paper. He's having us all on— maybe himself included—but behind the deep thoughts from Bughouse Square, there is always, however faint, the steady rumble of low-down mockery.

I wish Miller's self-educated hoboes were not more driven and harried than any college professor or machine tender. I wish once in a while somebody would come alive as simply human. I wish somebody would love somebody else, somewhere in all Miller's millions of words, just once, just a little, or at least let on that they felt somebody else was there. They never do. That is the basis of the indictment and the basis of the comedy. Do they really in *Gulliver* or Rabelais? I think not. *Don Quixote* is different? Yes, *Don Quixote* is different. That is why it is the only one there is. If we don't ask the impossible of Miller he is pretty satisfactory. Certainly he is an awful lot better than the dreary practitioners of the fashion this book founded, and it is unfortunate that their success should make him seem a little dated after twenty-seven years.

1961

37.

The Lost Vision
of Isaac Bashevis Singer

Recently I was working in a nightclub below Cooper Union. I had been out of New York for many years and it was thirty years since I had been in that neighborhood. Late in the wet night, a rainy moon in the sky, I went out for a breath of air and walked up the street looking for the Café Royale. I got to St. Marks-in-the-Bouerie, and walked all around it, trying to orient myself. There was no doubt about it, the Café Royale was gone and I couldn't even tell where it had been. Loneliness, nostalgia, the consciousness of age and the passing years, the ache was as much as I could bear. All that bright electric life was gone. How gone it really is, more lost than the noise of the elevated, long ago under the two o'clock in the morning moon, no one who was not there in the days when it was at its most splendid can ever know.

Yiddish culture is at a discount today. A lot of people seem to think it is counter-revolutionary if not positively anti-Semitic to speak the language. There is a curious tendency always to refer to the major Yiddish writers as Polish or Russian or German, to describe them in terms of the country of their origin or even in terms of their subject matter, however many years they may have spent in America. If this goes on one of the most valuable and, in actual fact, one of the strongest influences in American culture will be forgotten and drop out of sight. For the first quarter of the twentieth century New York was one of the literary and theatrical capitals of the world. Not only that, but at the time when American literature in English was struggling with the problems of American provinciality, one of the most intense sectors, the most intense sector really, of our literary life was characterized by its—to borrow a word from Stalin—cosmopolitanism.

When people ask me at lectures, "Mr. Rexroth, whom do you consider the leading American poet of the 1900's?" I love to answer, "Why, Stuart Merrill, of course. Who else?" He wrote in French. A good case could be made for the claim that the best writing done in America in the first quarter of the century was in Yiddish. I don't think it's really true, but it is sufficiently true to be passionately arguable in one of those passionate arguments that used to sprinkle the whiskers with sour cream in the Café Royale. The Café is gone, the arguments are gone, they've discovered sour cream in the bridge clubs of Ashtabula, and there's very little Yiddish literature being written.

But there is Isaac Bashevis Singer. If only he were left writing in Yiddish it would still be an important literary language. He is certainly one of the most remarkable American authors who has ever lived, as he is one of the most intensely Yiddish. Is Yiddish writing sinewy, grotesque, haunted, bitterly comic, deeply compassionate? Singer is close to being the most sinewy, grotesque, haunted, bitterly comic, deeply and desperately compassionate of all. Is most of it at its best, deeply rooted in the ecstatic brotherhood and fantastic folk culture of Hassidism? Singer is a very Zaddik; if he just believed in the efficacy of the Kabbalistic word, I am sure he could make Golems. His stories are Golems enough, they have an amazing life of their own for works of man.

We hear so much nowadays about alienation, we forget that its literary masterpieces, even when written by Jews, portray the alienation of the author from an essentially Christian culture. How little the dilemmas of Baudelaire, or Kierkegaard, or Nietzsche, or Sartre—or Heine—mean to a cultured Chinese or Indian! Isaac Singer is an alienated Zaddik, a Hassid who has found Pascal's abyss in the Zohar. The Farewell to the Sabbath, the dance under the new moon, something has blighted them, as something blighted the Mass for Baudelaire. Marc Chagall is jolly by comparison. Perhaps only Soutine, of all the Hassidic artists of modern times, shares so tragic, so abandoned and lost a vision.

Nowadays a lot of people know of the folklore of Hassidism only through the antiseptic anecdotes of Martin Buber. They are beautiful and clean, poignant and infinitely humane—and they might as well have been written by Albert Schweitzer or Rufus Jones. It is the other side of the violent, intense, locked-in life of the Polish ghettoes and villages we see in Singer. Buber has "faith"—a typically modern, enlightened faith. For all I know Isaac Singer may be a most devout Jew, but there is no "faith" in his stories and still less Enlightenment. For him, an alienated Rabbi Elimelik, "civilization" really is Gog and Magog. We hear so much about Tradition now. Who knows this Tradition better than Singer? Yet what survives for him, what is "usable" as the theologians put it, is just the witchcraft and the pain.

"Satan in Goray" and "Gimpel the Fool" are certainly amongst the most heart-piercing, penetrating, unforgettable stories ever written either in Yiddish or in America. Although I suppose

Singer's plots and characters and milieu could all be called sensational, they are sensational like *Märchen*, like Grimm's Fairy Tales, with the authenticity and closeness to physical reality and the ways of men of a folk tale told in a cottage on a winter night in a village in the backwoods of Poland. It is as though the Baal Shem Tov had seen a vision of Poland in 1940–45 before he ever set out on his travels, and sat down one night by candlelight and told his wife a long grotesque parable, there in his log hut in the Carpathian mountains—and never had gone on his mission. The trouble with all this liberal Neo-Hassidism is that it can't really cope with the insights and revelations of our cold, hopeless, sick time. There's a certain complacent Fabian Society optimism about it. Singer's can. It can even cope with its own disbelief.

Singer has many virtues, a wiry, inescapable style, an intensely personal, inimitable vision, a Machiavellian wit, but above all else it is the bracing, revivifying character of his insight that makes him important. I suppose it is a sort of message, "Life is a bitter tonic, but it cures death itself." I suppose he could be compared to Sam Beckett, or to the Bernanos of *Sous le Soleil de Satan*. But he is, really, a lot further along the road to the end of night than they are and he starts out from less auspicious and promising origins. Perhaps it is that, so far out along that road which we really, all fooling aside, know we each must travel, his people remain so unkillable, and their comradeship in humanity so inextinguishable, that makes him important. Perhaps that's it. Perhaps that is what makes him so much more indomitable an alienated man than most people who are only alienated from what we have come to call "Western Europe." Sounds like it should have "Defense Community" added to it, that term, doesn't it?

1957

38.
Citizen Fromm

If psychoanalysis is a medical specialty, popularizations are as pernicious as might be *The Little Osler, Or The Boy's Home Surgery*. If psychoanalysis is a department of literature, as some think, they are relatively harmless. Erich Fromm's *The Forgotten Language* is a collection of lectures delivered to the girls at Bennington and then to a group of medical students. Unless high schools have changed since my day, and I fear they may have, there is nothing in the book which should be over the heads of high-school students with a C average. Such popularizations are very merchandisable and presumably attract patients in droves, but are they valuable otherwise?

Dr. Fromm, with Karen Horney, is usually identified with Americanized post-Freudianism, the genial, or hunky-dorey school of psychoanalysis. Perhaps this is unfair. Dr. Fromm does not really seem to view life through the horn rims of an assiduous, New School-attending bachelor girl social worker, the rank and file of this powerful movement. I do not think he thinks of the cure of the mind in terms of the substitution of silk screens of Picasso over the mantel and Don Giovanni on the Deluxovox for the Dodgers and Hoppy in the *dénouement* of the American success story. He knows that what is wrong with modern man is not that he is not high-toned enough. He is more than that. But he is emphatically something not contemporary. He is an eighteenth-century man, a reasonable man. This gives his books, especially this one and the last two on religion and ethics, if not the unworldly aloofness of notes by a man from Mars, at least the sweet urbanity of Montesquieu's *Persian Letters*. He knows, as those who are too often linked with him seem not to have noticed, that our society is sick, deranged, demoralized, and that it is no good trying to heal the sick, deranged and demoralized by attempting to adjust them to it, even on its most civilized levels. On the other hand, he shows no evidence that he thinks anything is needed that could not be provided by a calm and reasonable old-time country practitioner or a good cynical priest. It is a little like watching Voltaire trying to exorcise an intelligent and thoroughly malignant dinosaur from his Swiss garden by the sole means of his dry, wise, but somewhat stereotyped irony. Voltaire could not write or understand tragedy. In *Psychoanalysis and Religion* Dr. Fromm equates tragedy with the realization of death. Voltaire believed in God in a mild, Deistic way, but he did not believe in the Devil. Younger men than Dr. Fromm or myself, but of our general class, born in one war, ruined in a second, fated to die with the rest of the species in a third, are uninterested in the existence of a Deity, but recognize that some pretty strong empiric evidence supports the Devil's case. Dr. Fromm's little analysis of dreams and unconscious symbolism, quite a masterpiece, really, of lucid, elementary exposition, misses the point. Freud may have said, changing the old philosophical saw, "Nothing in the unconscious which is not already in sensory experience," but, actually, dark unknown, possibly unknowable Titans struggle beneath the surface of man in all Freud's later metapsychological works. Even Jung's soft, herbivorous terrors are formidable enough. Dr. Fromm gives examples of dreams, simple things that begin with job difficulties and end with father fixations and such like. He analyzes the Oedipus cycle in terms of the matriarchal community versus the patriarchal State. At the end, like Marx with Hegel, he stands Kafka on his head to educe the Inspector and the Priest of *The Trial* as the "voices of the humanistic conscience"! This won't do. Perhaps Dr. Fromm is familiar with that world-wide International, the Third Degree. While one cop beats, tortures and curses the prisoner, another stands by, interferes at the last moment, and says, "Look, son, I'm your friend. I'd like to help you out of this jam and help you get back on your feet, if you'd just let me." That's the bastard to watch out for. He wrote Mr. Vishinsky's duets and gave the learned reports on the effects of foreign proteins in the Jewish bloodstream.

Something is awfully wrong with man and something is awfully wrong with his society. This is so obvious that people like Breton and Dali have made business careers out of purveying charlatan horrors as commodities to rich and idle women and *ballet regisseurs*. I don't doubt but that the average patient would be better helped by Dr. Fromm's sweet reasonableness than by over-sophisticated young doctors whose heads might be very Black Holes of Calcutta of existential anguish. I like Dr. Fromm. I like Diderot or Mirabeau or Beaumarchais, but over their shoulders peers the Marquis de Sade, just as the Comte de Maldoror peeks around the voluminous coattails of the author of *Les Misérables* and grimaces at the inventor of the Religion of Man.

Something is terribly wrong somewhere. Humanitarianism is not the answer. Dr. Fromm is a good citizen. I agree that if we were all good citizens of the community of love, or even the cooperative commonwealth, it would be easier to find the answer, but good citizenship alone isn't it. I don't think Freud found the answer. Certainly none of his descendants has. At least he knew the problem existed. The Greeks knew it, and Shakespeare, and a lot of others. When they wrote about it, we call it tragedy. Possibly psychoanalysis is only a rather naïve development of literature, at that.

1951

39.

Leslie Fiedler:
Custer's Last Stand

"Give it back to the Indians!" has been a catch phrase for disgust with the United States for generations, perhaps since a week or so after the first exchange of beads for real estate. In a trilogy of critical works, *Love and Death in the American Novel, Waiting for the End*, and now *The Return of the Vanishing American*, Leslie Fiedler has been developing the thesis that this is what is happening anyway, that American culture is reverting to a savage, or at best barbarous state, which is simply a modernization of the state of affairs that existed before Columbus. This is an amusing thesis, and it is easy to marshal facts and quotations to produce at least "a willing suspension of disbelief." The popular phrase originally used by Coleridge is apposite, because Fiedler is not writing anthropology or sociology, but literary criticism, not of poetry, true, with few, and then dubious exceptions, but of American novels. Still, he treats fiction as poetry—as a symbolic criticism of values. Speculation based on the analysis of myth and symbolism can make anything out of anything, as witness the long career of fads in comparative religion, from Max Müller or Bachofen to Carl Jung or Robert Graves. Myth, archetypes, mother right, what makes the arguments plausible is not scientific method, but obsession.

Leslie Fiedler is possessed by a number of obsessions which destroy his convincingness, except amongst people who don't know better. First, as is well known, is his favorite term of abuse,

"WASP." He uses it the way Stalinists used to use "Trotskyite," for the most incongruous assortment of writers and tendencies. Since he sees White Anglo-Saxon Protestants under every bed and in every woodpile, it is easy for him to so identify the main line of American culture with their works and to prove that this culture has been continuously challenged and is now collapsing from within. Ultimately this is an incurable distortion of vision due to membership in a small circle of extremely ethnocentric people—the self-styled New York Establishment, triangulated by the *Partisan Review, The New York Review of Books* and *Commentary,* and recently publicized abroad by a hilariously funny, Swiftian satire, by one of its leading members, Norman Podohretz's *Making It.* The United States is a big country, and this tiny set is not even an epi-center, but a small disturbance on an epicycle.

True, most of these people are neither Anglo-Saxon nor Protestant in origin, but rather outlanders who have been permitted into the inner citadels of Wasp culture as the Wasps themselves have wearied and wandered away. Their mentors, Kierkegaard, Henry James, Melville and the rest, it is true, saw life as a fore-doomed struggle of a rationalistic order, originating in the old Protestant theocracy, against the "dark forces" which had been driven into the unconscious. But this is a peculiarity of only a small sector of Americans.

The Mississippi drainage and the Far West have an older heritage, French, Indian and Negro. Whitman can be fully understood only in terms of his Quaker background, and there are thousands of descendants of pietists scattered across the country from Pennsylvania to Oregon. Chicago, Milwaukee, St. Louis, Cincinnati, besides being originally in French territory, were heavily settled by Germans, more socialist or Roman Catholic than Lutheran. So it goes. To the culture-bearers from New England the hinterland may have seemed populated by savages in 1840, as it still seems to the friends of Fiedler and Podorhetz today. Actually, the German, pietist and Populist, social-democratic culture of the Midwest cities, or the wave of communal colonies, from New Harmony to what became Sequoia National Park, both represent a great historical advance over New England. As for the frontier itself, only people like Francis Parkman found it shocking. Audubon did not. Mark Twain did not. The world of the Mountain Men, mostly renegade New Englanders and Virginians, may have resembled the Wild and Woolly West of Fiedler's imagination. Life on a cattle ranch bore scant resemblance to cowboy fiction—with the notable exceptions of Ernst Haycox and Gordon Young.

What is impressive about Mark Twain is the profound normality of his vision of the natural life. What he objects to is the New England *Geist,* and what he objects to about that is the cash nexus, disguised with spiritual pride. Only a crank could find ids and animuses writhing beneath his eminently sane surface. Only a professional humorist like Fiedler could present *Huckleberry Finn,* America's only great novel, as a homosexual romance.

This distortion of vision leads Fiedler to present his case in terms of some extraordinarily bad novels. He sees Barth's *The Sot-Weed Factor* as the beginning of a major movement in contemporary American literature—"give it back to the Indians"— a movement which has been continued by Thomas Berger, James Leo Herlihy, Ken Kesey and the neo-hippies. These are the heirs of the cowboys and Indians. Trouble is, there are still plenty of cowboys and Indians around, and they don't recognize themselves at all. It's the same story as Mailer's "The White Negro" essay about the Beats. Only a completely culture-bound white man could possibly think Negroes bore the slightest resemblance to Mailer's Greenwich Village race racketeers. Yet an essay I thought was satire when I first read it is believed religiously by thousands, including, of all people, Mailer himself.

The principal trouble with hobby-horses and crank notions is that they destroy taste and make discrimination impossible and lead to total misunderstanding of quite plain texts. Much of the Midwest Populist literature Fiedler reads as preaching savagery is simply an attack on the business ethic. Most startling is his use of a poem by Gary Snyder, which does curse the white man with an Indian curse, and which does renounce White America. It is a poem against the Vietnam war, and specifies in the title "the men in the Pentagon." Fiedler simply ignores this and equates it directly with Hart Crane's Pocahontas poem, a Lawrentian "back to the Dark Mother" piece of Romanticism.

There is something terribly Augustan and Eighteenth Century

about all this. In Lawrence's "The Princess" the girl goes down for water at a mountain stream and sees a wild cat across the water. All the terror of chaos overwhelms her as she exchanges stares with a poor little pussy, Tiamat rising from the Babylonish Underworld. I can't take it very seriously, I've camped with hundreds of Indians, and slept peacefully in canyons swarming with wild cats, I am just a Westerner, and I can't recognize the Dark Savage Forces that haunt Leslie Fiedler, but I must admit I find him frightfully amusing. His Huck Finn has afforded me almost as many chuckles as the original.

1968

40.

The Bollingen Series

Twenty-five years have slipped away since the Bollingen Series first started to come out, three or four years under the Old Dominion Foundation, and from then on under the Bollingen Foundation, a separate entity set up for the specific purpose by Paul and Mary Mellon. There are now almost ninety separate titles, some of them series of many books—the works of Paul Valéry and the works of Carl Jung, for instance. I own all of them, and the other day I separated them out from my library, where all books are arranged by subject. The effect was overwhelming. There has certainly never been another publishing enterprise like this.

Many of the books have cost more to produce than their retail price—*The Egyptian Texts*, for example. Others would be difficult indeed to get done today at any price. Over half the years the series has been in existence it has had books on the list of the Fifty Books of the Year, in addition to numerous other awards of merit.

From the very beginning many of the finest designers in the profession have worked for the series—Jacques Schiffrin and E. McKnight (Sandy) Kauffer until their deaths, and since then, Andor Braun, Bert Clarke, Paul Rand, Herbert Bayer, Joseph Blumental, P. J. Conkwright, Algot Ringstrom, Carl Purington Rollins, Stefan Salter and Joseph Weiler. Until 1961 the books were distributed by Pantheon, and Kurt and Helen Wolff probably had a good deal to do with advice on production, because the characteristic Bollingen design is not unlike their pre-Nazi German publications come true, with unlimited funds.

Not since the days when Claude Bragdon was designing books for the young Alfred and Blanche Knopf has a publisher achieved such an unmistakably individual design, characteristic and yet continuously varied in typography, binding and jackets. Bollingen books are as easy to recognize as the uniform, dark blue Oxford University Press volumes, and yet each title has its own dress, expressive of itself.

There used to be a story, quite apocryphal, around publishing circles that Paul and Mary Mellon, talking with Carl Jung, said, "We don't know what's the matter with us." Jung answered, "You have too much money." Paul Mellon said, "It's not my fault. What can I do about it?" Jung said, "Give it away." Mellon replied, "That's easier said than done. I don't know how to give it away effectively," and Jung said, "Give it to me; I'll give it away for you." This was thought very funny in the more despicable post-War II literary cocktail parties. It's quite untrue, but it does bear a kernel of truth. Looking back now over almost one hundred titles and twenty-five years it is obvious that the Bollingen Series constitutes an important pivot in the swing of Western culture to a new taste quite contrary to the one dominant between the wars.

When the series began, the world was sliding once again into catastrophe, the same catastrophe from which it had never recovered in 1918. The interbellum years had been years without interiority, years of rational organization of values measured by things. What the Russians vulgarized as Socialist Realism was dominant everywhere in literature. The American Scene Painters were still riding high. The intellectuals were all either fellow travelers of one variety of Marxism or another, or violent anti-Marxists, obsessed with the paranoias of jilted mistresses. Here and there an odd man out called himself a Buddhist, or a pacifist, or became a Trappist, but even the dream world of the surrealists or the neo-scholasticism of Jacques Maritain were rationalistic, authoritarian and mechanistic to the core. Read today, the manifestoes of the surrealist leader André Breton sound like hysterical Haeckel, high on hash. Although most people haven't found it out yet, what came to a close in the period from the Spanish Civil War, the Moscow Trials, to Hiroshima and Nagasaki, was the age of mechanism, the reign of reification. A not unimportant force in closing that historical door has been the Bollingen Foundation.

Whether D. T. Suzuki, Mircea Eliade, Heinrich Zimmer, Joseph Campbell or William Blake or Coleridge, there is a kind of relentlessness about the consistency of the Bollingen program. What is this program? A steady drive toward reclaiming interiority, reinstating values that cannot be reduced to quantities. And it's all been done so handsomely. The old order may have been bankrupt and grubby, but it was still almost all-powerful when the Bollingen Series began to marshal its elegantly caparisoned forces.

No one has ever put it better than Teilhard de Chardin, when he said that the revolutions of the past two hundred years have been struggles for political and economic liberty, but that the revolutions of the latter part of the twentieth century would be struggles to give meaning to life. "Not the rule of men," said Engels, "but the administration of things"—but the rearrangement of things does not produce its own value. What is it all for? For this, a purely rationalist materialism, whether Diderot, Marx or Freud, provides no permanently satisfactory answers.

We are living in a time when answers are being demanded in prayer and contemplation in monasteries and ashrams, in turmoil and repression in the colleges, and in violence and fire in the streets. The program of the Bollingen Foundation has been an adventure for significance, a quest for meaning, just as much a part of the struggle for revaluation and refounding of a collapsed Western civilization, as any of the headline-making disturbances which have become a characteristic mode of life of this society, whether "expansion of consciousness," *negritude*, free option in styles of dress, the mystical revolt, painters like Mark Tobey and Morris Graves and their descendants, poets like Allen Ginsberg, Gary Snyder, Philip Whalen, Leonard Cohen, Joni Mitchell, Bob Dylan. The connection is closer than Paul Mellon may imagine. Many of the most scholarly Bollingen publications, now that they are being re-issued in paperback, are an integral part of the counter-culture, the alternative society. In the words of a member of my own Poetry and Song workshop, "The Ballad of Tom Jefferson":

Po boy, jes a settin in the winder
A workin the *I Ching*
When the pigs come and hauled him away.
O cast them yarrow sticks and flip them coins
The oracle reads so plain
In this hate world there's truth to the test
So children come ye hear.

I doubt if Carl Jung, Richard Wilhelm or Mr. and Mrs. Mellon anticipated exactly this comeuppance of the publication in English of Wilhelm's the *I Ching*.

Some of these books are unlikely ever to be equalled— *African Folktales and Sculpture* by Paul Radin and James Johnson Sweeney, a most brilliant idea, and perhaps the greatest book bargain of the century. In addition, the combination of profoundly searching folk tales and beautiful sculpture is a most concrete showing forth of *negritude*, more objective than all the speeches of Leopold Sédar Senghor, however estimable those may be. Think of the books that have challenged the very fundamentals of the old culture—*The Art of Indian Asia*, by Heinrich Zimmer and Joseph Campbell; *The Tao of Painting*, by Mai Mai Sze; the beautiful books on Navaho religion; the collected Daisetz T. Suzuki's *Zen and Japanese Culture*; Carl Jung's works on alchemy; Kathleen Raine's *Blake and Tradition* —books like these, although genuinely popular with the educated public, could not be produced commercially at anything but prohibitive prices. And there are the lavishly illustrated scholarly works in many volumes. The Egyptian series, the

Samothrace excavations, and Goodenough's *Jewish Symbols,* are the sort of things that once were sponsored by Royal Societies and now are hardly ever published. There are the complete works of Carl Jung, of Paul Valéry, of St. John Perse, André Malraux's *Psychology of Art,* Hugo von Hoffmansthal, the Mellon Lectures at the National Gallery of Art, seventeen of them to go to date, the complete Plato and most of the important books of the school of comparative religion inspired by Heinrich Zimmer, Joseph Campbell, Mircea Eliade and others, as well as major classics never done in English, like the *Muqaddimah of Ibn Kaldoun,* one of the world's major histories, the *Eranos Yearbooks,* collections of the discussions held at Ascona on the northern shores of Lago Maggiore, now in their sixth volume in English and their thirty-sixth in German, 1933–67—conferences in the history and meaning of the spiritual life of man in all times and places.

What an impressive thing it is, this vast array of books, dedicated to the creative rather than destructive subversion of a materialistic, competitive, acquisitive society. It has been the fatal flaw in the social unheavals of our time that they have lacked objectives which were in themselves structures for a satisfactory alternative society, a scale of values around which men could live without preying on each other. Lacking a new humanism which could meet the unsatisfied and fundamental demands of humanity, social change in the twentieth century has usually slipped back into a reinstatement of the most drab and the least satisfying spiritual, or rather anti-spiritual, values of the nineteenth century. The Bollingen Series has been a vast enterprise in practical utopianism, the search for values for a society in which all men might live creatively with the assurance gained both from their fellows, from within themselves and from association with nature that this creativity was meaningful.

It's all been done graciously, too, with a minimum of sweat and bureaucracy. Long ago I got the idea of doing the other major history then still untranslated, the *Historical Memoirs,* or perhaps it should be called the *Historical Encyclopedia* of Ssu-ma Chien. I talked to one of the senior advisors for a couple of hours, and he said, "Go ahead and set it up." I would translate from the French of Chavannes (about half the original work) and the rest with a couple of Chinese assistants, a project of several years' duration, all arranged so simply and pleasantly. Then I discovered to my horror that somebody else had already devoted a good deal of his academic life to the job and I withdrew in haste. There are plenty of gentlemen in foundations, but *qua* foundation, graciousness is not the besetting virtue of most of them. The things you have to fill out always make me lose my temper, and with it, my interest, which is why I have to work for a living—if you call it work. Mark Twain said he never did a lick of work after he left the riverboats. But I have never forgotten that conversation, and now, looking over 25 years of accomplishment, I would like to repay my compliments to Paul Mellon and his co-workers. The Bollingen Series and the Foundation are more than very civilized. They have proved to be very civilizing. In no trivial way they have modified the *Zietgeist*.

What is this all for? Who these days is satisfied? The young, like Diogenes—"I am looking for a satisfied man." What values guide the satisfied—the non-grasping, non-authoritarian, the non-invasive?

1967

41.

Allen Ginsberg in America

At the *Howl* trial in San Francisco the prosecutor asked one of the witnesses, "You say this book is not pornographic. What kind of a book would you call it?" The witness answered, "It could best be compared to one of the prophetic books of the Bible, especially Hosea, which it resembles in more ways than one." The prosecutor, taken aback, dismissed the witness.

It is very true—Allen Ginsberg is in the direct line of the

nabis, those wild men of the hills, bearded and barefoot, who periodically descended upon Jerusalem, denounced king and priesthood, and recalled the Chosen People to the Covenant. If any writer in America is true to his tradition, it's Ginsberg. Behind him stretches away for generations the prophetic, visionary and orgiastic tradition of Hassidism. He is a Zaddik. Immediately behind him stands Whitman and the founders of communal groups from Oneida to New Harmony, from the Schwenkfelders to the Mormons, those noble souls who almost won, who almost established America as a community of love. It is the Whitman of "Passage to India" who appears to Ginsberg in a supermarket. Immediately in Ginsberg's own childhood, as he says in *Howl,* was what we used to call "the revolutionary movement" before it became a minor department of the Narkomindel, the Russian Foreign Office, when the region in which he grew up, Passaic and Paterson, was a land of promise as well as a place of the "dark Satanic mills" of Blake, where thousands of Jewish and Italian and Appalachian migrants hoped to build Jerusalem in New Jersey's green and sullied land. Unless Ginsberg is understood as a religious leader of the same kind as his younger colleague, Gary Snyder, he cannot be understood at all. Although it was his fame and his loyalty to his old friends from Columbia, who used to get drunk in the San Remo on MacDougal Street, that launched the actually very small Beat movement, he was anything but a beatnik, and it is only as the counter-culture has caught up with him that he has come to play his full role.

Just as the Ginsberg of ten to fifteen years ago was an *hallucination publicitaire* of the news weeklies and picture magazines, so Jane Kramer's Ginsberg in *Allen Ginsburg in America* is a *New Yorker* "Profile." This is a strange animal which resembles the window mannequins in Saks, the movie stars of the Silents, or the creatures who advertise whiskey in the periodicals with the most expensive advertising rates. Amongst poets the most scathing term of contempt is *"New Yorker* verse," even though some of the leading writers in the country have been published in its pages. There is a kind of Winnie the Pooh whimsy that spreads over everything and turns it all into something synthetic made of polyesters and cloying soybeans. Jane Kramer is unquestionably a woman of very good will indeed.

She obviously worked extremely hard to be just, sympathetic and illuminating in her three-part *New Yorker* "Profile" that makes up this book. In the process she obviously developed great affection and respect for Ginsberg. Yet it's all unreal. Her description of the sessions of the leaders of the great Golden Gate Park Be-In, which was the Coming of the Kingdom of the Flower Children before the Mafia took over the Haight-Ashbury, reads like nothing so much as Pooh, Piglet, Rabbit, Owl, Eeyore, Tigger, Kanga and Roo all running around with their clothes off, high on pharmaceuticals beyond the fondest dreams of Huxley, Watts and Leary rolled into one. Said Dorothy Parker, "Tonstant Weader thwowed up." I know all these people, most of them very well indeed, and believe me, they are in deadly earnest. There is nothing whimsical about what they propose to do to the old culture. The counter-culture may be distorted and turned into its opposite or coöpted by the voices of the Establishment, and of course when Big Business in the form of the Mafia discovered that it could sell methedrine and heroin to adolescents as enlargement-of-consciousness sacraments of a new religion, they discovered the most profitable counter-revolution in history, but none of this is what Ginsberg or Gary Snyder or Lenore Kandel or the other people Jane Kramer writes about are about.

Probably the best journalistic picture of Ginsberg available is Paul Carroll's many-page interview in the April 1969 issue of *Playboy,* and the real kernel of that is Allen's little discourse on the ecological breakdown that threatens the extinction of the human species within a comparatively short time, and the necessity for an ecological revolution against the life-destructive forces that are corroding everything about us. The point is Ginsberg is a very serious man. He actually believes with Whitman and with Whitman's master, "I am come that ye might have life, and that ye might have life more abundantly." He may be mistaken as he has made many mistakes along the way that he is now trying to correct and at the end he will probably be crucified in some socially acceptable way, one of the ways of the American Way of Life, but it won't be for not trying. It is quite impossible to domesticate a person like this, even in the most sophisticated stately homes of Scarsdale where *New Yorker* "Profiles" go when they die.

This is not really to put down *Allen Ginsberg in America*. It is unquestionably written with a full measure of affectionate sympathy and a large half-measure of understanding. Perhaps deliberately it is designed to domesticate Ginsberg, to smuggle him into the glass-table breakfast nook surrounded by the conservatory where he will turn the crisp bacon and coddled egg and crispies into honey and locusts and the sugar cubes—well, you know what Timothy Leary does with sugar cubes. I suppose this is all to the good. If the junior élite embrace Ginsberg because he is lovable, who knows what will happen? There is nothing false about Jane Kramer's lovable Ginsberg, there's just a lot more to him than that, as there was more to Hemingway than shadow boxing in Abercrombie and Fitch.

I see I have done just what bugs Allen, written of him as a sociological phenomenon rather than as a great literary artist. Oh well. Jeremiah and Isaiah are great poetry as well as great prophets. Ginsberg's verse broke the iron crust of custom of the self-styled Reactionary Generation, deprovincialized American verse and returned it to the mainstream of modern international literature. So, Allen, you're a great literary artist.

1969

42.

The Authentic Joy
of Philip Whalen

I have often thought of doing a book called *The Laughter of Buddha*. In the Mahayana and Hinayana Sutras together there are about ten places where Buddha laughs. At the most subtly trivial circumstance or at—the same thing—the revelation of ultimate reality. A disciple picks a flower along the road and smells its perfume, or a vision is revealed of the infinitudes of infinities of the universes, each with its Buddha, and The Enlightened One laughs with enlightenment. Baron von Hügel loved to point out that an abiding joy, the habitude of good humor, was considered by the Vatican in the canonization proceedings that authorize the veneration of a blessed or a saint as one of the essential characteristics of beatitude. This is what Philip Whalen's *On Bear's Head* is all about. For Philip, being is joy. He has no epistemological problems because for him ontology is not just joyful; it's funny. In a transcendental sense? Yes, but in a mundane one, too.

> Soap cleans itself the way ice does,
> Both disappear in the process.
> The questions of "Whence" & "Whither" have no validity here.
>
> Mud is a mixture of earth and water
> Imagine WATER as an "Heavenly" element
> Samsara and nirvana are one:
>
> Flies in amber, sand in the soap
> Dirt and red algae in the ice
> Fare thee well, how very delightful to see you here again!

Nowadays Buddhism is like the weather. Everybody's talking about it, but how many people are doing anything? Some people are born authentic, some people achieve it, some have it thrust upon them. As poet and person Philip Whalen simply is. He is about as thoroughly authentic an individual as human physiology is capable of producing. D. T. Suzuki, Christmas Humphries, Alan Watts, even Gary Snyder, many modern Japanese view askance. When Philip Whalen, in his red whiskers, looking like a happy Ainu bear-god, walks down Omiya-dori in Kyoto's weavers' quarter, every face lights up with that old-time Buddhist joy, even though most of the inhabitants are Left Communists, militant atheists, Koreans and Untouchables. He is the kind of person Japanese wish all Westerners were, the good Japanese, that is. There's plenty that like Organization Men. I have in fact seen Philip ambling past the market stalls and running into a march of demonstrating strikers, and everyone smiled and waved and he waved back. That's the way you feel when you read his poems. You want to smile and wave back. Gary Snyder, who in fact the people in the same neighborhood *do* accept as a scholarly yamabushi, a wild hermit monk come down from the mountains, has written a poem called "Smoky The Bear Sutra." It is more like his friend Whalen's poetry than anything else he has written, and in a sense it's about Philip.

Don't get the idea that Philip Whalen is some kind of clown and that his poems are just jokes. He is a greatly learned man, more in the mainstream of international avant-garde literature than almost anybody else of his generation, a man of profound insights and the most delicate discriminations. It all seems so effortless, you never notice it, as you never notice until it has stolen up and captivated you, the highly wrought music of his verse. It all sounds so casual and conversational, just as a lot of Mozart sounds like a country boy whistling along his way to the swimming hole.

How intimate his poetry is, and how closely and deeply connected with place. He is as intensely Northwestern as the painters Morris Graves and Mark Tobey. This abides. Yet each place he goes envelops the poems of that place with a luster of specificity like the nimbus around the picture of a Buddha or a Christian saint. San Francisco, the mountains and sea of the West, Japan. Each poem occupies its own poetic world and the reader finds that world risen about him. This is a very Chinese theory of poetics—that each poem should present an inescapable poetic situation. "The banana leaves tear in the rain." It is the south in the monsoon season. "Heavy incense smoke lowers under the gilded ceiling." A palace. "The painted lute lies by the pearl curtains." A concubine. "Nothing is left in the candlestick but a thread of ash and tears of wax." They are exhausted with too much sex. This is a formula anybody can learn. Philip Whalen doesn't work by formula. He works by total realization, very simply.

Reading *On Bear's Head,* this big book full of beautiful poems, some of them in Whalen's own inimitable calligraphy, it is easy to understand why a poetry like his plays the enormously important role it does in the alternative society, the new world that is being born from the womb of the old. Whether on the printed page, in poetry readings, in rock lyrics or the songs of folk and protest singers, or in the *cafés chantants,* a new moral universe is coming into being, growing up like the lotus from the mud out of the old savage world of the twentieth century, that soon a better day will call the age of pre-historic man, or there will be no soon, and no day at all. What distinguishes Philip Whalen is what distinguishes a very few of the singers—Joni Mitchell or Anne Sylvestre. He doesn't seem to have to struggle up from the mud. He just blossoms naturally. I doubt if he calls himself a Buddhist. He doesn't have to shout or take off his clothes or smoke marijuana on television or even ring little cymbals. He just walks along Omiya-dori saying good morning to the people selling grilled eel or sushi rice rolls or pickled fern tips. Two blocks away the bush warblers sing and make love in the transcendental rock and gravel gardens of Daitokuji, the great complex of Zen monasteries.

1969

43.

Smoky The Bear Bodhisattva

One of the surviving or junior members of the pre-war Reactionary Generation, the Old Left Establishment, one of the numerous clones of Philip Rahv, once referred to Gary Snyder, Philip Whalen and myself as "members of the bear-shit-on-the-trail school of poetry." Was it Lionel Trilling? Was it Leslie Fiedler? Was it Norman Podhoretz? I can't remember; they all look alike to me, and, as Lenore Kandel says, an hour after you have eaten them you are hungry again. Regardless, the charac-

terization was appropriate and even just. As a description of
spokesmen for a way of life only dimly discernible by a two-
hundred-inch telescope from Morningside Heights or the roof
of a thirteen-story office building on Union Square circa 1930,
it is the complaint of the senile establishment that the counter
culture has no ideologists, no critics, except their own renegade,
Paul Goodman. What they mean by ideology in criticism is
prose that quotes predigested Freud and misunderstood Marx
and concerns itself with a verbalized relationship of a completely
urban society in the bygone industrial era. No bears shit on the
grass, alas, in Central Park.

Gary Snyder is unquestionably the leading ideologist and
critic of the counter culture, but he is that, not discursively, but
as a poet whose values are exposed in the factual experience of
the poem with the presentational immediacy of concrete happen-
ings. The ideology is the perspective. The criticism is in the
arrangement. The dead culture is challenged not by rhetorical
judgment but by unassimilable occurrences. The Old Guard's
reaction to Gary Snyder is much like their reaction, when they
were a very young guard, to Laura Riding. She wrote the best
poetry of her time, but since it implicitly challenged all the presuppositions of interbellum culture, that culture found her totally
indigestible and forgot her. Even the bright young homosexuals
of the country house weekend soviets who when she came to
England sat at her feet to learn the ABC's of modernistical
versification, ran away when they found out what she meant.
They fled from her who sometime did her seek.

Allen Ginsberg is assimilable. We can always make room in
the canon for Hosea. The prophet, the *nabi,* is a standard ap-
purtenance of the Solomonic court. Ginsberg must struggle continuously to keep from being digested. Even so he is one of
America's Hundred Best Celebrities. Whalen minds his own
business and is scarcely aware that the dead world exists. Snyder
is a master of challenge and confrontation, not because he seeks
controversy but because his values are so conspicuous, so plainly
stated in the context of simple, sensuous, impassioned fact that
they cannot be dodged. Young people make up the huge audiences at a Ginsberg reading to be exhorted. They come to the
almost as large ones of Gary Snyder to learn. Who else will

teach them? When Snyder some years ago in the Early Flower Children Days visited one of the first communities of love in the wilderness, he said, "Gee, you ought to build a couple of latrines." An otherwise nude girl wrapped in a torn lace curtain said, "What's a latrine?" Snyder went and got a shovel. If thee does not turn to the inner light, where will thee turn? Over the entrance to every respectable quarterly and the *New York Review of Books* is a sign in letters of gold: "Bears are forbidden to shit in this office" which translates *"Mene mene tekel upharsin."*

Snyder is the principal controversialist of the counter culture because he simply refuses controversy altogether. He acts on the assumption that the old world is totally, irrevocably, stone dead. He confronts it simply by being there. Why does he stay around? The bodhisattva's vow is, "I will not enter Nirvana until I can take all sentient creatures with me." But the bodhisattva doesn't consciously make a vow. He is a bodhisattva out of transcendental indifference. As far as he is concerned he is just plain old Smoky the Bear.

The dead society was urban, its culture the pleasure of a clerkly caste. Allen Ginsberg cries, "Woe, woe to the bloody city of Jerusalem!" Snyder, like Benedict of Nursia, or the yamabushi of Japan, goes to the wilderness. His values are those of the wilderness, of the lynx on the branch, the deer in the meadow. The confrontation is total. There are no bears amongst the roses, only a critic who supposes things false and wrong.

I once long ago said to Gary that Buddhism was the assumption of unlimited liability for the community of love, and Gary said, "The best way to put that is unlimited interiority in the community of love." For the Buddhist vision is the empirical, prime reality. Nirvana is samsara. The world is the transcendent. Illusion is illumination. The disciple holds up a flower and Buddha laughs, and all the Buddhas of all the Buddha worlds of all the infinities of infinities light up and laugh. The point is flower. How right the interbellum culture was to make a saint of that sick man, Kierkegaard. There is no interiority there, only a horrified utter exteriority. "Who is Buddha?" "I think I'll cook bean cake for supper." In the necklace of Shiva every diamond reflects every other and is itself reflected.

Twenty years before ecology became a fashionable evasion with the public and a profitable lie with Shell Chemical Gary Snyder, still in college, was talking about the ecological revolution. In fact the first time I ever met him we talked all night about it while some wandering girls from Reed College listened in rapture. He came into my flat in San Francisco very brown, in boots and blue jeans. "Looks like you'd spent the summer in the mountains," said I. "Yes," he said. "In the Northern Cascades." "I used to work up there," I said. "My first job for the Forest Service was at Marblemount on the Skagit River. My boss was a wonderful guy named Tommy Thompson. It was his first year as District Ranger." "What did you do?" said Snyder. "I packed mules to build a lookout on Mount MacGregor. It was the first lookout in that country." "That's where I was," Snyder said. "I was in the lookout. This summer was Thompson's last year with the Forest. He's retiring." Snyder has great respect for trees. Can a tree become a Buddha in some future incarnation? This is a tree viewed from the perspective of karma. The tree already is a Buddha. Ecology is not a religion but a science. Science, say the professors, is value neuter. This is the essence of Western civilization: *All intellectual and physical activity tends to approach the condition of being totally value neuter*. Newton's laws are all reducible to Carnot's Third Law— from Carnot Carnap's inexhaustible exegesis of moral entropy. Marx called it the cash nexus. We fight fire with fire. *Ecology is the science of values*. A college student on vacation sitting in a fire lookout in the Cascades, Gary Snyder was evolving in his head an ecological esthetics. The poem is the nexus of the biota, the knot of macrocosm and microcosm, a jewel in Shiva's necklace. But the poem is a perspective on a person and a person is a totalized perspective on all the others. For a world epoch Shiva dances; for a world epoch he dreams. We think of this as the time of Shiva's dancing. It is not. The world of limited experience is the dream of being. What we call being is illusion, the dream of Shiva. It is an instant or a million times a million years before he wakes. Knowing, acting, loving, you are Shiva, but you dream.

"Far East"—"Far West" Snyder calls two sections of his first collected poems, *The Back Country*. It's there he found wisdom, where the antipodes merge. The Indian alight with fasting seeking a name at the edge of the mountain snow. Which Indian? American Indian? India Indian? Or the mad mountain monk Han Shan whose Cold Mountain Poems Gary Snyder has translated, or the wilder mountain monks—yamabushi—of Japan, or Old Coyote, coming down the smoke hole, or the Siberian shaman full of mushrooms, flying over the North Pole. Only those who do not deny the web of beings have vision. It's not just that Snyder has learned from the songs of the American Indian translated by Frances Densmore or the shaman odes of early China. It's that he's lived a certain kind of life, a life that lingers on all over the world waiting for the television screen to go blank and the skyscrapers to fall. Is this "an apocalyptic world view"? Snyder is an eschatologist as seen by the denizens of apocalypse. Apocalypse is taking place in the world of grasping. For those who have put away grasping it is not there. "Don't own anything you can't leave out in the rain," says Snyder. For those who turn to the extended family merged in a tribal society from which all acquisitiveness is disciplined away by the only opponent of grasping—contemplation, apocalypse will not matter. The community of love will survive in the mountains and on remote islands and some places in the cellars of burnt-out cities, or the whole planet will go out like a light, or all the million insoluable problems will solve themselves in a technological society where only a new tribalism can be an efficiently functioning social order. "Are you ready for Armageddon?" say the Jehovah's Witnesses when they ring your bell on a Sunday morning. It's always Armageddon. Lenin said his Bolshevik state would realize itself in the application of the philosophy of American efficiency experts and the development of electricity. The Buddha word, the myths of Northwest Indians, the I.W.W. Preamble and the technology of electronics. What is Buddhism? What shall we have for supper?

Snyder's poetry and his prose, collected in *Earth House Hold*, are full of small dramas of an utterly non-combative character played out in naturally limited microsocieties. Men in the mountains, at sea, in monasteries and ashrams, and in the special little ashram he and his Japanese friends developed on a lonely, volcanic island between Kyushu and the Ryukus living on fish and yams and spending a good deal of their time in the hard work that makes all other work easy—contemplation. Karma means work, and contemplation is the karma that changes the signs from negative to positive and finally erases them in the empty circle that ends the Zen pictures of the boy hunting the buffalo.

I do not believe that there is a single individual who has more influence on the youth who leave the dead society for the counter culture than Gary Snyder. He makes explicit what the musicians play and sing. He doesn't get the publicity; the journalists and the sociologists scarcely know he is there. Jerry Rubin, Stokely Carmichael, Rap Brown, Bobby Seale, David Dellinger—these are all readily recognizable by the *Time* researchers because they inhabit the same world, the flickering simulacra of the television tube. The journalists and the sociologists create the revolution in their own image. The lictors of hell, are they sentient beings, or merely automata created especially for the purpose?

Gary Snyder and Masa Uehara were married on the lip of the crater of a very active volcano on a tiny island in the midst of the bright, empty Pacific—viii. 40067 (*reckoning roughly from the earliest cave paintings*).

1970